IMAGES
of America

BEAUMONT

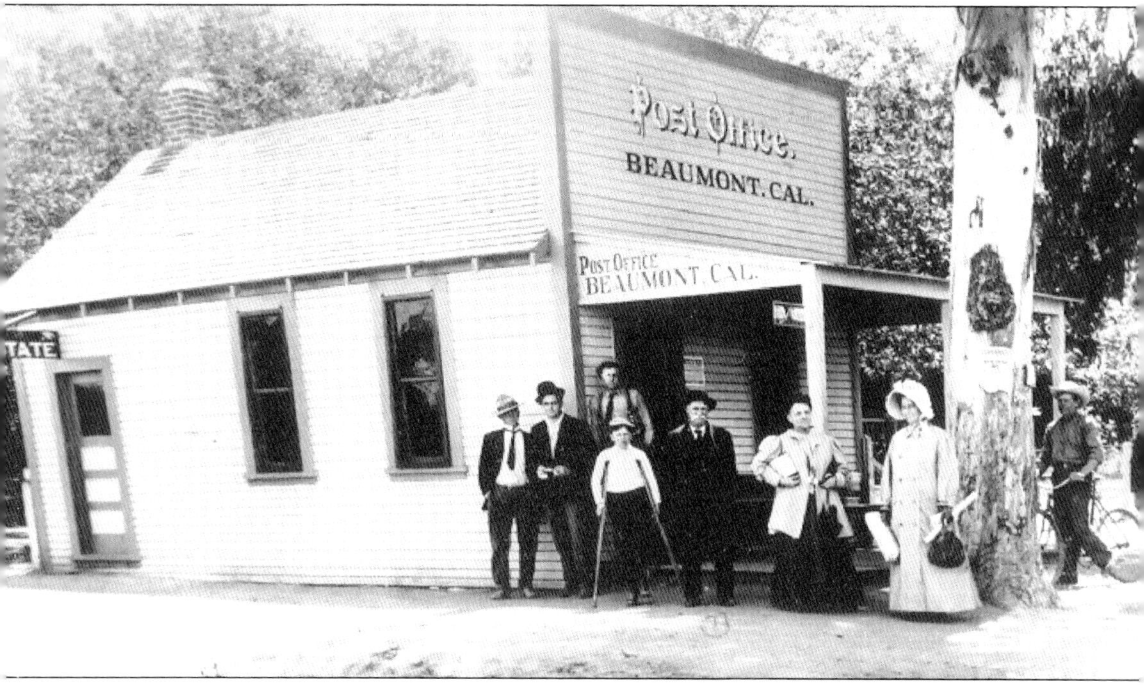

This photograph was taken of Beaumont's first post office around 1880. It was located on the southwest corner of Egan Avenue and Fifth Street near the train station, diagonally across from where the second Beaumont bank was built in 1923. The bank still stands today. The group posed in front appears to be proud of their post office. (Courtesy of Jim Lester and Joan Taylor of Beaumont Chamber of Commerce.)

ON THE COVER: This is a photograph of the Beaumont Hotel, built in the vicinity of Beaumont Avenue and Fifth Street in the late 1880s by the Southern California Investment Company under the leadership of Dr. Sigler. The premium items for fostering real estate booms included impressive hotels and ample water and land, and Beaumont was no exception. The Beaumont Hotel, later named the Edinburgh Hotel, burned to the ground in August 1935. (Courtesy of SGPHS.)

IMAGES
of America

BEAUMONT

Kenneth M. Holtzclaw and Mayor Jeff Fox

ARCADIA
PUBLISHING

ISBN 978-0-7385-4713-8

Published by Arcadia Publishing
Charleston, South Carolina

Printed in the United States of America

Library of Congress Catalog Card Number: 2006934436

For all general information contact Arcadia Publishing at:
Telephone 843-853-2070
Fax 843-853-0044
E-mail sales@arcadiapublishing.com
For customer service and orders:
Toll-Free 1-888-313-2665

Visit us on the Internet at www.arcadiapublishing.com

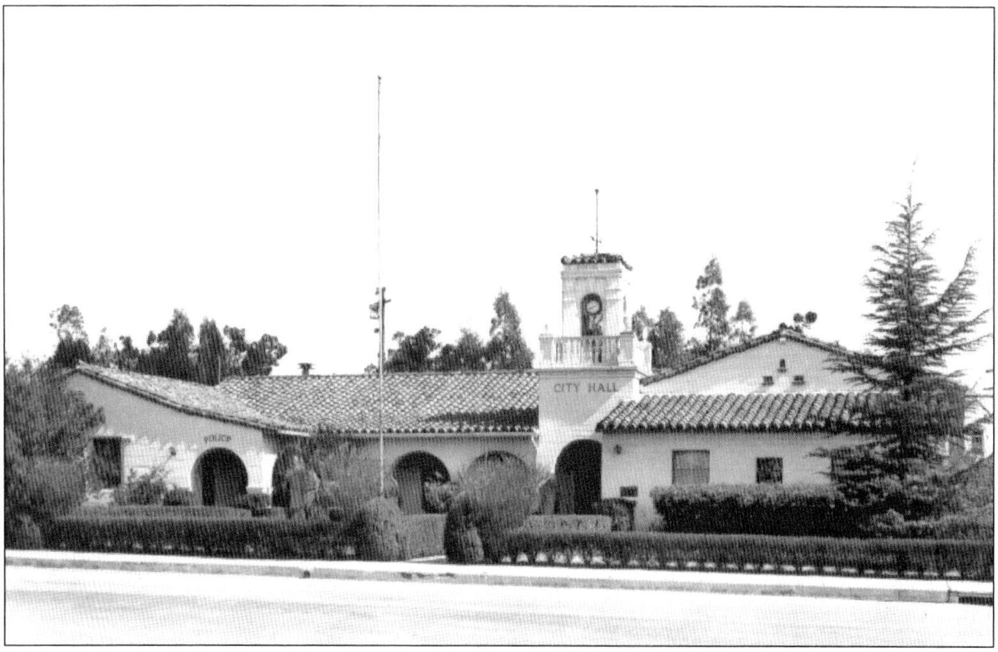

Pictured here is the old Beaumont City Hall at 500 Grace Street before its relocation to Beaumont's Sixth Street grammar school building in the mid-1980s. City hall originally shared the building with the Beaumont police station. Since the city's offices were moved to Sixth Street, this structure has housed the school district offices. (Courtesy of Nara Haskell.)

Contents

ACKNOWLEDGMENTS

When a photographic book like this is compiled, it usually the result of a joint effort of a number of people, and that is certainly true in this case. Therefore, I would like to acknowledge and thank those who helped in its compilation. Marilyn Vonderheide, manager of the Laura Mae Stewart Foundation (LMSF), contributed the images that make up chapter five. I am indebted to her and the LMSF for their contribution. Sue Smith, a longtime resident of Beaumont, contributed the photographs that make up chapter three, images that add significantly to the understanding of Beaumont's contribution to paleontology. Steve Lech, Riverside County historian and author, provided vintage photographs as well as helpful advice. Nara Haskell, ex-president of the San Gorgonio Pass Historical Society (SGPHS), supplied invaluable vintage photographs throughout the book.

Others to be thanked are Jim Lester and Joan Taylor of the Beaumont Chamber of Commerce; Clara DiFelice of the Beaumont Library District; Bill Bell of the Banning Public Library; Bill Lopez of the *Record Gazette*; Steven Morgan, president of Precisions Stamping, Inc., of Beaumont; Marianne Bailiff, longtime resident; Jim Barrett, fourth-generation resident; Mary Ellen Caldwell, mother of astronaut Tracy Caldwell; Bud Mathewson, businessman and local historian; Homer Shockey, ex-president of SGPHS; Donald and Susan Echlin, Beaumont residents; Norman McGary, acclaimed artist; and Betty Lewis.

INTRODUCTION

It is both useful and interesting to trace the development of an area's history. To better understand current conditions and future options for Beaumont, it is important to look at its past. Beaumont lies in a valley plain at the summit of the San Gorgonio Pass and is cradled between Mount San Gorgonio in the San Bernardino Mountain Range to the north and Mount San Jacinto in the San Jacinto Mountain Range to the south. Among the early Native American inhabitants who once roamed or lived in this area, there were no foreign intruders in the area's early history. However, the pass was doubtless a favorite corridor from the desert to the ocean for Native Americans of other areas, so there was some intermingling with outside tribes. But understandably, the private serenity of natives living peacefully at the summit was not to last because of foreign intrusion to follow.

Arriving first were the exploring Mexicans, then the Spaniards, and finally the Europeans. Spanish expedition reached the area around 1774, and by 1824, Franciscan Fathers of the San Gabriel Mission established an adobe mission outpost north of the summit. Parties from the mission made long trips to the Salton Sea to obtain salt, as salt refineries had not yet been established. They allegedly used the mission outpost as a wagon stop to and from the Salton Sea, but it was eventually abandoned. In 1843, Gov. Pio Pico had granted Rancho San Gorgonio to Santiago Johnston, but after he failed to develop it, the rancho was abandoned and later homesteaded by Pauline Weaver. His homestead included the abandoned mission outpost adobe, as well as the property that now encompasses the Highland Springs Resort.

Parts of Weaver's homestead were sold on October 10, 1853, to Dr. Isaac Smith, a retired U.S. Army surgeon, and to William Edgar, another ex-army surgeon. Dr. Smith built a home at Highland Springs, and Edgar established a farm nearby with a winery. Wine was produced from grapes grown on his farm; one of the area's first farming endeavors. Edgar Street in Beaumont still bears his name.

Four men—Leland Stanford, Collis Huntington, Mark Hopkins and Charles Crocker—launched their Southern Pacific (SP) Railroad venture in 1860. The route, through the pass via the summit area, had been surveyed and approved, and by 1862, President Lincoln had authorized the construction of a railroad to the West Coast. However, the railroad would not appear for over another decade, but regular stage service through the pass did begin in the same year. The first Wells Fargo stagecoach left Los Angeles to La Paz on September 6, 1862, spurred by the discovery of gold at La Paz on the Colorado River. It was a six-passenger stagecoach and was pulled by a six-horse team. The first wave of settlers moved into the summit area with the stage.

Smith's Ranch soon became Smith's Station, serving as a local stage stop and providing lodging for passengers. Other stage lines followed over this particular route. Noble Ranch to the east in Banning became another stagecoach stop, later bought by James Gilman when it became Gilman stage stop. The most famous stage driver to pass over this route was Wyatt Earp. Stage companies were popular, and numerous ones evolved. However, it was not long until the "Great Iron Horse" would arrive upon the scene, dull their venturous activity, and eventually put them all out of business.

In 1875, even before there was a town in the place called Summit, the railroad established a station there—a small, red structure. The first passenger train came through Summit in 1776. The railroad continued to play a major part in Summit's history. In 1884, George Egan bought most of the property encompassing the summit area and proceeded to lay out a town site that he named San Gorgonio. He established a ranch, grew grapes, and built a winery. Later he sold all his holdings to the Southern California Investment Company, which after the real estate bust in 1888, struggled to stay above water before a San Francisco bank took over.

In 1907, after an unsuccessful attempt to develop the town by the investment company, Kenneth Smoot and Claredon Eyer bought all of the unsold lots in town as well as 3,500 acres north of town. They began an extensive advertising campaign and changed the name of the town from San Gorgonio to Beaumont. They established the Land and Water Company, actively installed lines to serve new residents, built the elaborate Beaumont hotel, and rented a special SP train from three to five cars long to carry prospective buyers to Beaumont. Land in town was offered from $50 to $200 per lot. The promotional and sales program was very successful.

The population of Beaumont at the time was between 200 and 300. Houses were scattered sparsely throughout the town, with the majority of the lots being vacant. The major buildings of Beaumont included the railroad depot, the Beaumont Land and Water Company building, and three hotels called Hotel Beaumont, Summit House, and Del Paso Hotel. But Beaumont continued to grow, and on November 18, 1912, it was incorporated as a city of the sixth class. A rapid influx of new residents after World War II brought its population to over 3,000 in 1950, and it has increased by slightly over 1,000 people per decade since then, until the recent real estate boom, and today it has exponentially risen to an estimated population of over 23,000.

One

Early Beaumont Years

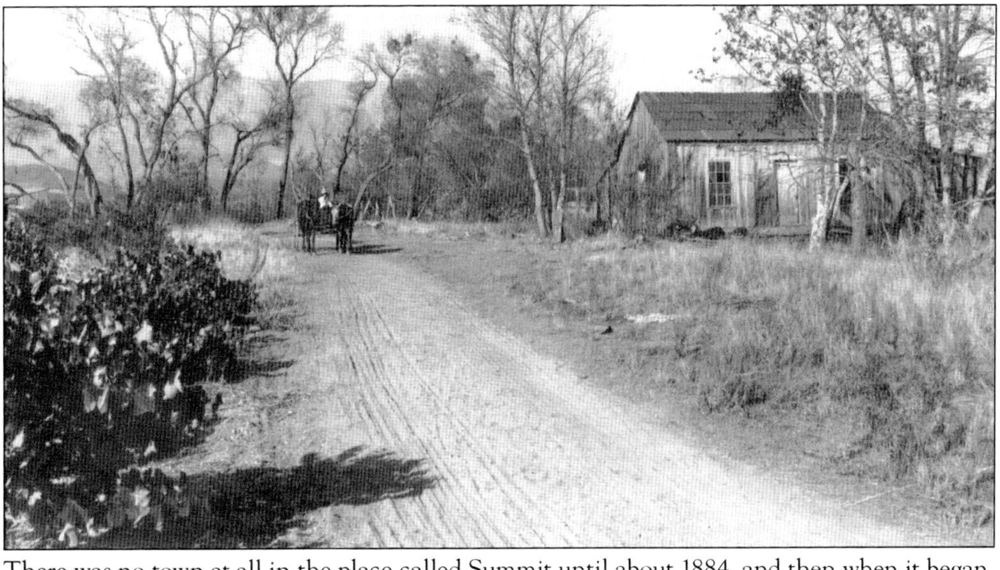

There was no town at all in the place called Summit until about 1884, and then when it began, it was known as San Gorgonio. Notwithstanding the fact that there was no town until 1884, a small, red railroad depot and telegraph office was established there in 1875. A man named George C. Egan bought railroad land and procured other lands so that he owned practically the whole town site in and around the present town of Beaumont. He built a house, seen here, north of the town site and established a ranch there. (Courtesy of Nara Haskell.)

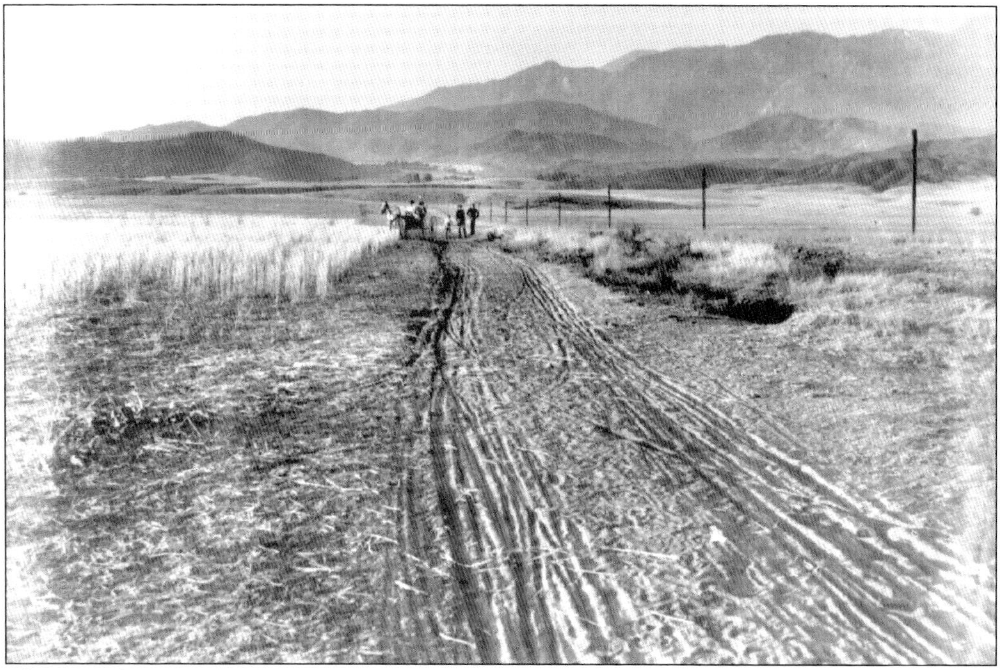

This is a photograph of San Gorgonio Avenue looking north during the early stages of its development. In 1884, George Egan laid out the San Gorgonio town site and this view represents a bit of his initial endeavor. Note the absence of trees at this time. They would not appear until shortly later, when the town site came under new ownership and extensive tree planting occurred. (Courtesy of Nara Haskell.)

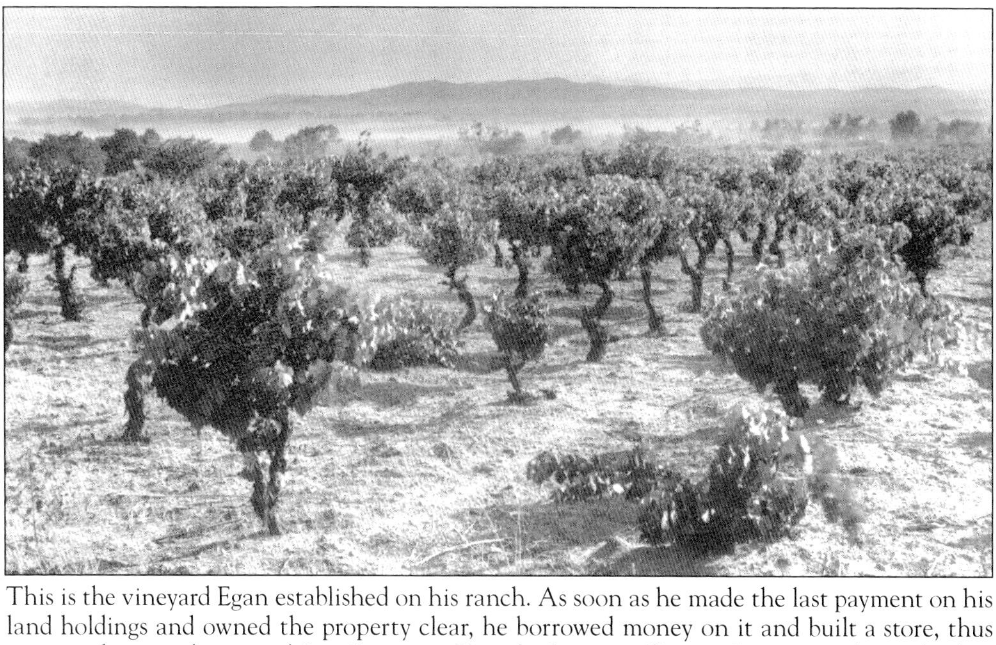

This is the vineyard Egan established on his ranch. As soon as he made the last payment on his land holdings and owned the property clear, he borrowed money on it and built a store, thus starting the town he named San Gorgonio. Egan had a post office in the store and was the first postmaster. Also, around the year 1884, a man named Parrish built a tiny place south of the railroad. (Courtesy of Nara Haskell.)

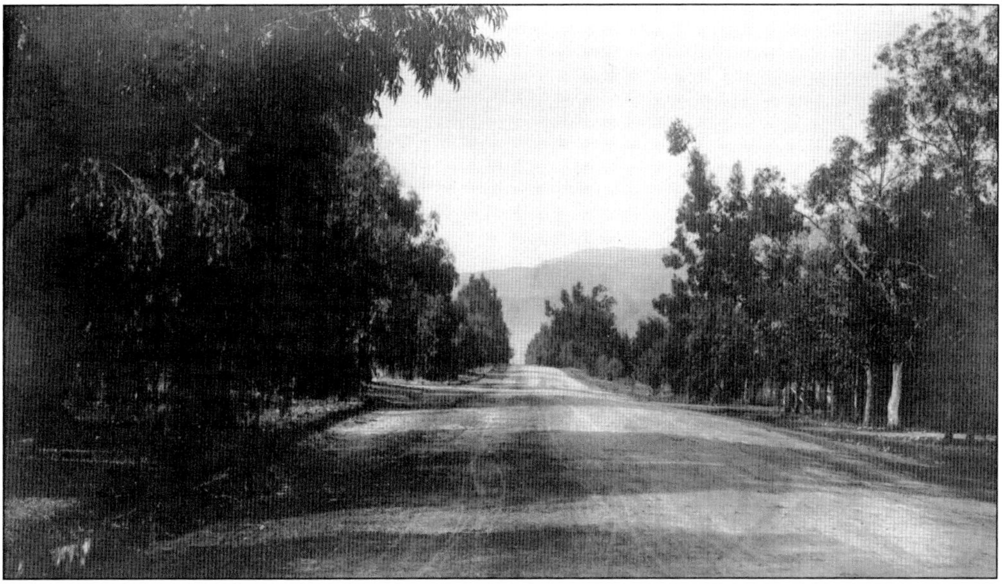

In 1886, a company called the Southern California Investment Company purchased all of Egan's holdings at San Gorgonio and changed the town's name to Beaumont. The name was adopted in 1887. The company proceeded to "boom" the town. They planted eucalyptus, pepper, and other shade trees along about 20 miles of streets. Seen here is Beaumont Avenue looking north with eucalyptus rather than today's large deodar trees. (Courtesy of Steve Lech.)

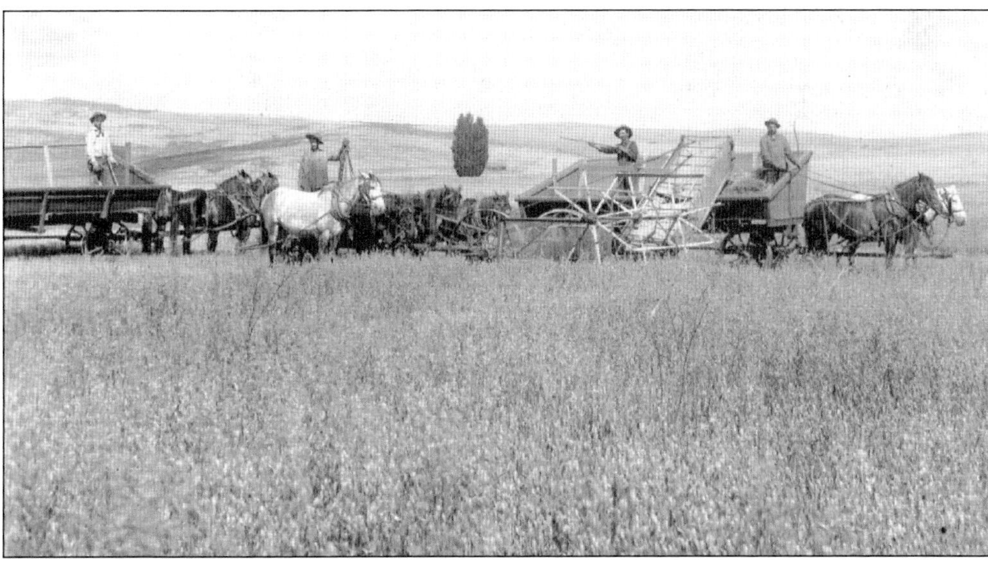

At this time, the chief industry was raising grain and hay, which was dominated by Reznor Stewart on his 2,200-acre hay ranch. Seen here is a farming crew harvesting oats. Little fruit had been planted by this time. In 1888, the real estate boom burst, the Southern California Investment Company struggled, and its financing bank took over its holdings. Stewart continued to farm. (Courtesy of Marilyn Vonderheide and LMSF.)

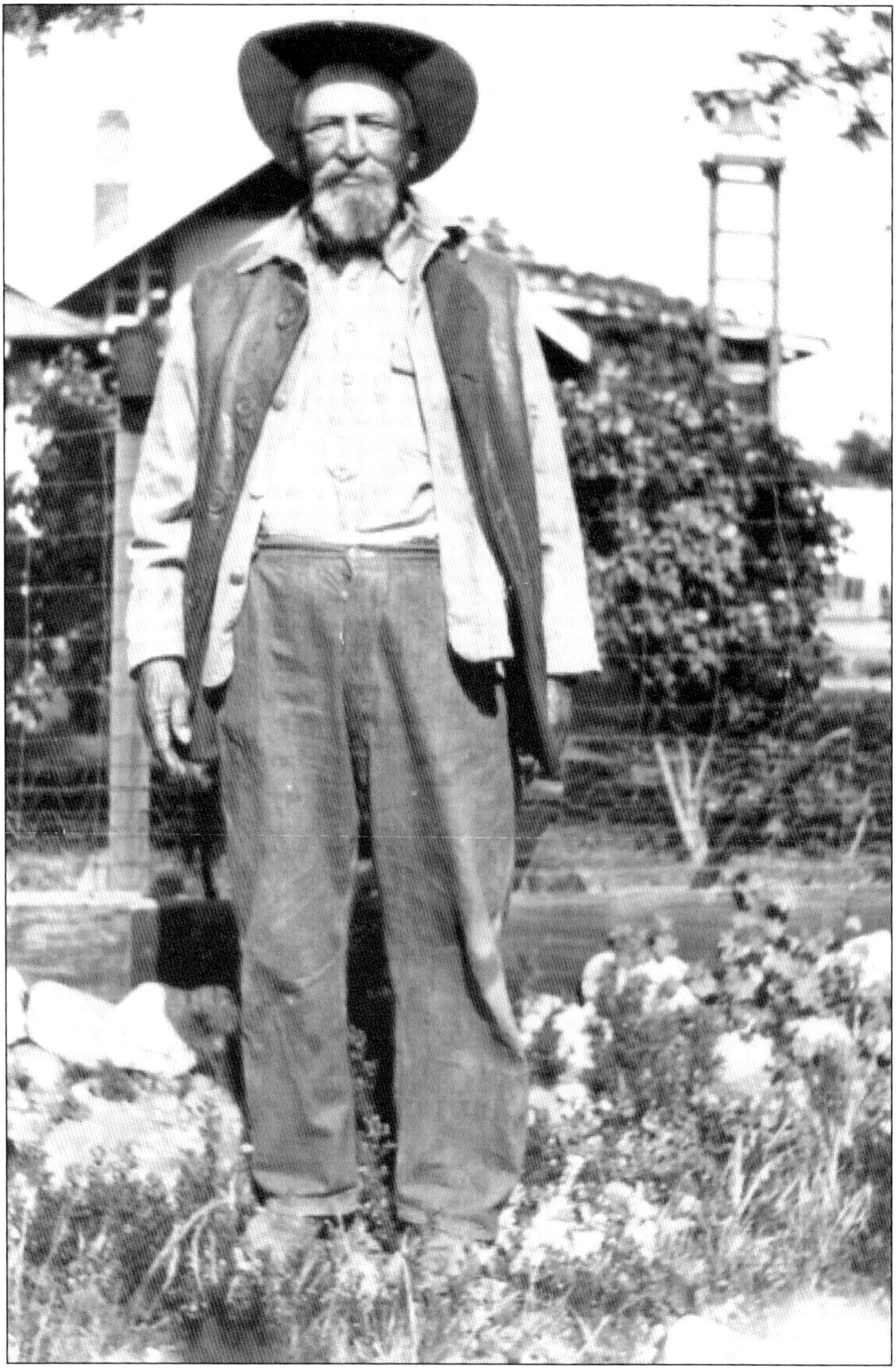

Reznor Perry Stewart came here in the mid-1800s before the real estate bust of 1888. The original homestead that he had taken in 1883 south of Beaumont blossomed to over 2,200 acres when he purchased land from the Southern Pacific Railroad. The casual stance captured in this photograph is typical of his relaxed demeanor. Regardless, he worked hard at farming his large acreage. (Courtesy of Marilyn Vonderheide and LMSF.)

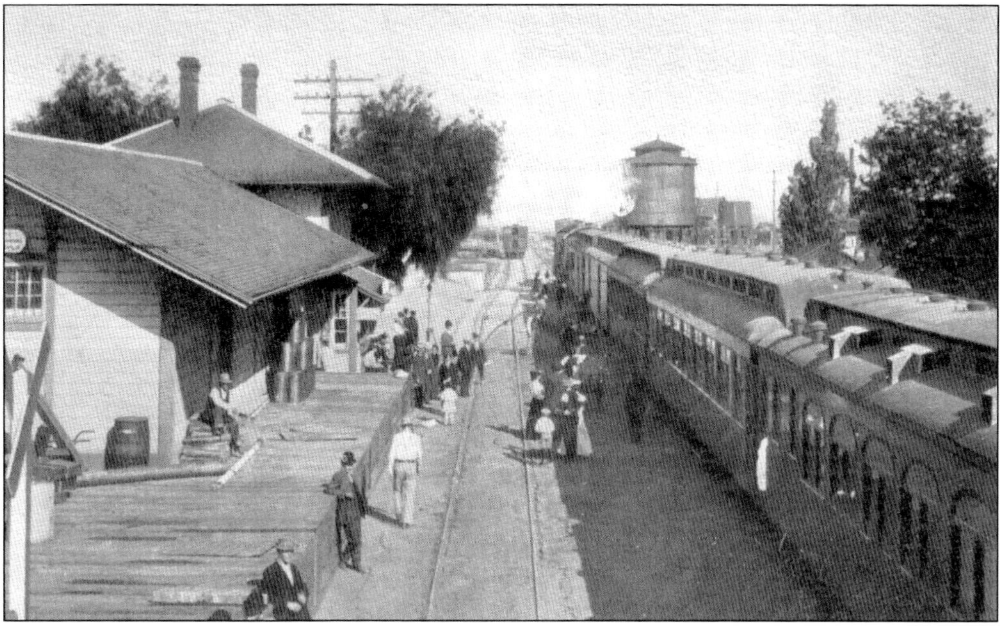

In 1890, Beaumont, though crushed under the weight of failure of two years before, had grown somewhat. The railroad built a larger depot, seen here, in 1887. At this time, the business portion of Beaumont included two stores, a saloon, a post office, a livery stable, three hotels, a large grain warehouse, a schoolhouse, and two churches. (Courtesy of Steve Lech.)

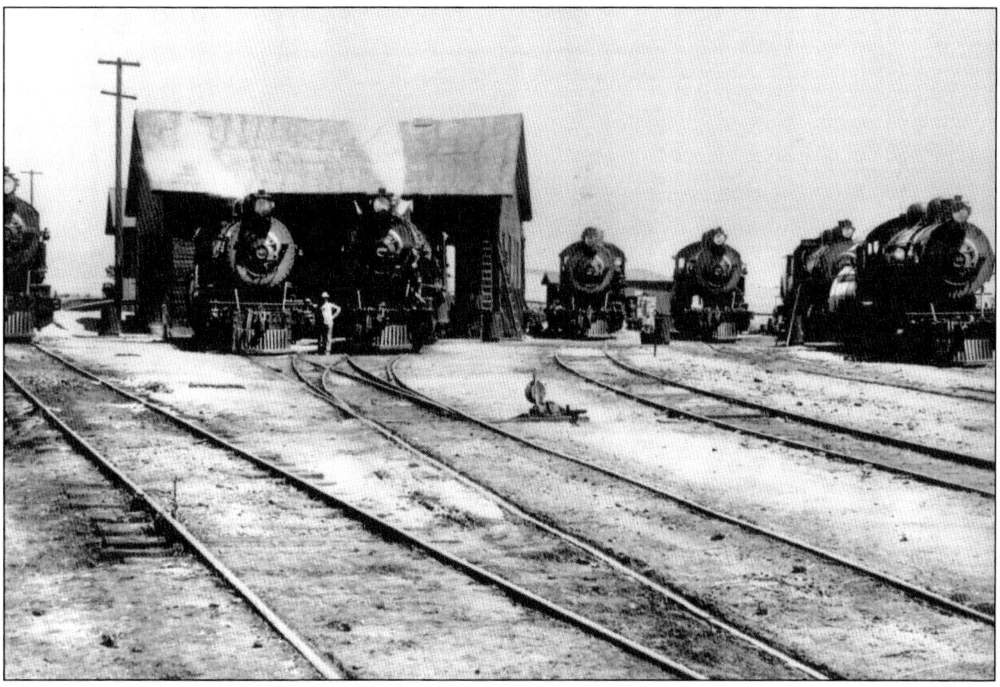

Soon after the large train depot was built, about 1887, its little roundhouse was moved to Banning, and a much larger one built in its place. Seen here is the roundhouse in Beaumont, which was important in keeping the railroad functioning well. Other improvements were made around the depot area in subsequent years. (Courtesy of SGPHS.)

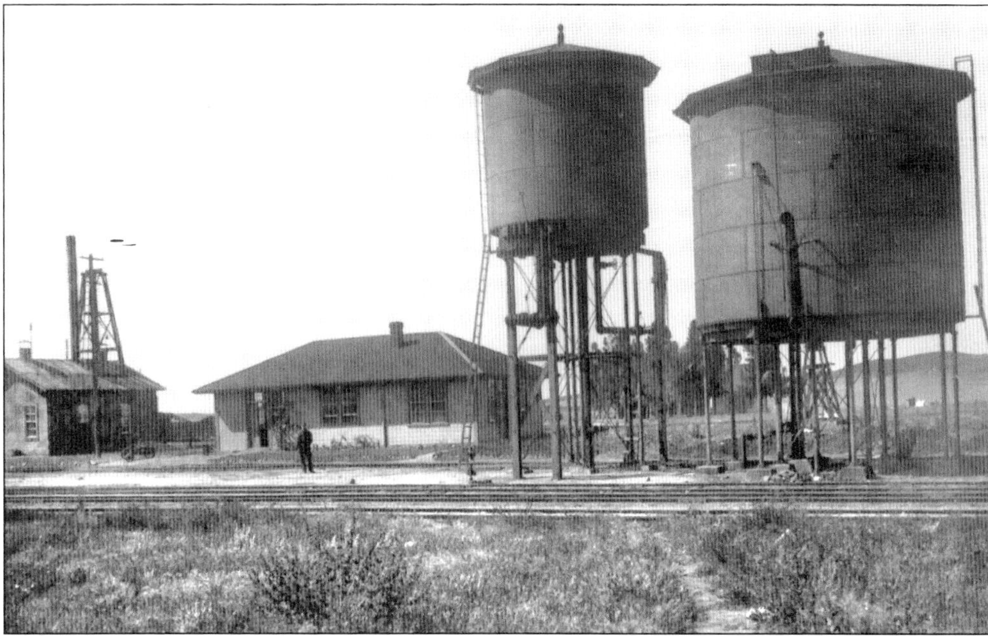

Soon after the new roundhouse was constructed in 1887, a new larger water tank was added due to more water being required to service another train that was added to the line. Behind this large tank is the framework of a windmill used to pump water from a well for the tanks. The house in the center belonged to Mr. and Mrs. Roy Adams. Roy was an employee of the railroad. The shop at the left was still standing in 1982. (Courtesy of SGPHS.)

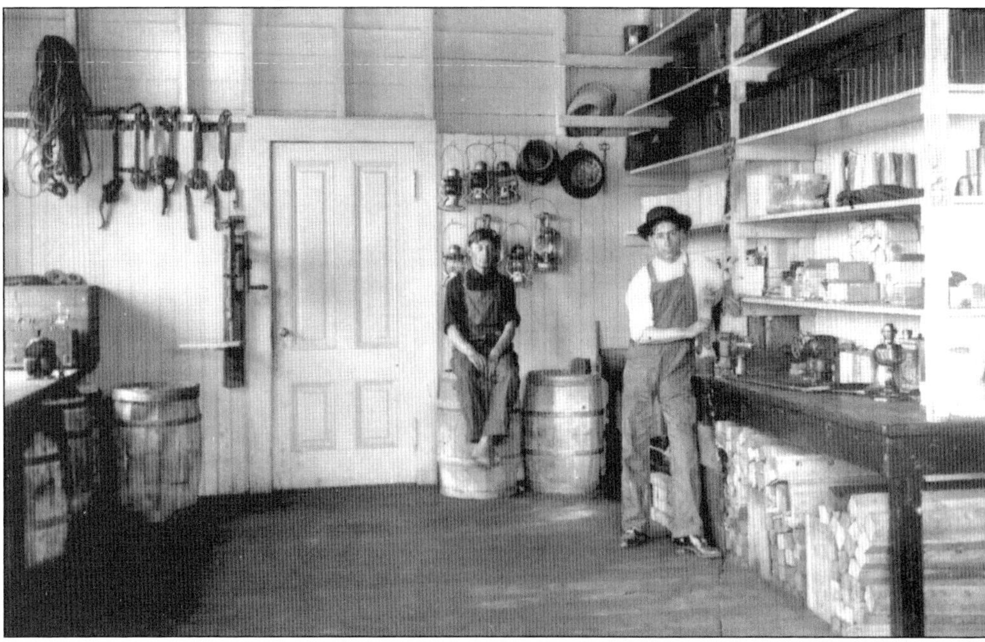

Pictured is the inside of one of the roundhouse storage rooms where lanterns and other needed items were amassed. The storage rooms also served as tool sheds and workshops for some of the employees, two of whom are posing here. The storage rooms maintained an essential function for the roundhouse, which kept the trains serviced and running. (Courtesy of SGPHS.)

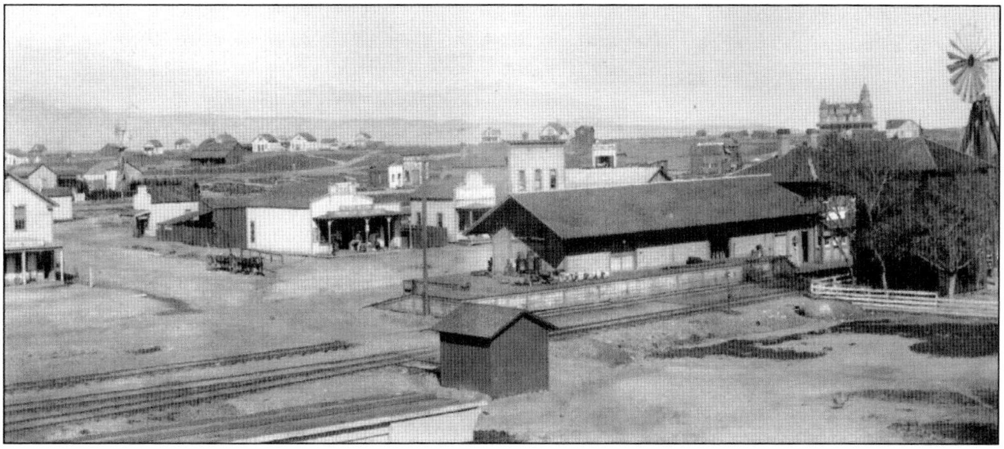

This is a panoramic view of Beaumont during its early era. A point of interest is the Beatty House, at left, which later became the Summit House, Beaumont's first hotel. Also notice Egan's new store across from the Beatty house, which faces the depot on Egan Street, taken for his name. Nearby Grace Street was named after his daughter. Hotel Beaumont is seen in the distance at right. (Courtesy of Donald and Susan Echlin.)

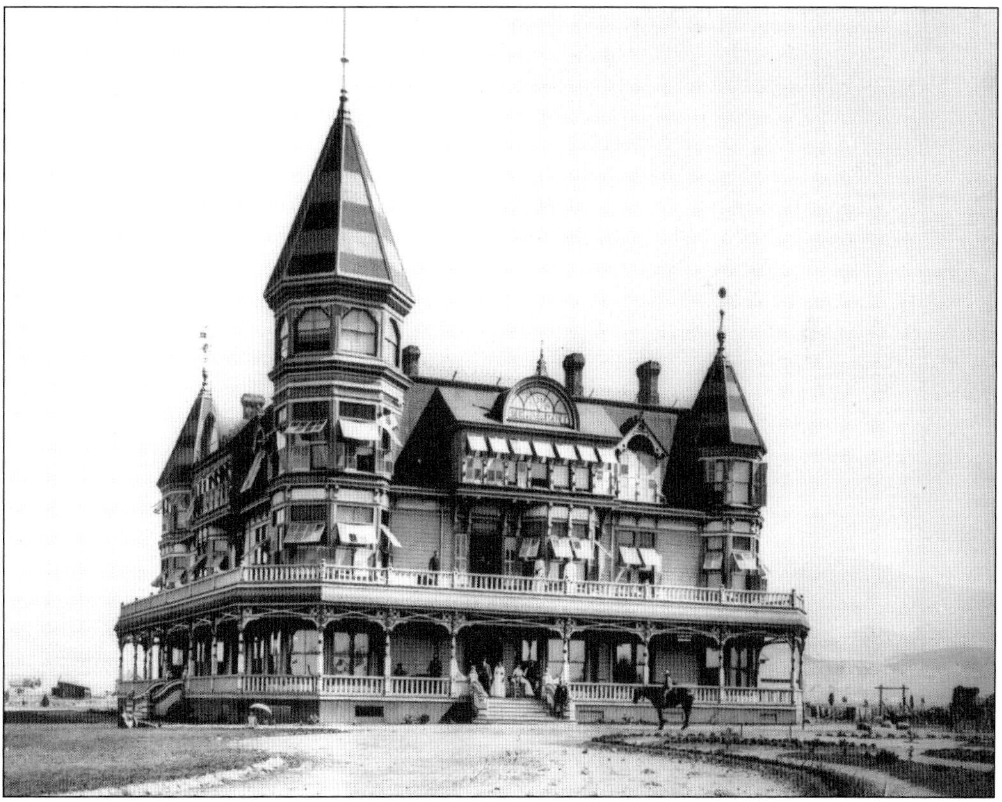

One of the most expensive improvements the investment company that purchased Egan's property at San Gorgonio made in 1887 was to construct Beaumont's third hotel, the Beaumont Hotel, at a cost of $40,000. This and structures elsewhere were built to attract potential land buyers during the booming years. After the 1888 bust, it stood unused for years. It was renovated and reopened in 1907 as Edinburgh Hotel, but in 1909, it was destroyed by fire. (Courtesy of SGPHS.)

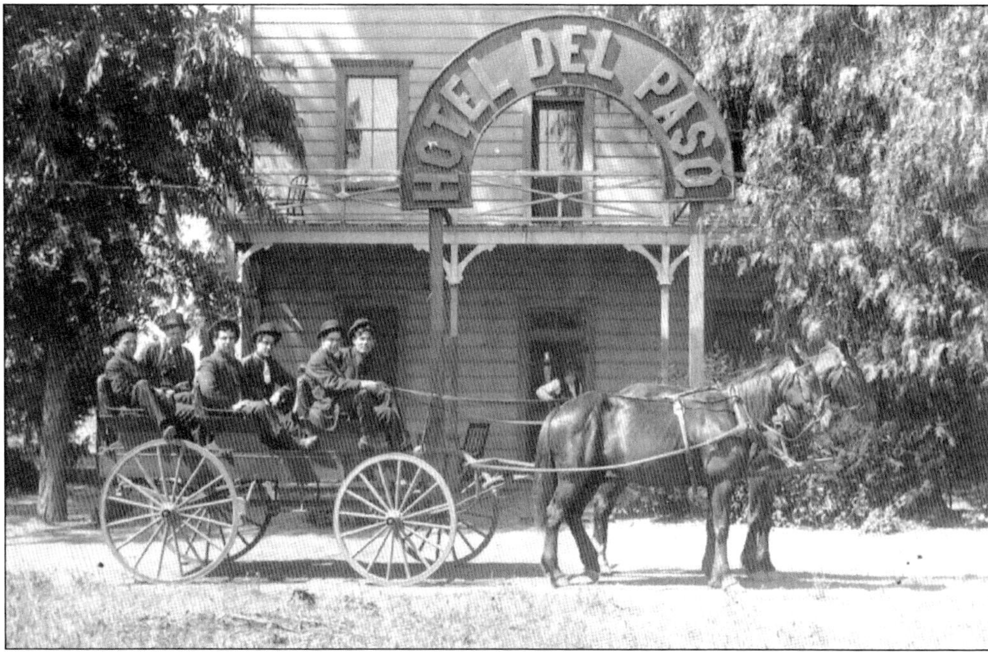

The Del Paso Hotel, seen here, was constructed in 1886, two years before the real estate bust. It was the second hotel built in Beaumont and was owned by Mrs. M. M. Fisher. Scenes like this were not uncommon around early hotels, because real estate speculators were rampant during the boom years, and they often treated their clientele like royalty, as seen here with a buggy tour. (Courtesy of Nara Haskell.)

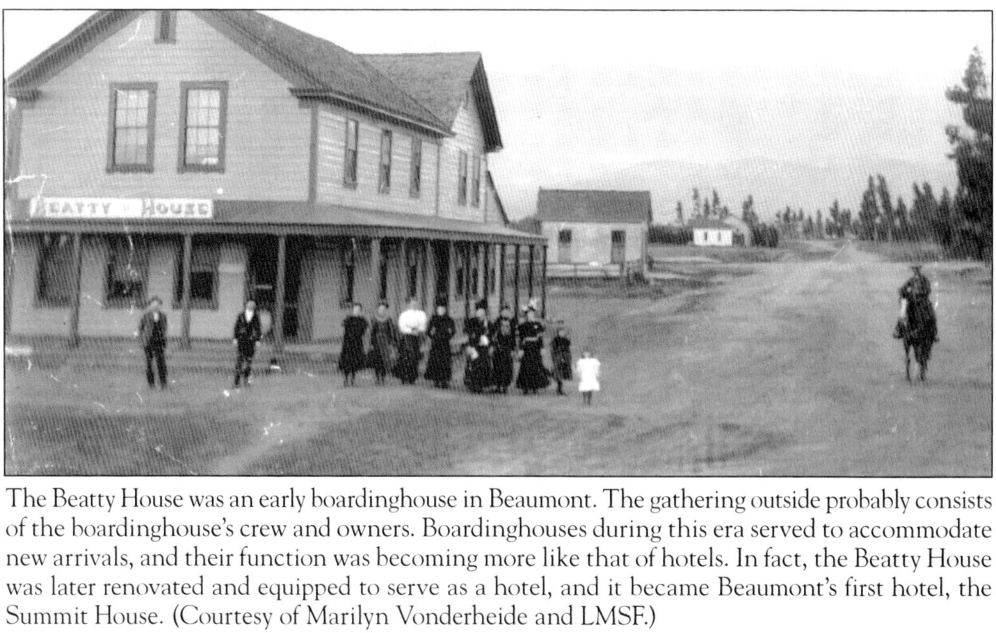
The Beatty House was an early boardinghouse in Beaumont. The gathering outside probably consists of the boardinghouse's crew and owners. Boardinghouses during this era served to accommodate new arrivals, and their function was becoming more like that of hotels. In fact, the Beatty House was later renovated and equipped to serve as a hotel, and it became Beaumont's first hotel, the Summit House. (Courtesy of Marilyn Vonderheide and LMSF.)

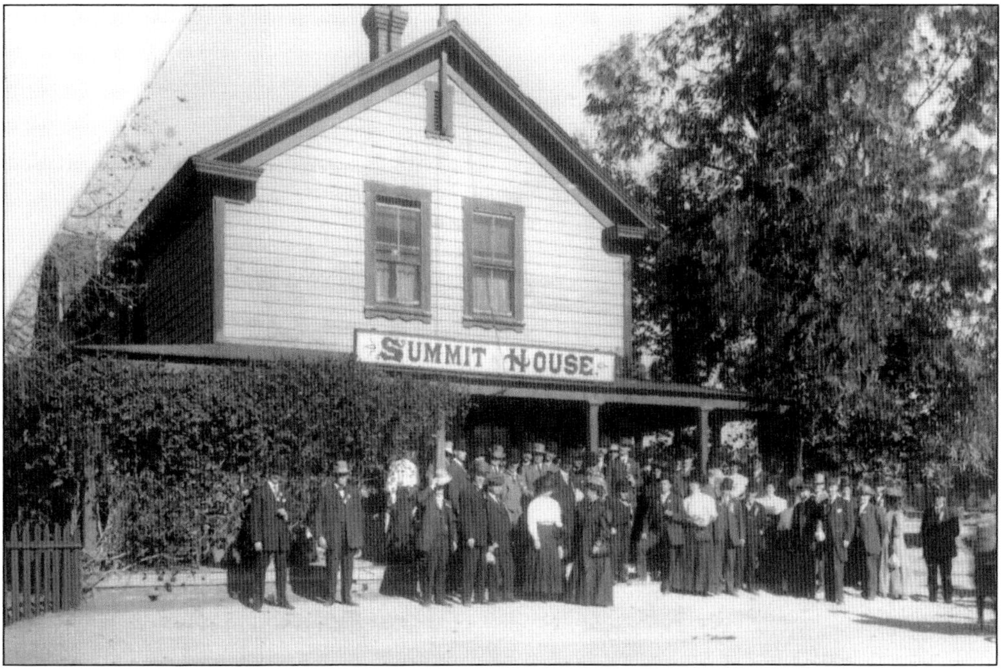

The Summit House was established in 1884 by Frank Mindler. It catered to large groups that needed lodging in Beaumont on special occasions. Seen here in front of the hotel are members of the Southern Editorial Association, who held their meeting there. Often Smoot and Eyer's prospective land buyers would also be housed there. (Courtesy of SGPHS.)

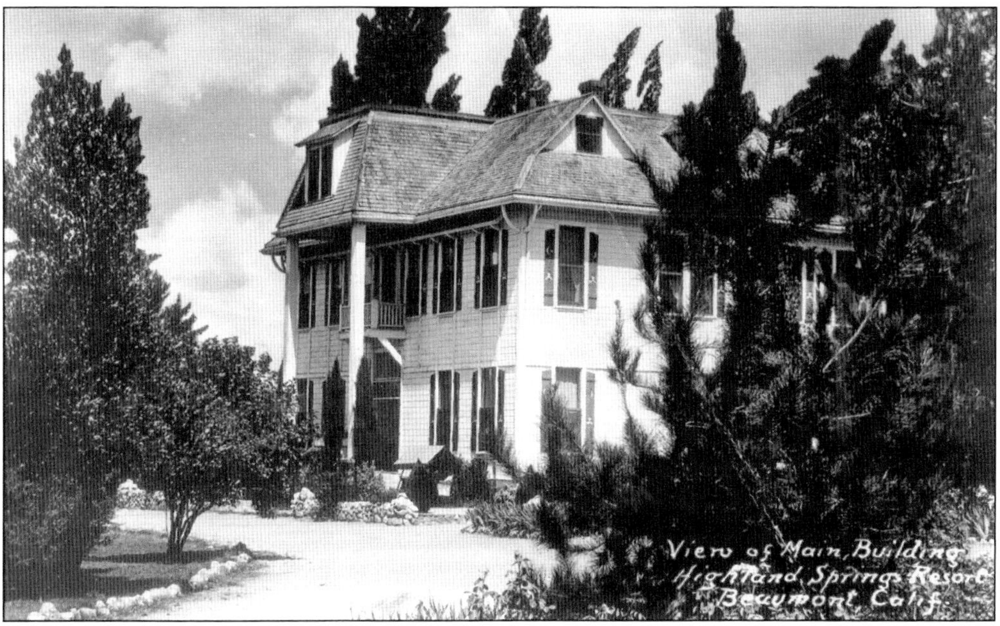

In 1884, Smith's Station, a stage stop in northeastern Beaumont, was bought by a company of capitalists. Seen here is the large three-story house they built. One of the owners, a man named Veile, opened it as the Highland Home Hotel. It was another important structure in Beaumont that was used to lure potential land buyers to the area. (Courtesy of Steve Lech.)

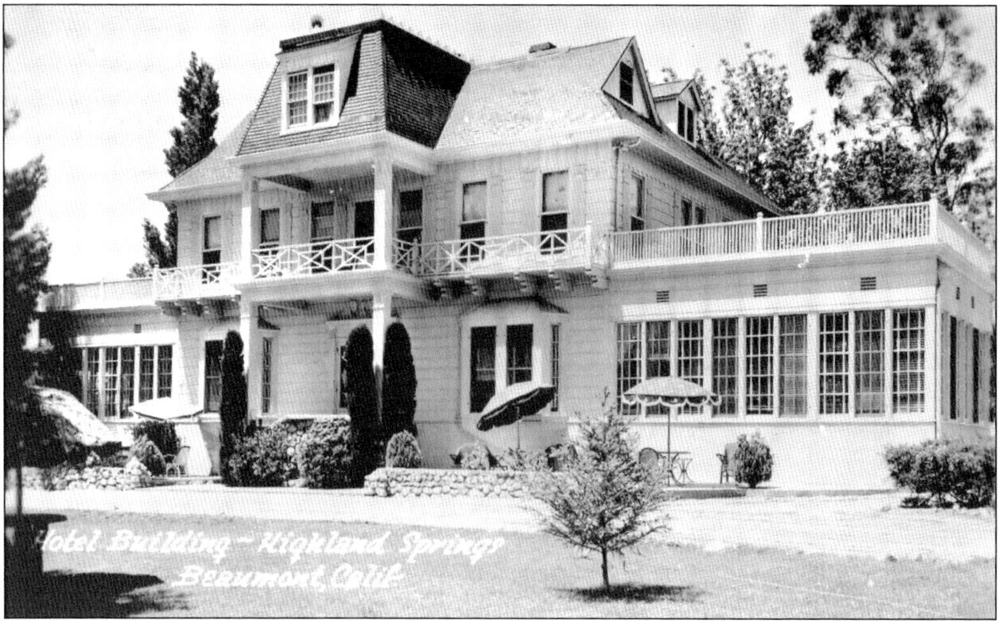

Around 1888, Palmer and Halliday of Santa Ana bought the Highland Home Hotel and proceeded to set out quite a large acreage of fruit trees. In 1921, the hotel was sold and renamed Highland Springs Hotel. It is seen here after it was refurbished with an addition built on both its right and left sides. It since has burned down. (Courtesy of Steve Lech.)

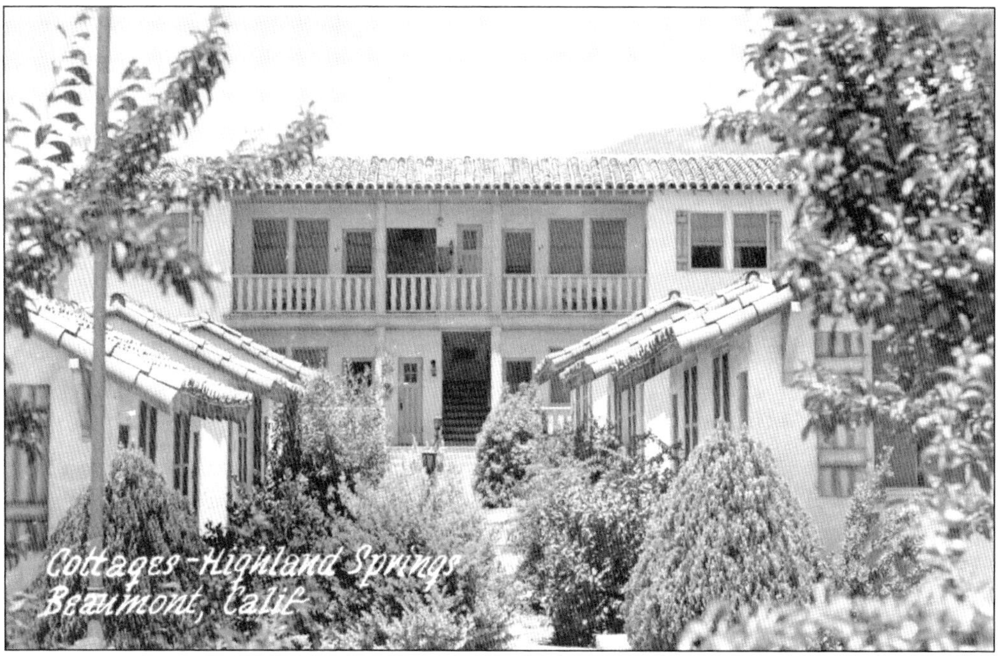

This is a group of cottages that still stand on the old grounds of the Highland Springs Hotel even though the hotel is gone. Highland Springs was a popular place, and many even came here from great distances. The cottages were deemed a necessity in order to accommodate the visiting crowds. Highland Springs remains a popular resort today. (Courtesy of Steve Lech.)

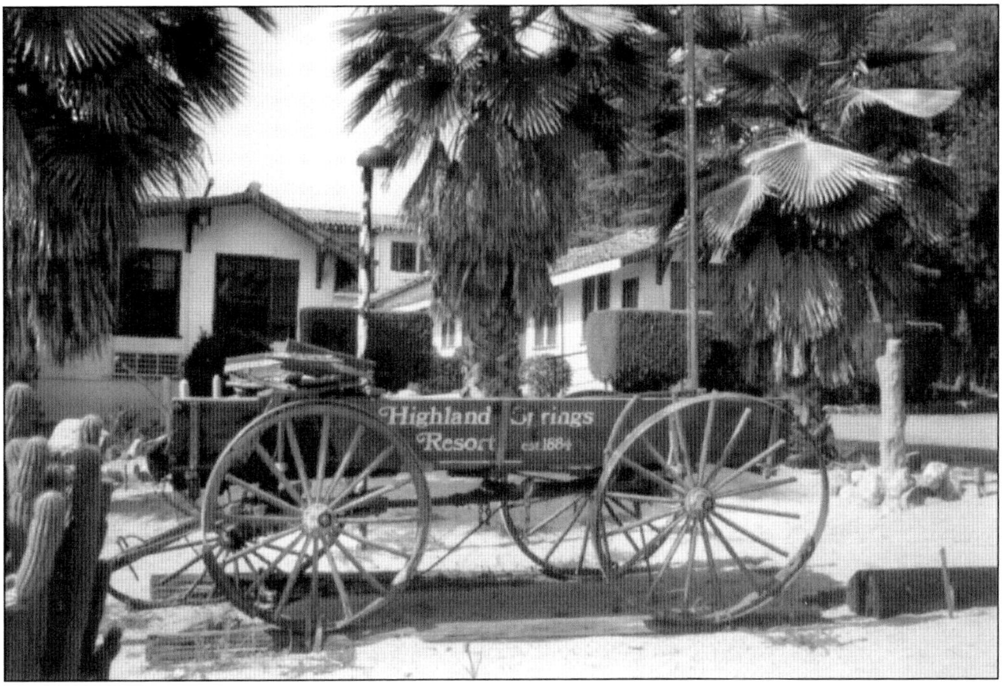

Behind this old buggy advertising the Highland Springs Resort, several of the resort's bungalows can be seen. Some tourists come here to visit and vacation, and others come to attend the conferences that are sometimes held at the resort's facilities. The essence of the park is its splendor, the 100-year-old pines, and its history, which dates back to 1884. (Courtesy of authors.)

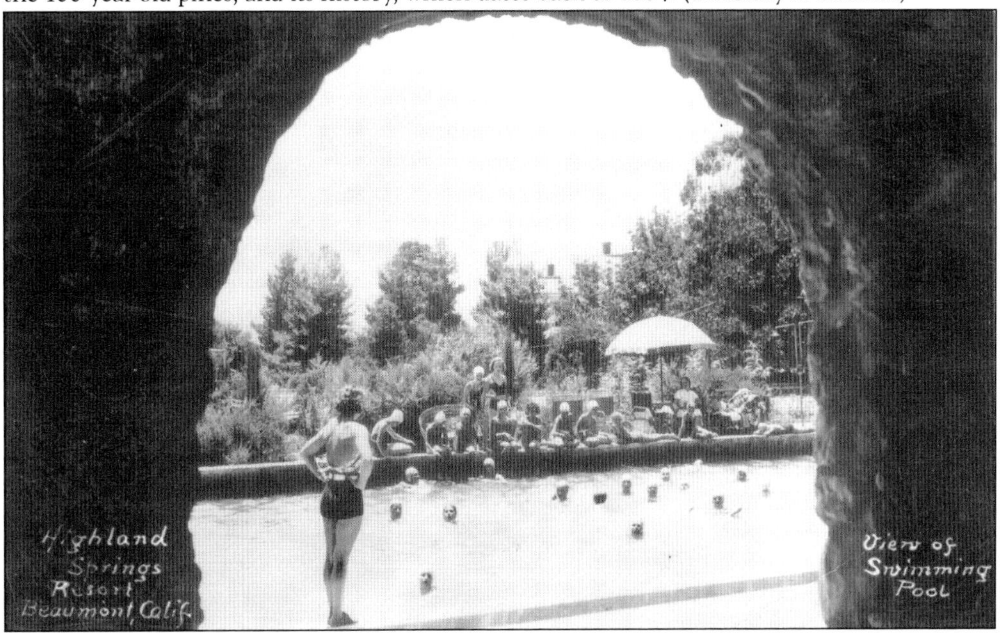

This is an early view of the swimming pool at the Highland Springs Hotel, which is occupied by a large group of ladies that appears to be doing a regimented pool activity. Seen through the arch of the pool building, it is certainly apparent how popular the pool was at Highland Springs Resort. (Courtesy of Steve Lech.)

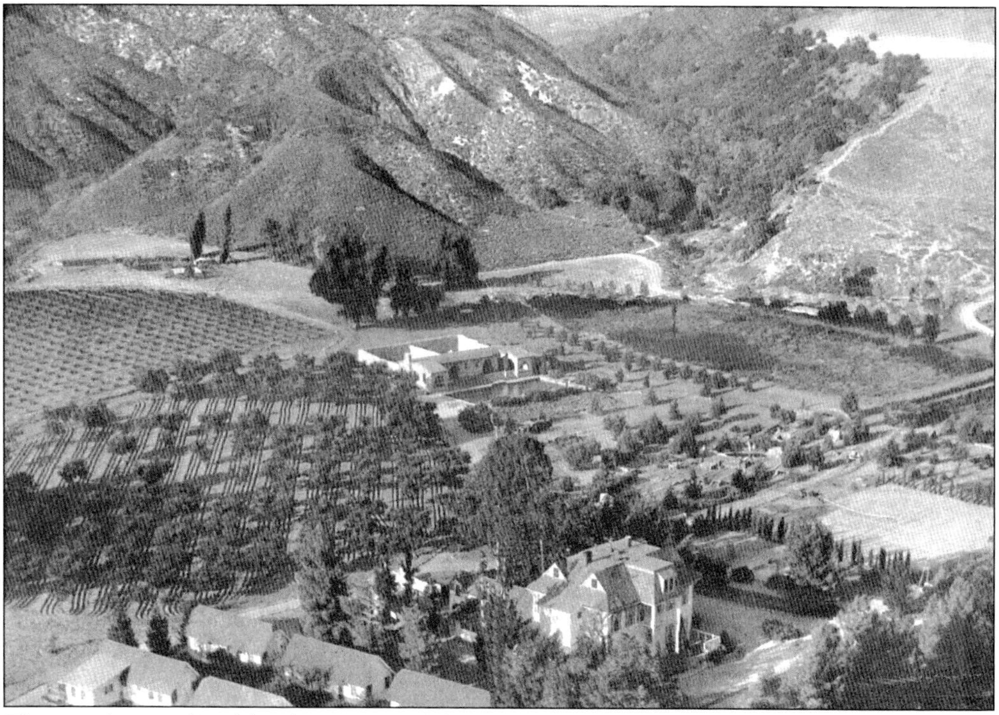

This aerial view of Highland Home Hotel shows the area sometime after 1888, when Palmer and Halliday had already bought it. The pool, which is surrounded with fruit trees planted by the new owners, can easily be seen in the center of the photograph. The fine fruits obtained from these orchards were so choice that they were awarded a prize at the World's Fair in Chicago in 1893. (Courtesy of Steve Lech.)

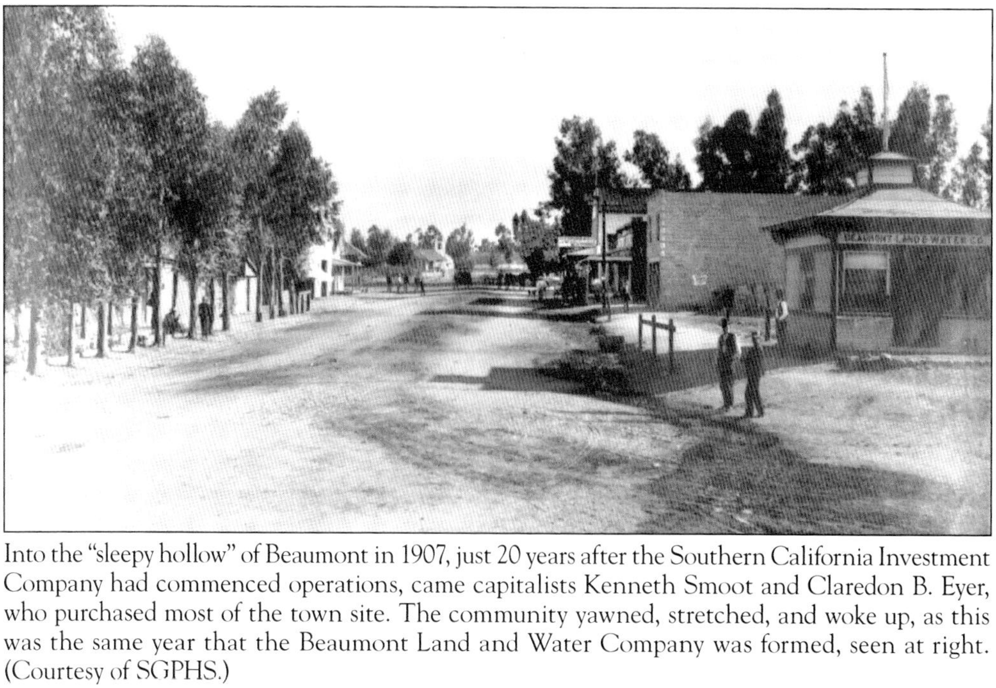

Into the "sleepy hollow" of Beaumont in 1907, just 20 years after the Southern California Investment Company had commenced operations, came capitalists Kenneth Smoot and Claredon B. Eyer, who purchased most of the town site. The community yawned, stretched, and woke up, as this was the same year that the Beaumont Land and Water Company was formed, seen at right. (Courtesy of SGPHS.)

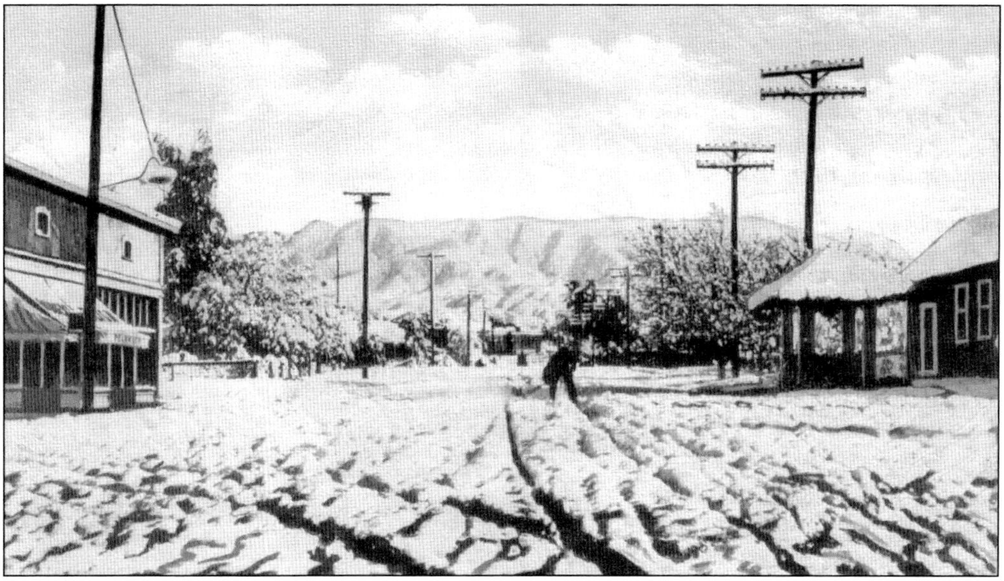

This is an early snow scene in Beaumont. The canopy-type roof on the early Land and Water Company building at right denotes its meager beginning. It was originally formed to acquire water and lure back land sales. Shortly after Smoot and Eyer arrived, they not only purchased most of town site but also approximately 3,500 acres north of town. (Courtesy of Nara Haskell.)

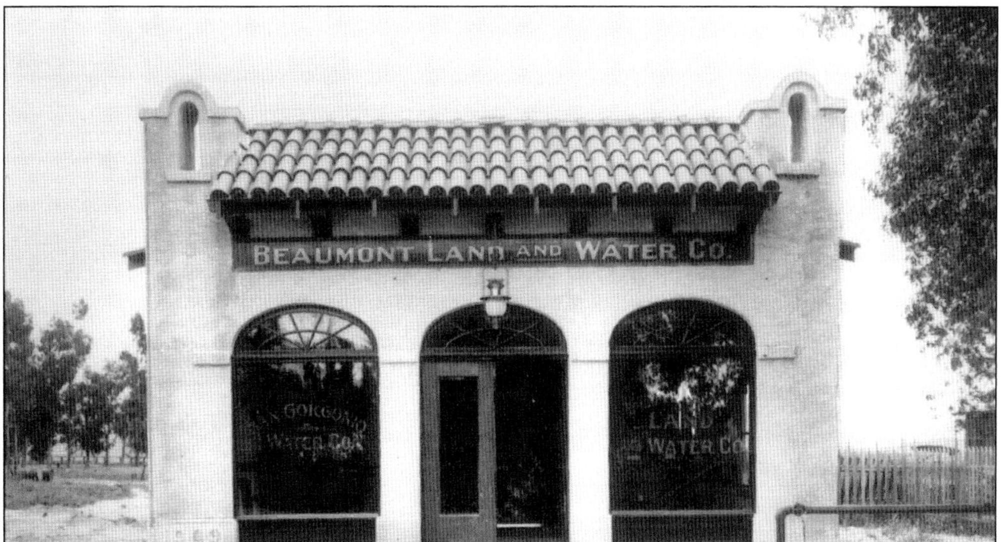

Around a decade after the bust of 1888, real estate began to recover. This is an image of the new, attractive water company building that Kenneth Smoot and Claredon Eyer built, with Smoot becoming president. After an unsuccessful attempt to develop the town by an earlier entrepreneur, the two were determined to succeed. They were not dismayed by the bugaboo of "no water," which had prevented other capitalists from investing in Beaumont. (Courtesy of SGPHS.)

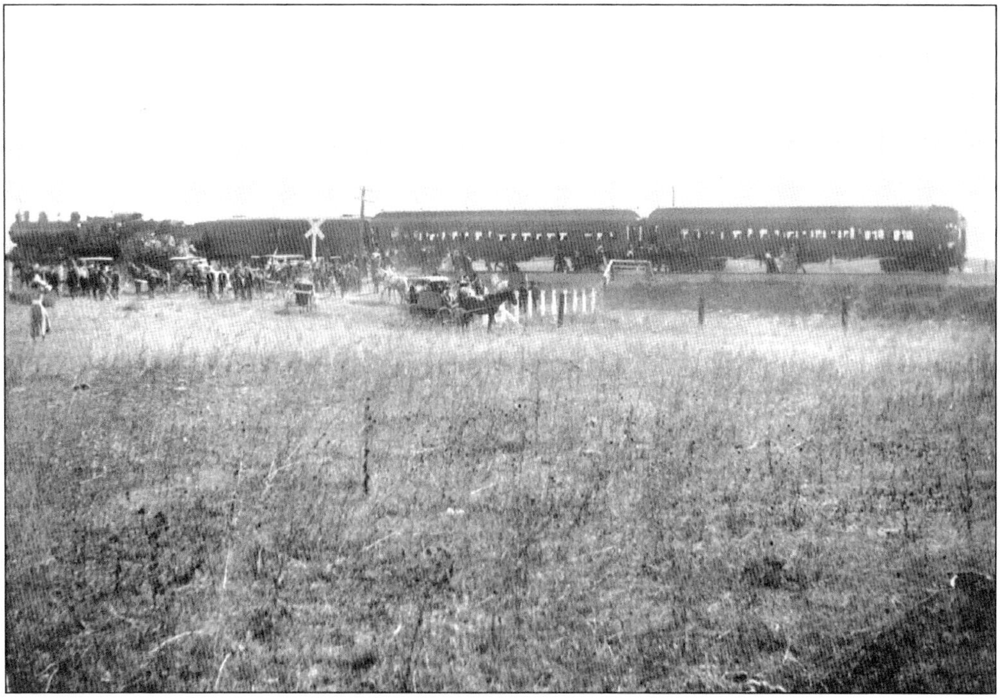

This photograph depicts a Los Angeles, three-car excursion train that was occasionally rented by Smoot and Eyer to bring potential land buyers to Beaumont. Horse-and-buggies are seen leaving the train site loaded with interested land buyers. They were taken to the locations where land was sold and even given a barbecue for lunch. (Courtesy of Nara Haskell.)

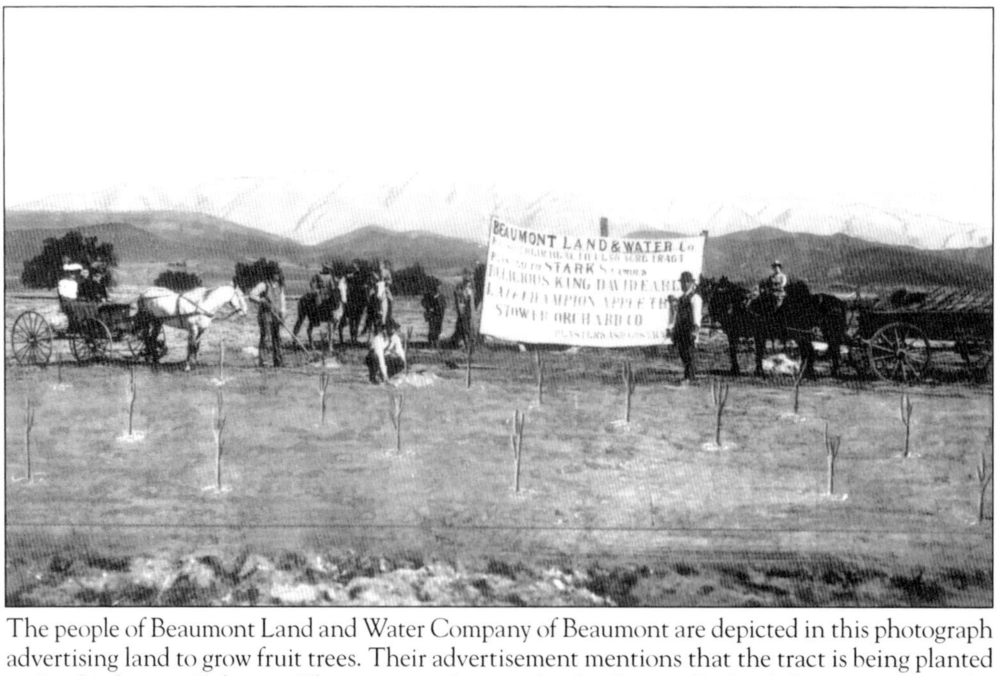

The people of Beaumont Land and Water Company of Beaumont are depicted in this photograph advertising land to grow fruit trees. Their advertisement mentions that the tract is being planted to Stark's famous Delicious Champion apple trees by the Stover Orchard Company. Note the young apple trees that have been planted in the foreground. (Courtesy of SGPHS.)

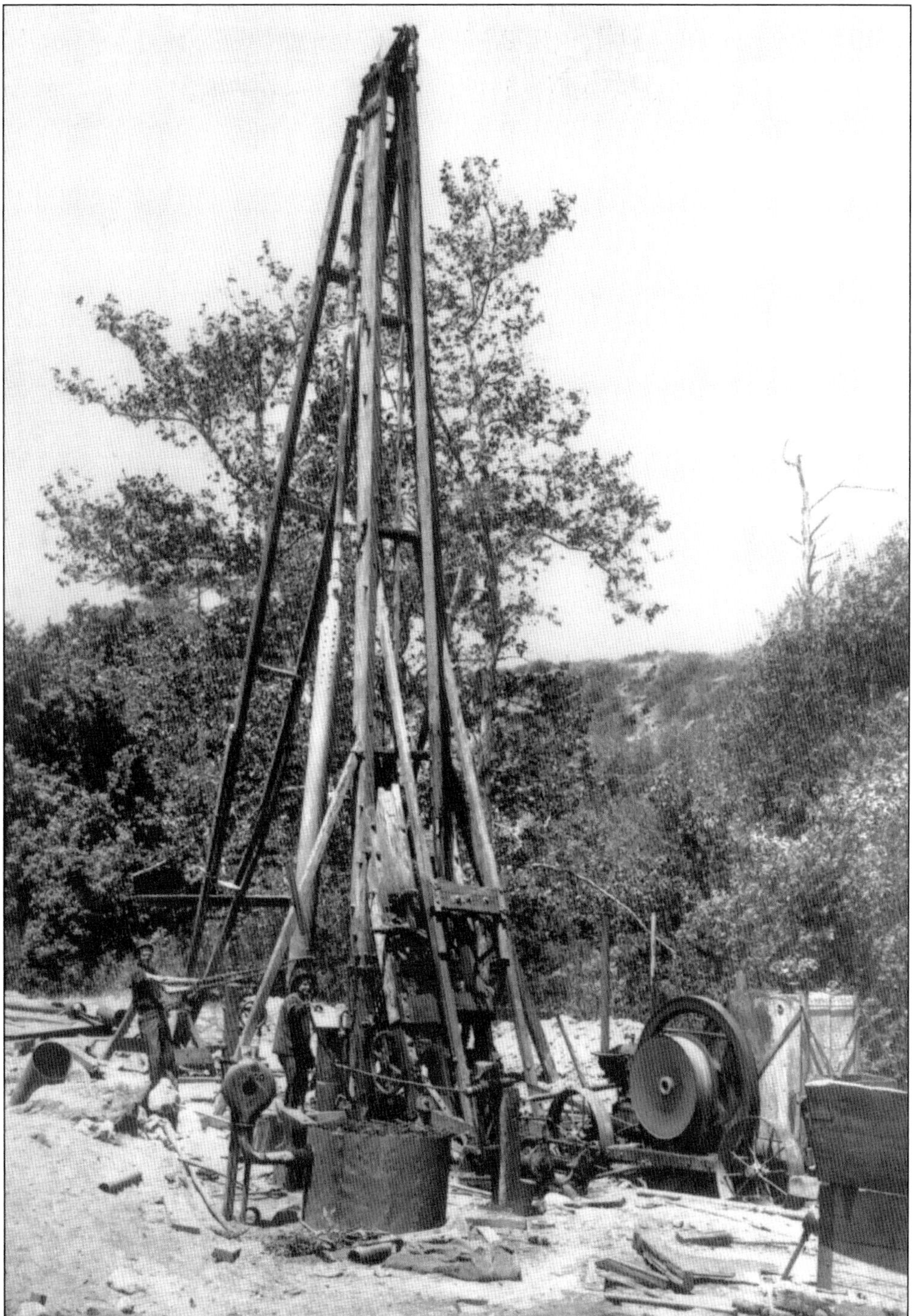

At the beginning of the 20th century, water-well drilling was quite a chore due to the fact that there was no sophisticated well-drilling equipment as there is today. Seen here is a wood-constructed derrick used in Edgar Canyon for drilling for water. Although rather crude compared with today's equipment, it did get the job done. (Courtesy of SGPHS.)

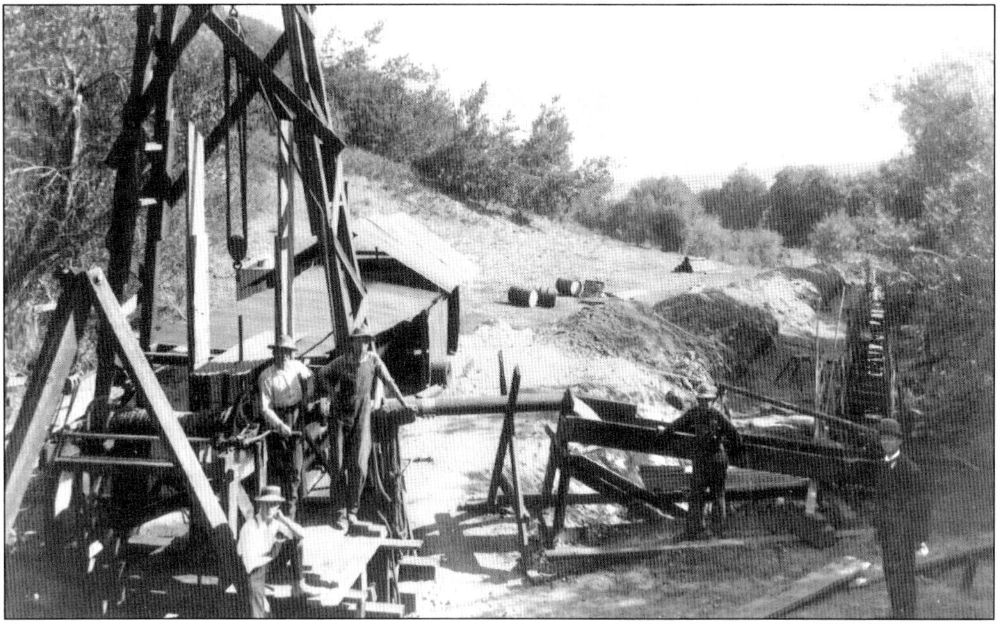

The Beaumont Land and Water Company drilled water well No. 2 in 1908 in Edgar Canyon north of Beaumont. It was 346 feet deep and 12 inches in diameter. This photograph depicts the workers proudly exhibiting the flow of water brought forth from their labors. They were happy for this one, because the first well was drilled in the valley and was unsuccessful. This venture promoted relocation of the drilling operation to Edgar Canyon. (Courtesy of SGPHS.)

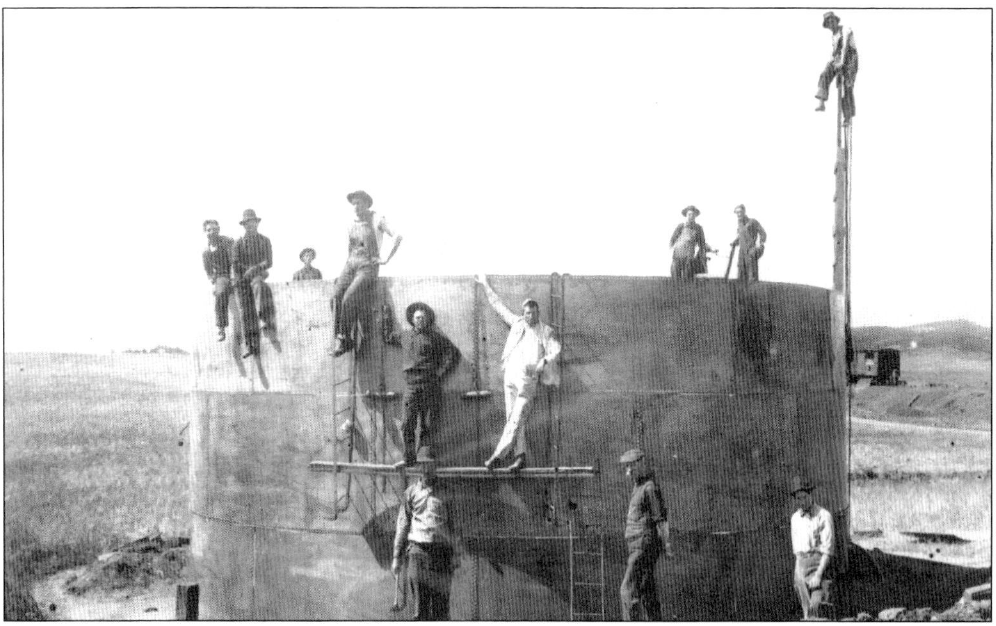

It can readily be seen that water was quite available in Edgar Canyon. By use of a Weir gate, water could be directed into a flume for transport to Beaumont or either routed to a nearby reservoir for storage. Ample water was an important consideration for buying farmland in the area. Shown here are a group of anxious workmen awaiting the first flow of water to their new tank. (Courtesy of Nara Haskell.)

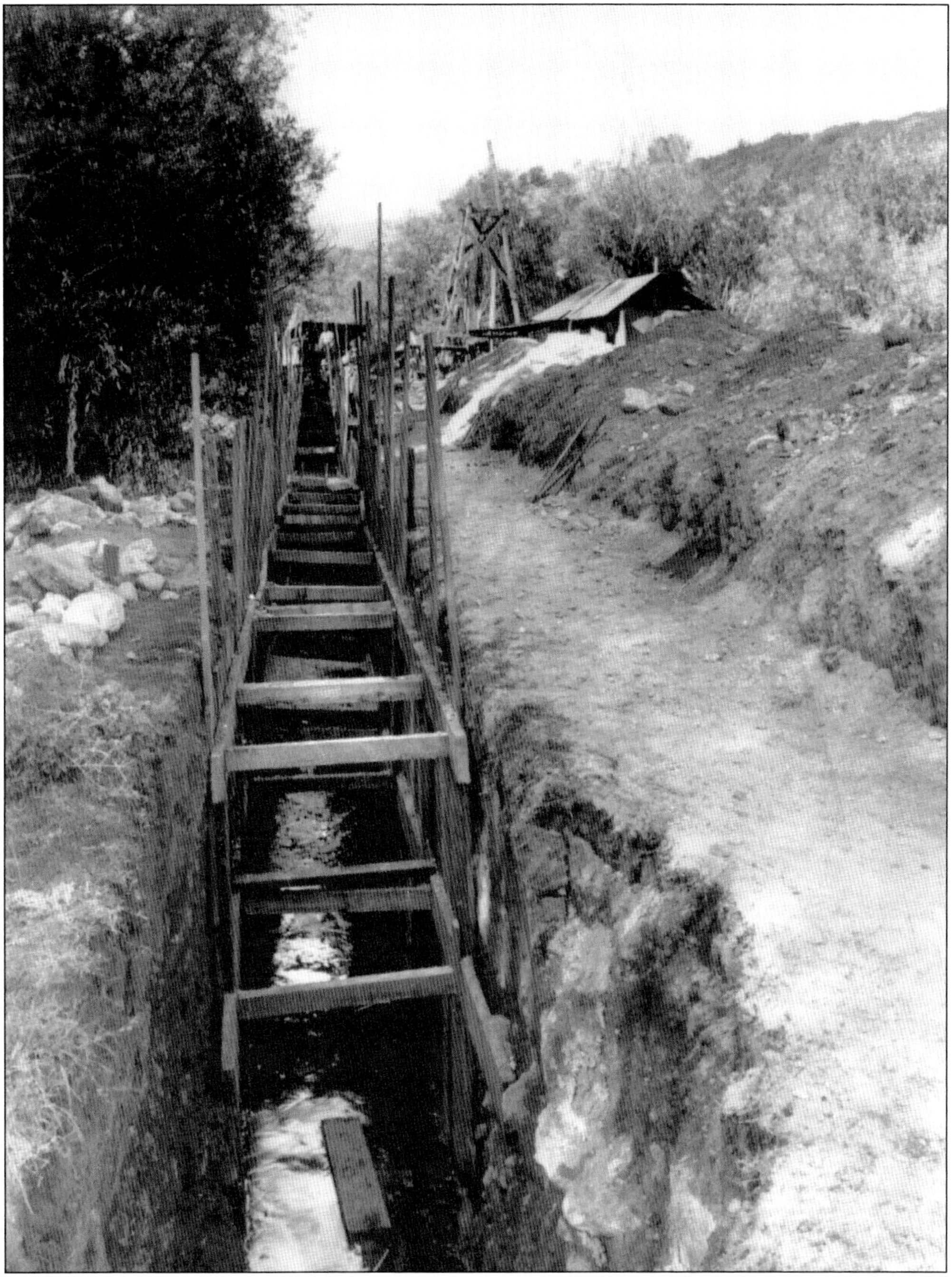

When well No. 2 was sunk north of Beaumont, it produced an adequate supply of water to the town, and a canal flume was built to bring it to Beaumont. The complexity of such an undertaking involved shoring up the canal wall, as can be seen in this photograph. (Courtesy of SGPHS.)

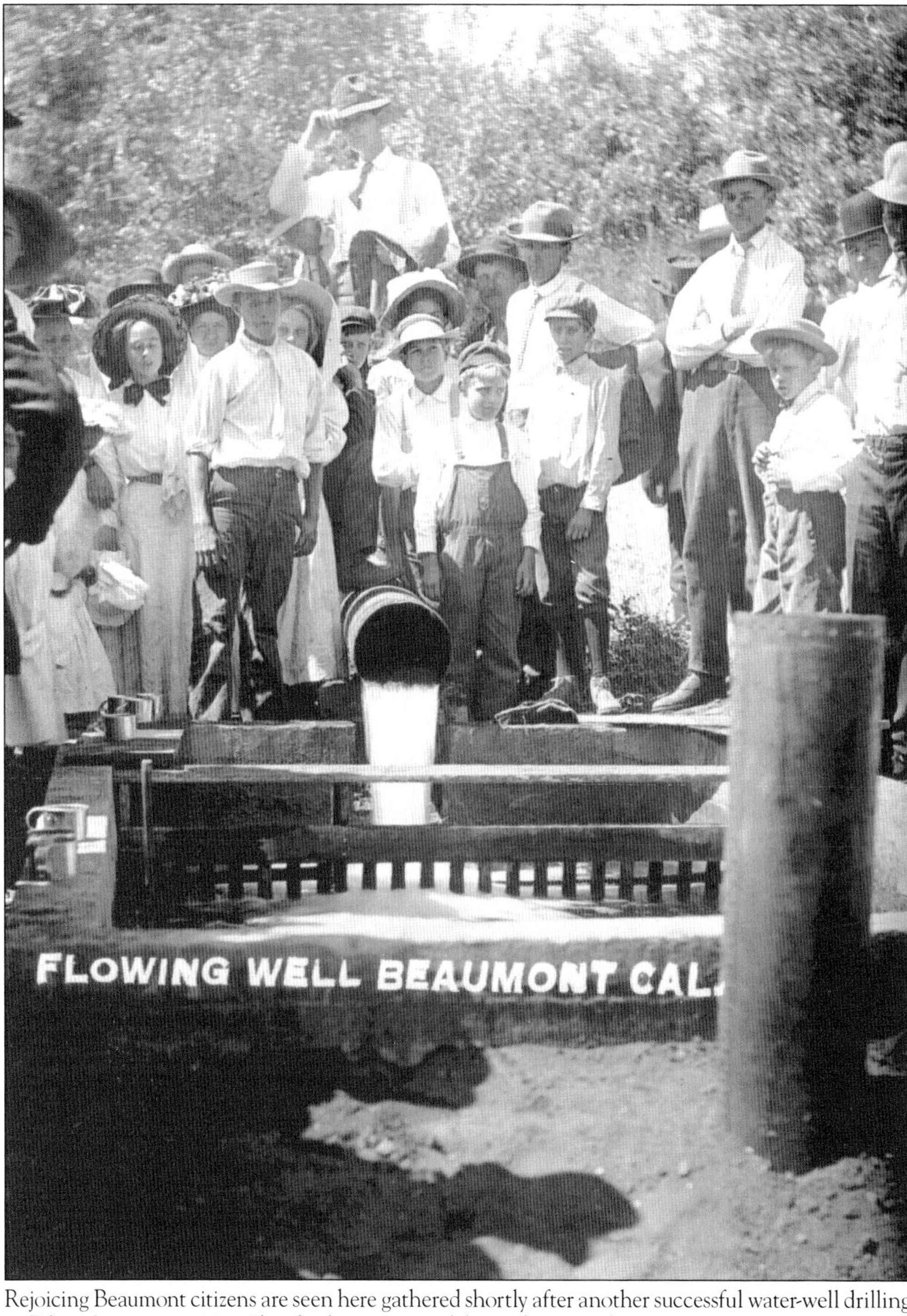

Rejoicing Beaumont citizens are seen here gathered shortly after another successful water-well drilling in Edgar Canyon in 1908. They had reason to celebrate, because this event guaranteed more water for their town. It flowed from the well pipe and was fed directly into a flume that brought water down the canyon either into a holding reservoir, where it was stored, or into another flume to be directed to Beaumont. Four more wells would follow. (Courtesy of Nara Haskell.)

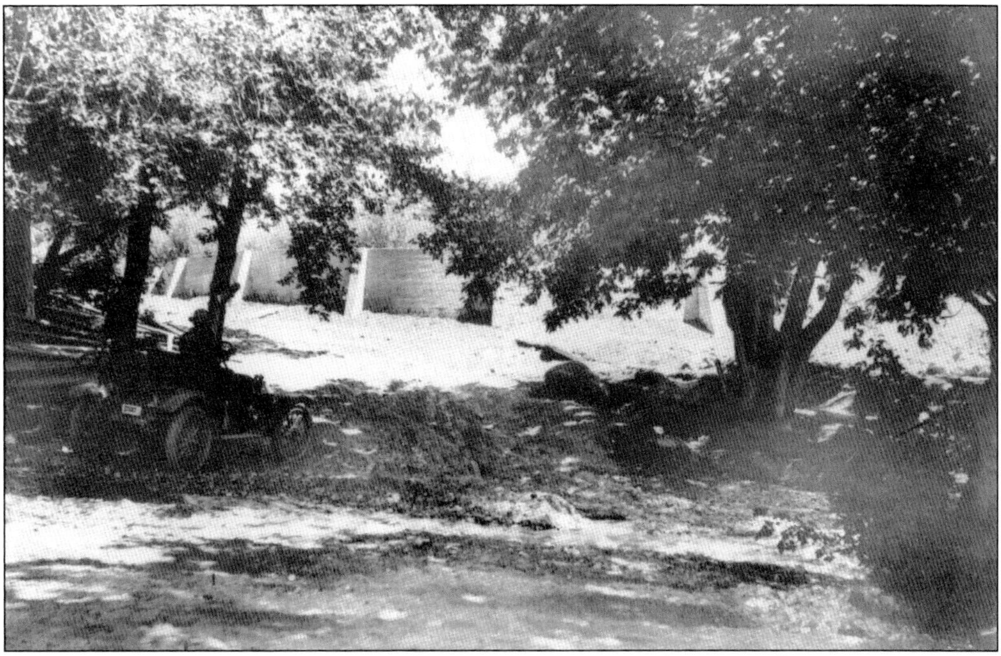

Seen here shielded behind the trees is the reservoir, constructed in 1911, where water was stored in Edgar Canyon after it was brought down from the wells on higher ground. The Beaumont Land and Water Company assured prospective real estate buyers that water was available for farming and could verify this fact when they brought them here to see it firsthand. (Courtesy of Nara Haskell.)

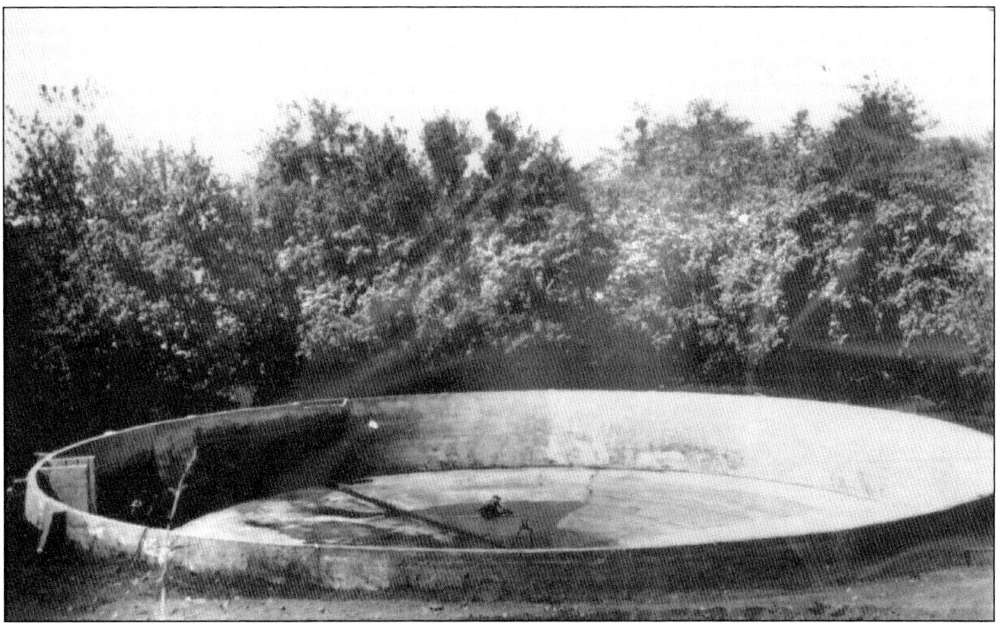

This photograph was taken of the 1911 Edgar Canyon Reservoir looking down from above. The size of the reservoir can be seen, and the small image of a man sitting in the center exemplifies the large volume of water it could contain. Beaumont, like Banning, relied on reservoirs to store water. (Courtesy of Nara Haskell.)

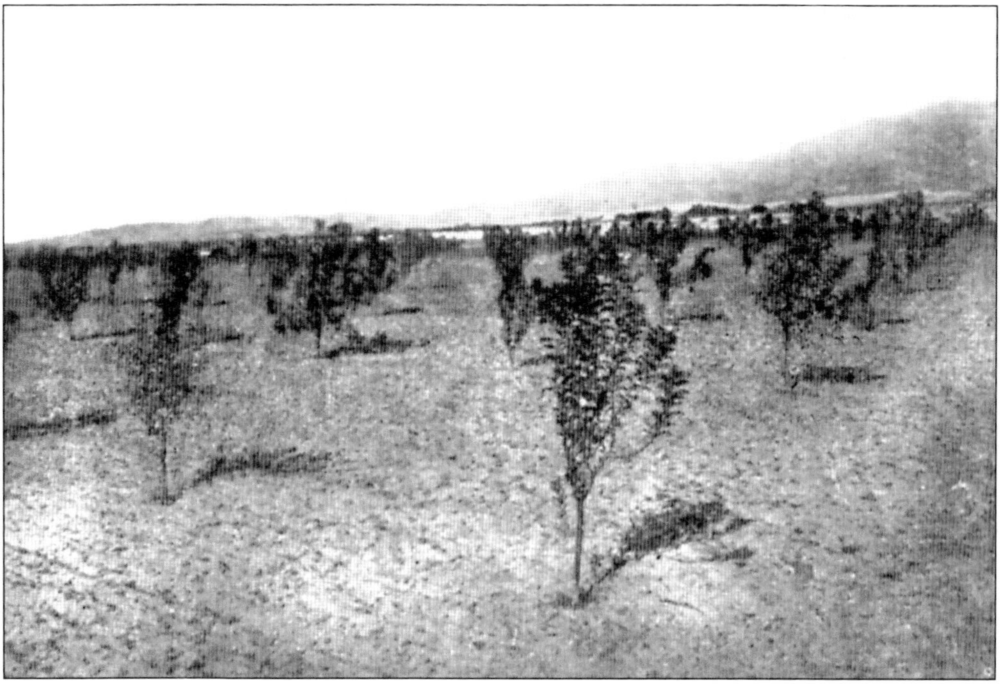

This young apple orchard is just one of many that were coming into production in the northern acreages of Beaumont after planting started to accelerate. Apples were the most popular fruit grown in the early years of production; however, cherries, peaches, and plums subsequently were grown as well. (Courtesy of Steve Lech.)

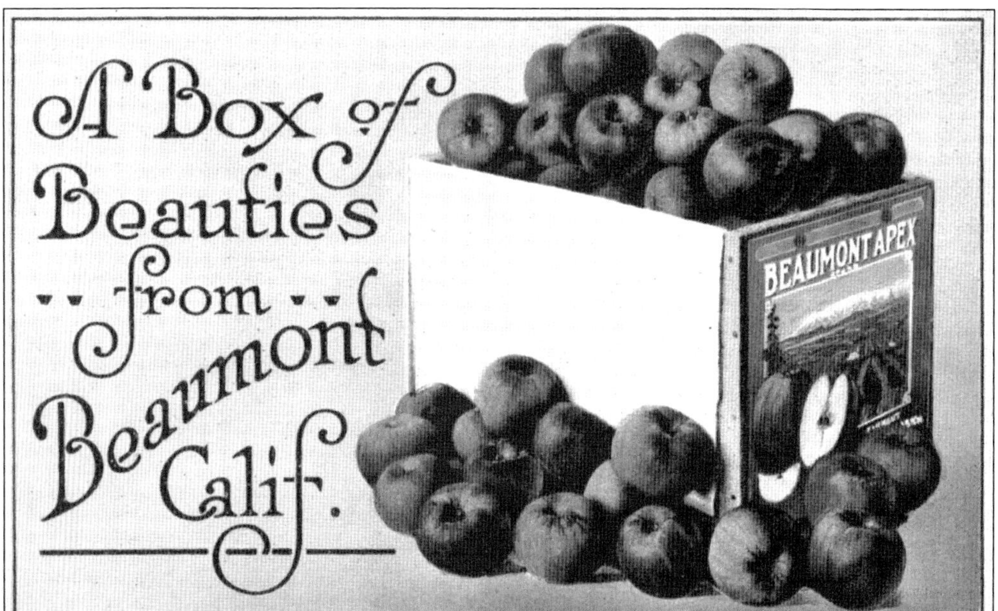

Beaumont became a well-known grower of apples and cherries. This is an advertisement of one of Beaumont's popular apple brands, Beaumont Apex. Fruit grown here was once awarded a prize in the World's Fair in Chicago and became recognized quite extensively. (Courtesy of Steve Lech.)

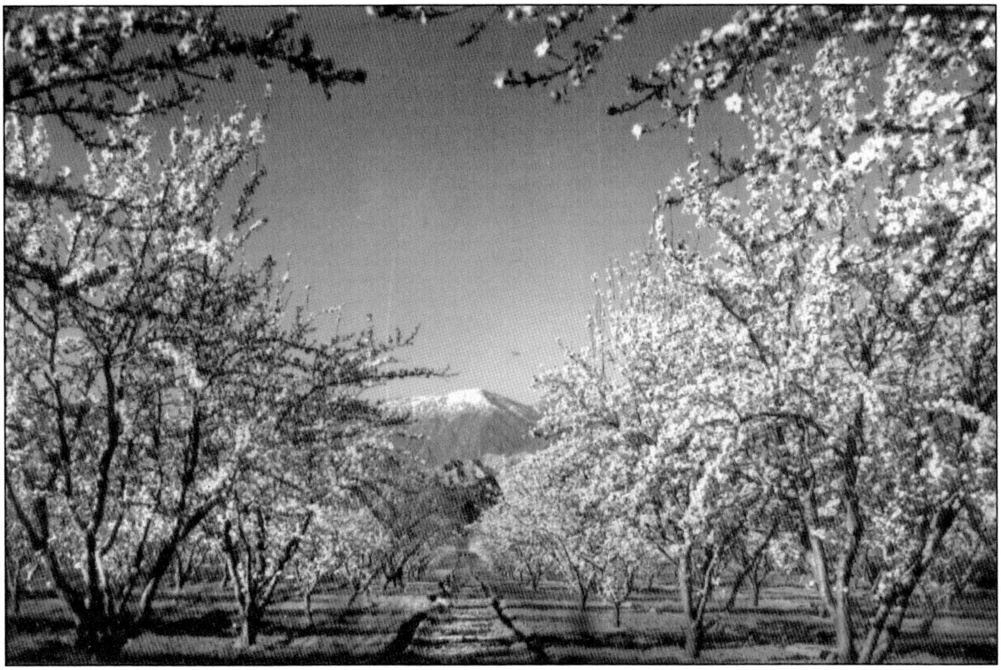

The orchard in bloom in this photograph of Edgar Rancho, north of Beaumont, was not an uncommon sight, as growing fruit was becoming a large-scale operation in the valley. It was estimated that there were over a 1,000 new trees planted in the area, excluding the old orchards. Many of the new trees were of varieties of apples. (Courtesy of Norman McGary.)

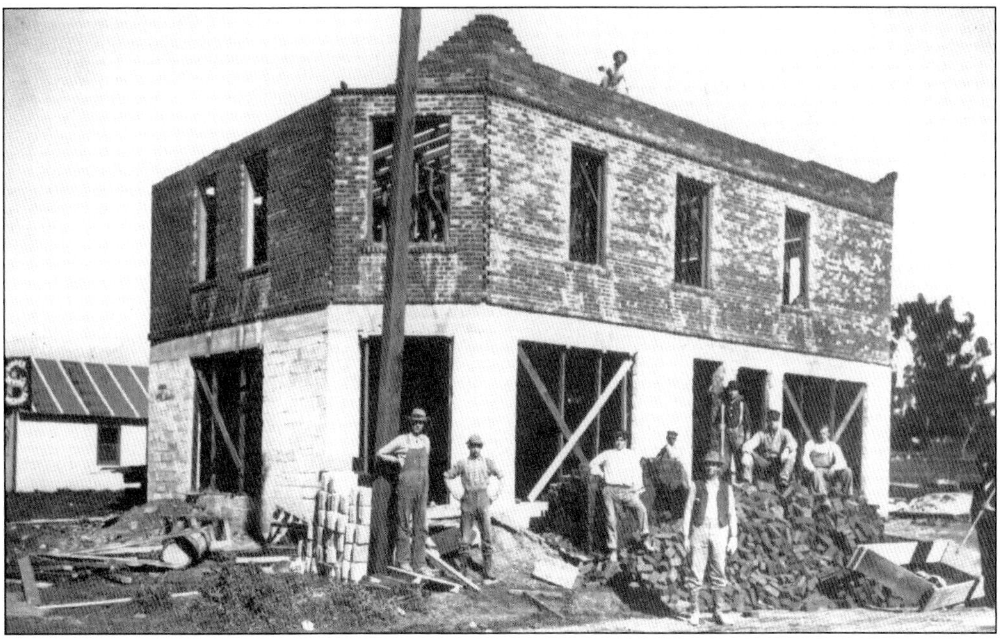

Before the beginning of the 20th century, the acreage at Highland Springs was bought by Palmer and Halliday of Santa Ana, who planted acres of fruit trees, including olives, cherries, peaches, and grapes. This and other ventures in Beaumont spurred the need for a bank. Seen here is the first bank in Beaumont, under construction in 1909. (Courtesy of Nara Haskell.)

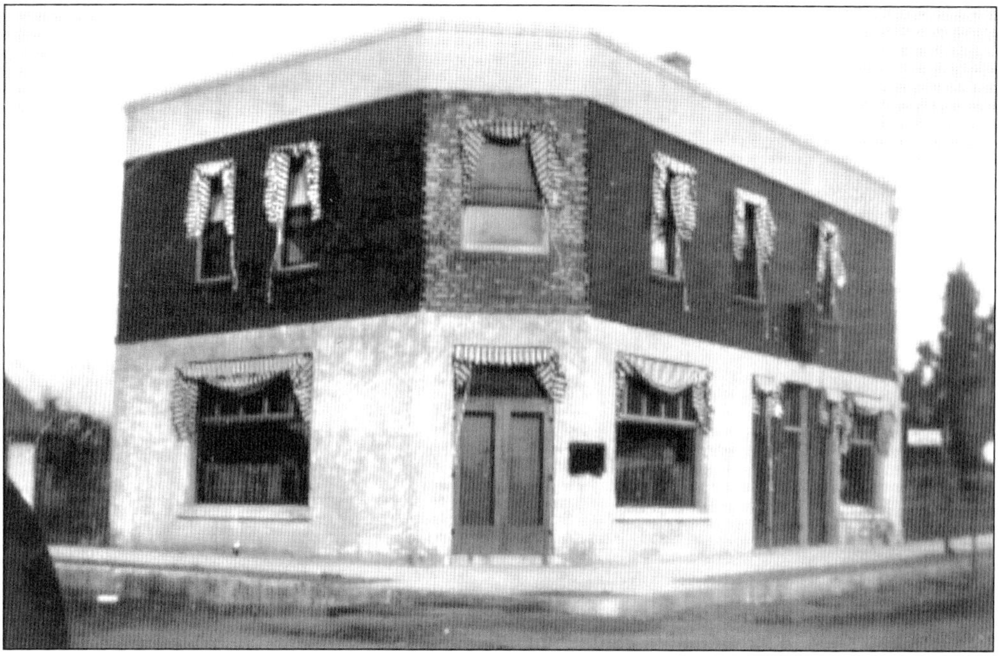

In 1910, just three years after the Beaumont Land and Water Company took over, the population of Beaumont reached 1,100, and establishment of a bank became inevitable. The first bank of Beaumont was built on the southeast corner of California Avenue and Fifth Street, as seen here. It was founded in 1909 and by 1911 was in full operation. Reznor Stewart was one of its founders and its president for several years. (Courtesy of Marilyn Vonderheide and LMSF.)

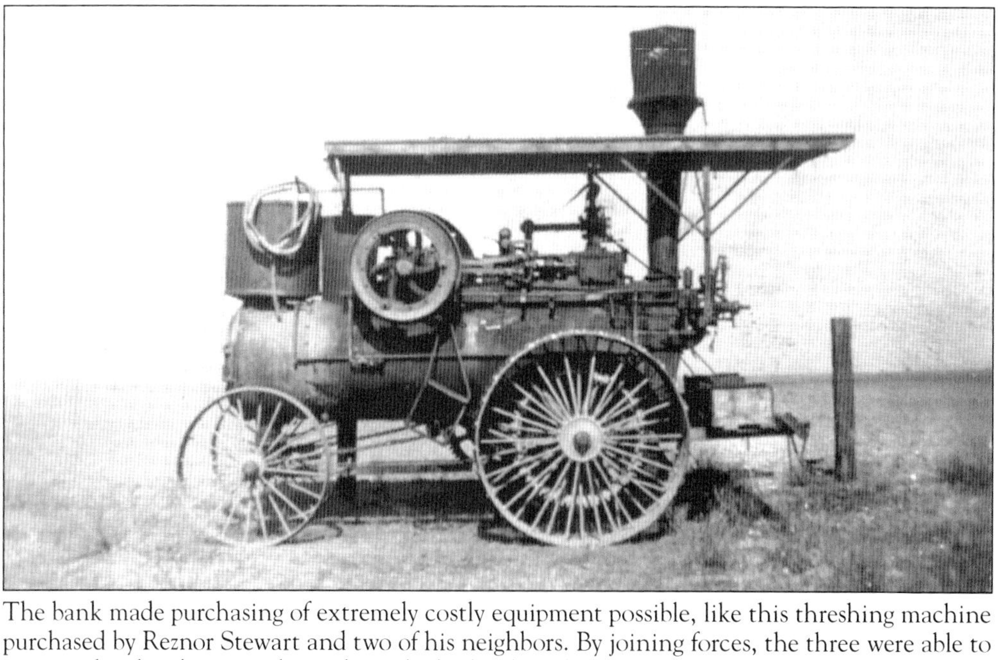

The bank made purchasing of extremely costly equipment possible, like this threshing machine purchased by Reznor Stewart and two of his neighbors. By joining forces, the three were able to acquire the threshing machine through the bank and also obtain other expensive equipment that was desperately needed to harvest barley grown on a large scale. (Courtesy of Marilyn Vonderheide and LMSF.)

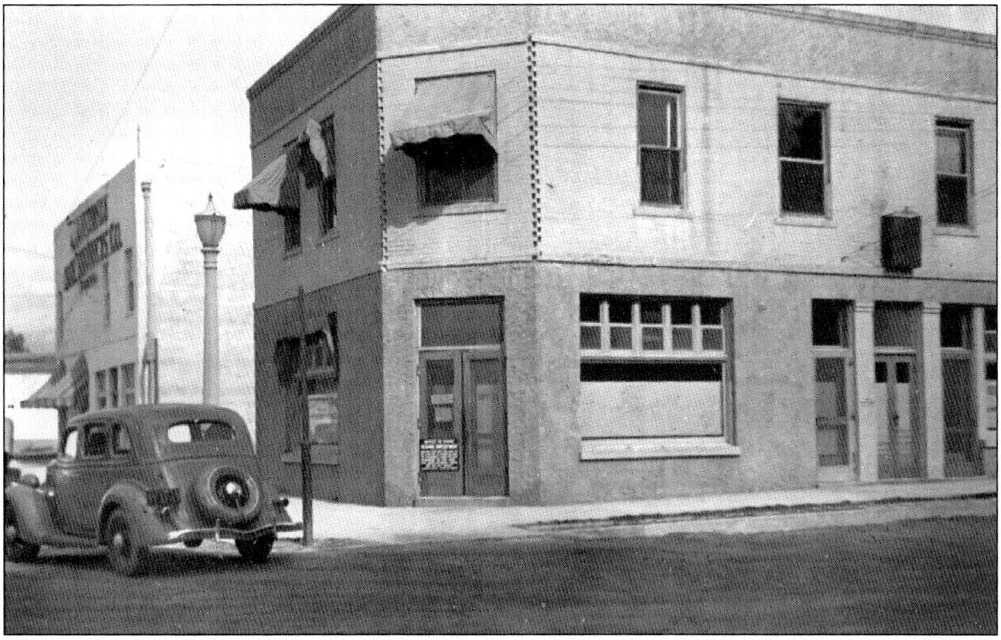

The second bank of Beaumont was built in 1923 at a new location on the northeast corner of Egan Avenue and Fifth Street and became the new home of Beaumont Bank, which previously was housed in the first bank building on the southeast corner of California Avenue and Fifth Street. As indicated here, the first bank building eventually was occupied by another business. Notable is the 1936 Ford sedan, which dates the building to over a decade after the second bank was constructed in 1923. (Courtesy of SGPHS.)

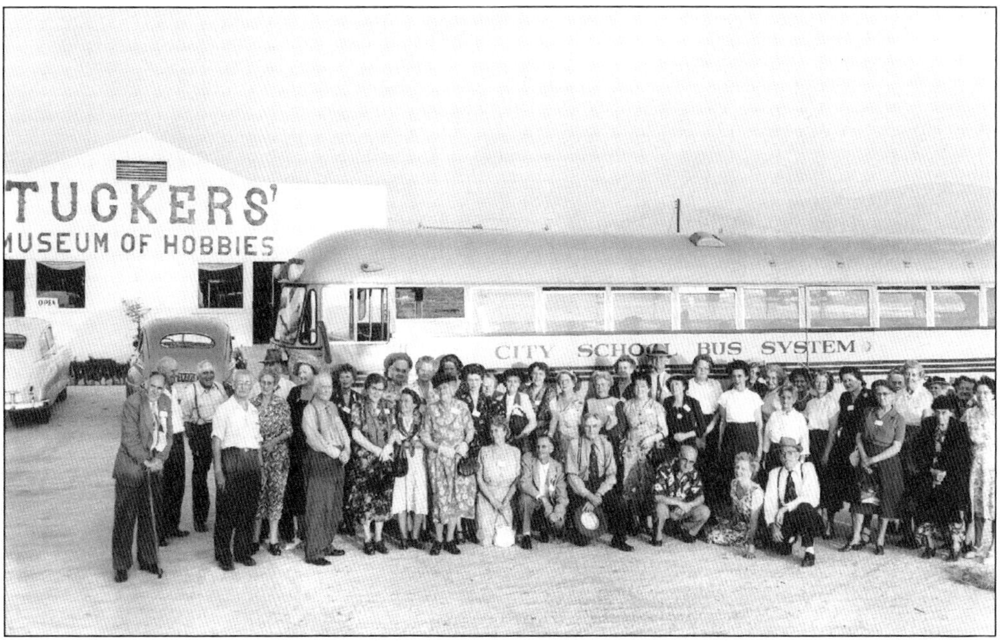

It is evident from this photograph of a large group of visitors that Tuckers' Museum of Hobbies in Beaumont was an active site. It is interesting to observe that Beaumont pioneer Guy Bogart is among the group, standing fourth from the left with his wife at his side. (Courtesy of SGPHS.)

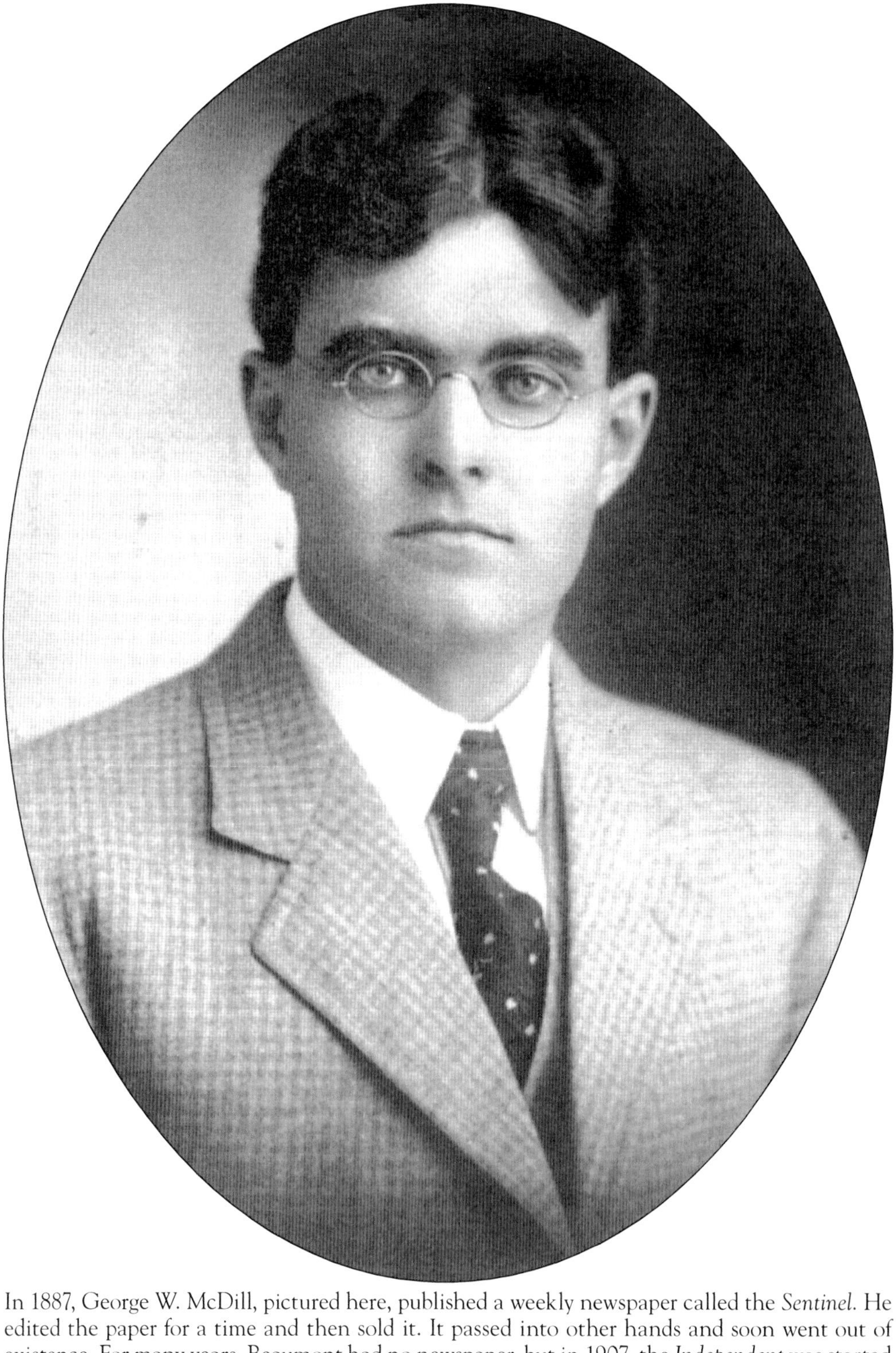

In 1887, George W. McDill, pictured here, published a weekly newspaper called the *Sentinel*. He edited the paper for a time and then sold it. It passed into other hands and soon went out of existence. For many years, Beaumont had no newspaper, but in 1907, the *Independent* was started but only had a brief existence. (Courtesy of Nara Haskell.)

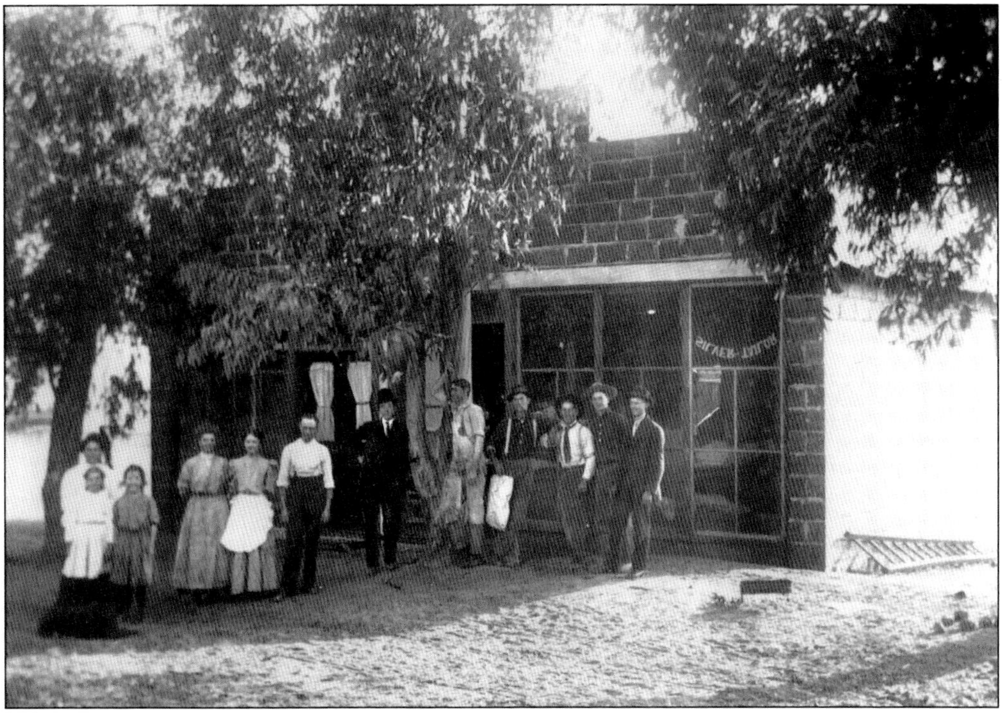

It was not until 1908 that the *Gateway Gazette*, with Arthur J. Burdick as editor, was established. In front of the *Gateway Gazette* Building is the *Gateway* staff gathered for this photograph in 1911, several years after it was started. In 1909, another paper, the *Beaumont Leader*, was first published. Two weeklies later followed. (Courtesy of Nara Haskell.)

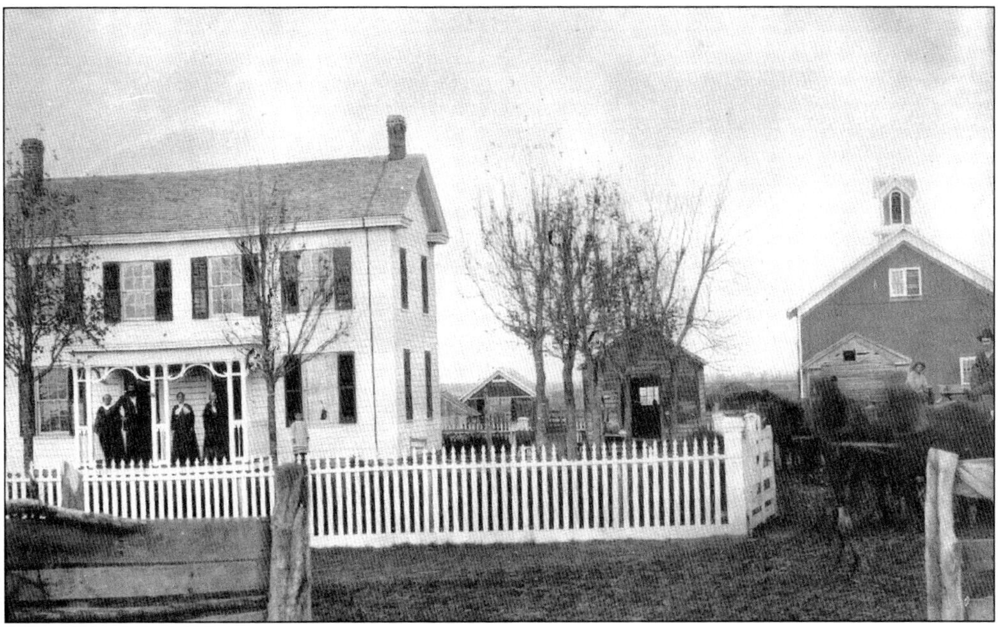

This is the Martin family ranch house that was located where the Peacock Valley subdivision is today. Family members pose on the porch. Note the two-horse buggy leaving through the open gate at right. (Courtesy of Nara Haskell.)

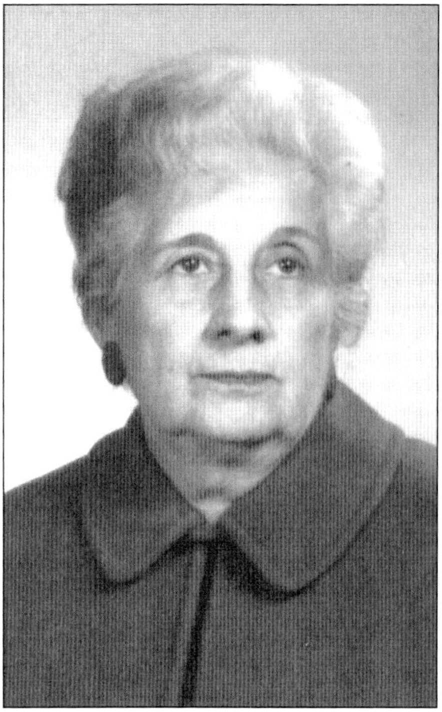

During Beaumont's early development, George Egan had a post office in his store and was Beaumont's first postmaster, although a man named Lamb unofficially handled the residents' mail, which was thrown off the trains for a short time before Egan's appointment. This is a portrait of Ellen Martin, who later became Beaumont's postmistress and held the position for many years. (Courtesy of Nara Haskell.)

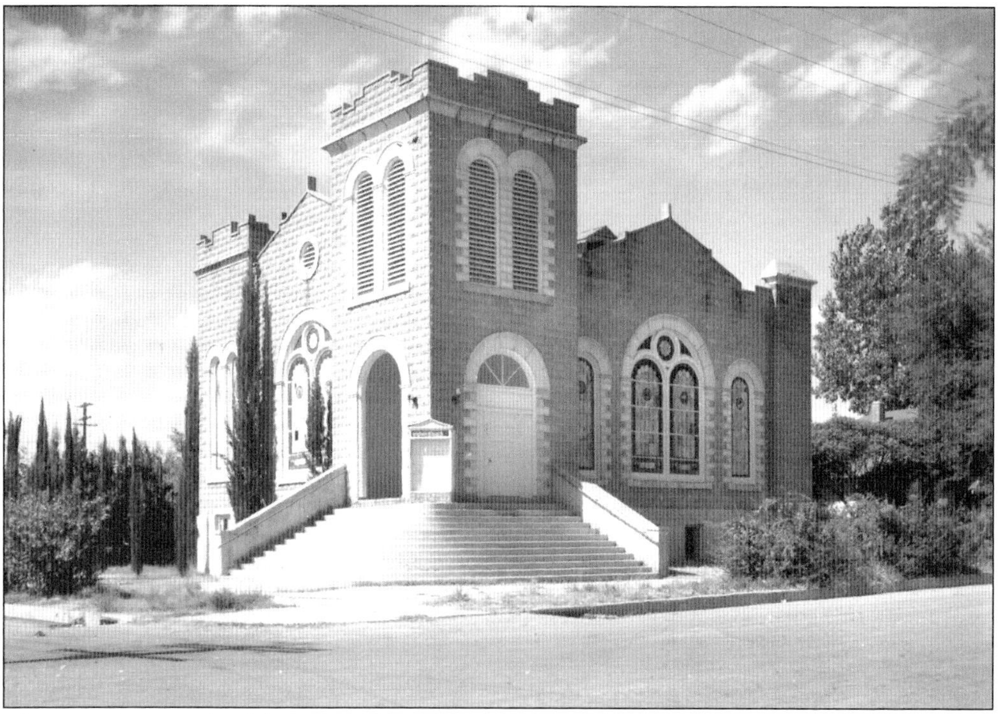

This is a photograph of the ornate block church that today stands on the corner of Egan and Seventh Streets. It was built by John J. McCoy in 1885 as an Episcopal church. Numerous other buildings in and around Beaumont were constructed with this same type block, although some are no longer standing. (Courtesy of Steve Lech.)

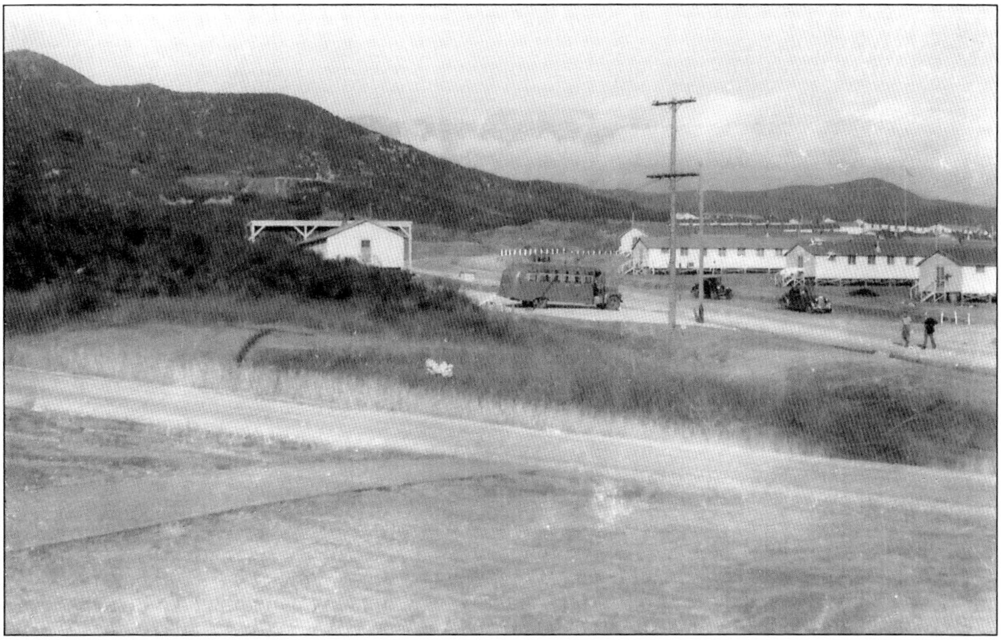

This 1944 photograph shows General Patton's hospital in Beaumont, which was renovated by U.S. Navy corpsmen after he abandoned it to begin his North African campaign. The hospital compound covered about 100 acres. It was used to accommodate wounded navy personnel brought in from the Pacific war zone. (Courtesy of Homer Shockey.)

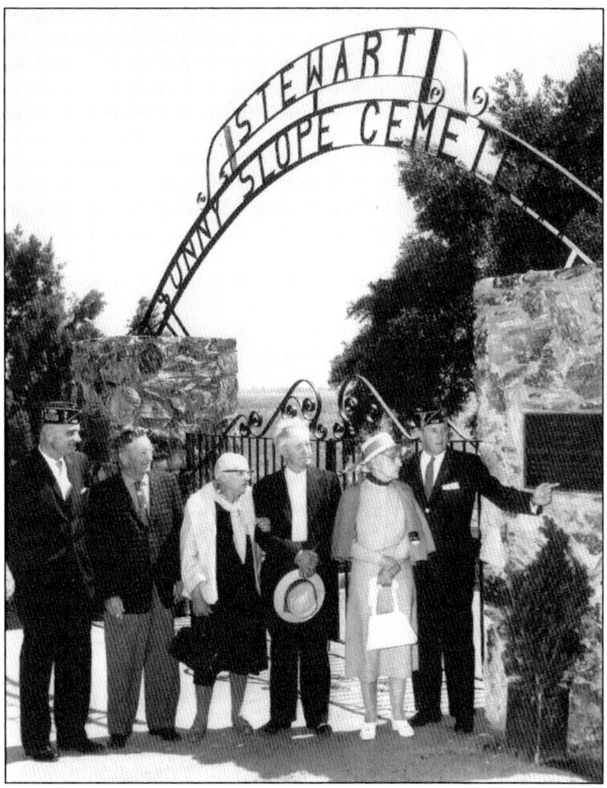

This is a group at a dedication ceremony after the donation by the Stewart family of another seven acres to the Stewart Sunny Slope Cemetery, as well as the current pump and pressure system. Its original six acres were donated to the City of Beaumont in 1888. Pictured here from left to right are Paul Miller, Clarence Lewis, Clara Stewart Beasley, Earl E. Beasley, Laura Mae Stewart, and an unidentified man. (Courtesy of Nara Haskell.)

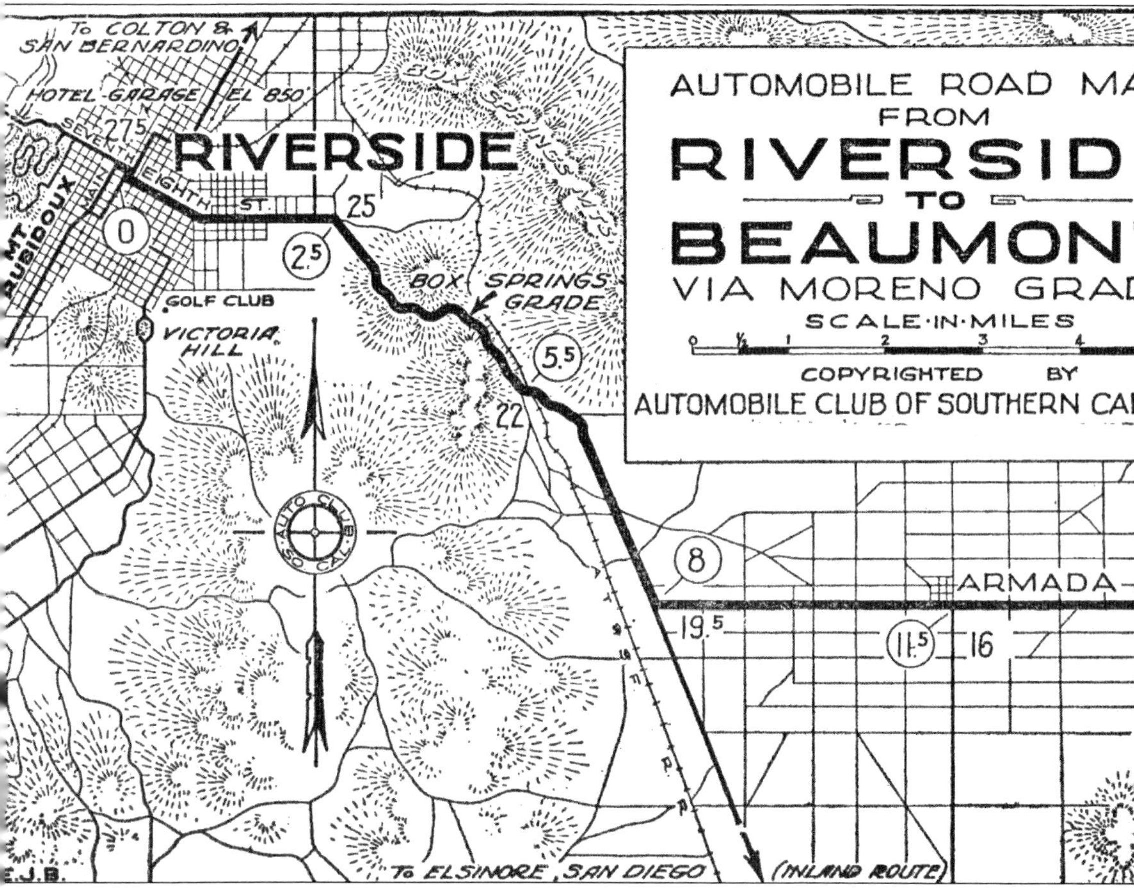

This early road map produced by the Automobile Club of California shows the road between Riverside and Beaumont prior to construction of current Highway 60 from Moreno to Beaumont.

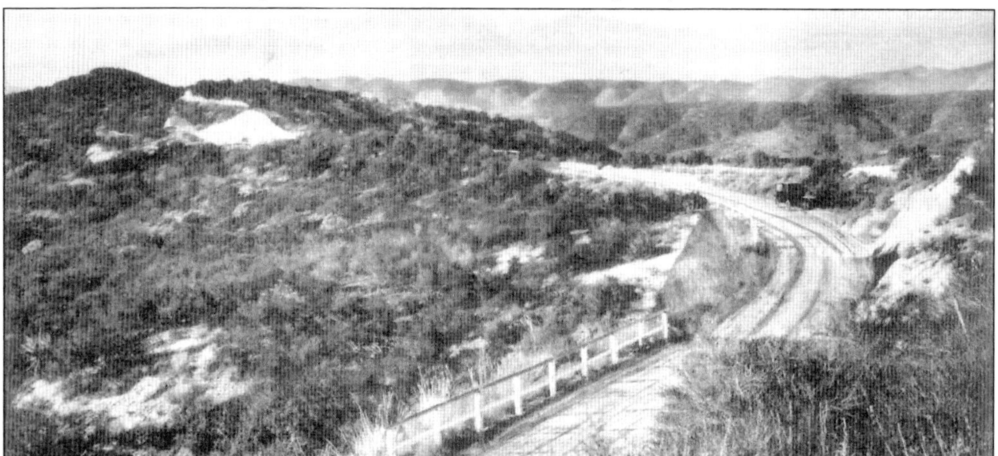

This is a section of Jack Rabbit Trail near Beaumont. Its humble origins began when John J. McCoy, Frank A. Tatley, and M. V. Park, armed with bundles of lath, some white cloth, two axes, a carpenter's level and a grading pole, laid out the road. Light travel over the short stretch was established in 1895. (Courtesy of Steve Lech.)

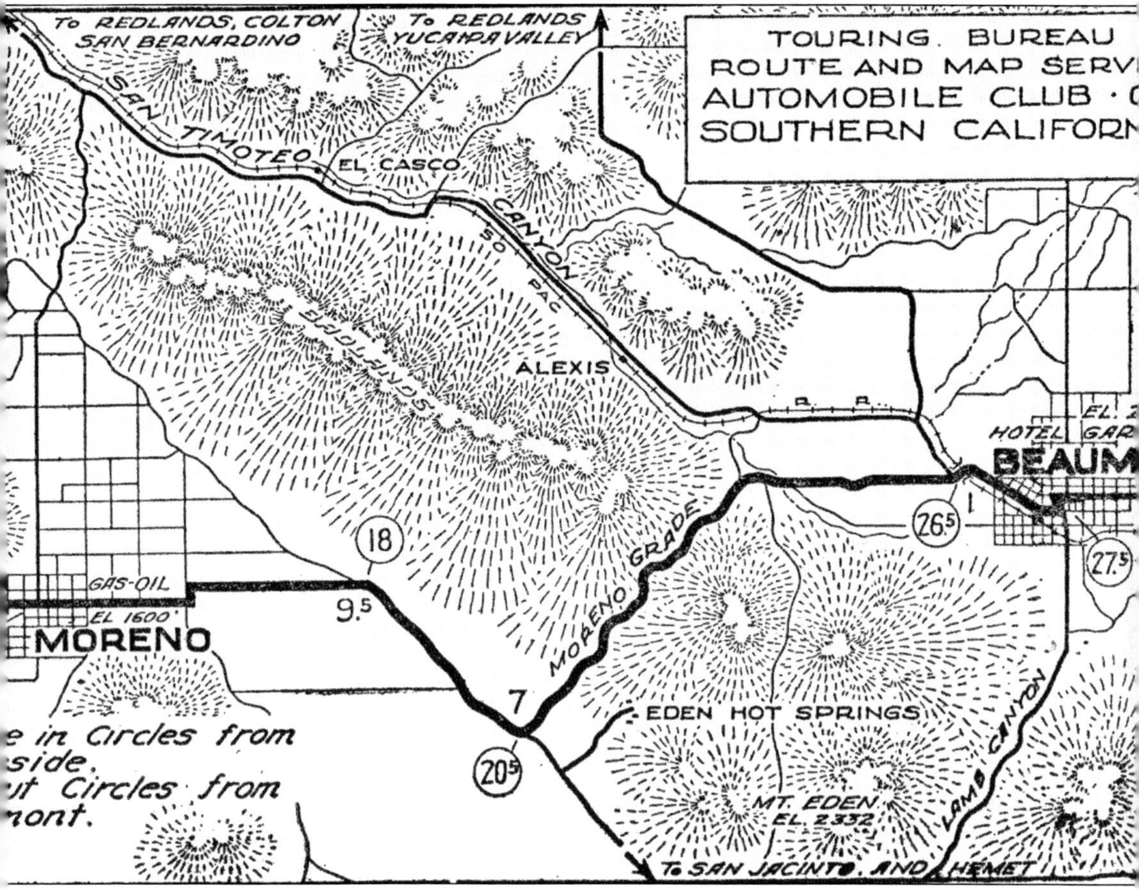

Before its construction, Beaumont was reached via Moreno Grade (Jack Rabbit Trail), a treacherous four-mile section on the right of the map. (Courtesy of Steve Lech.)

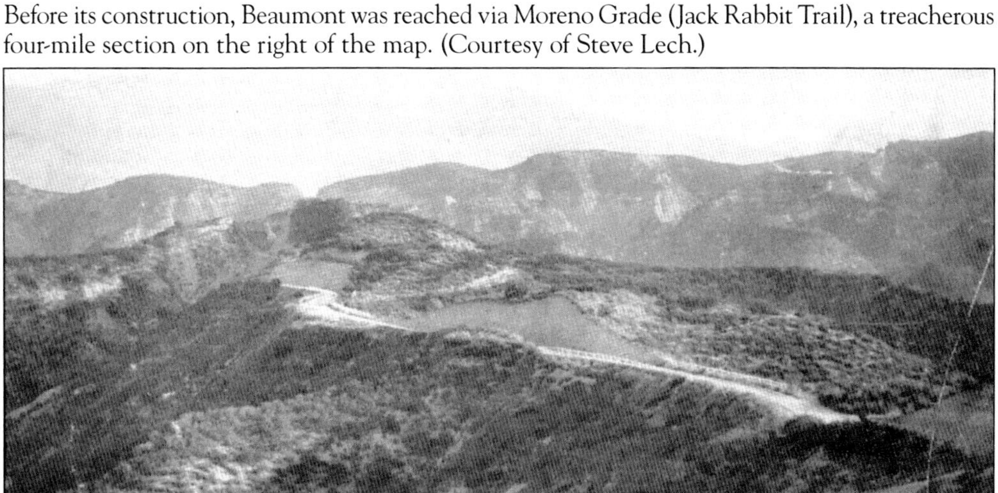

This is a section along Jack Rabbit Trail further along through the area called the Bad Lands. The route was first called San Gorgonio Drive and later dubbed Jack Rabbit Trail by a Riverside newspaper, a name that remains. Even though light travel was established in 1895, it was not until 1935 that the road was paved. (Courtesy of Steve Lech.)

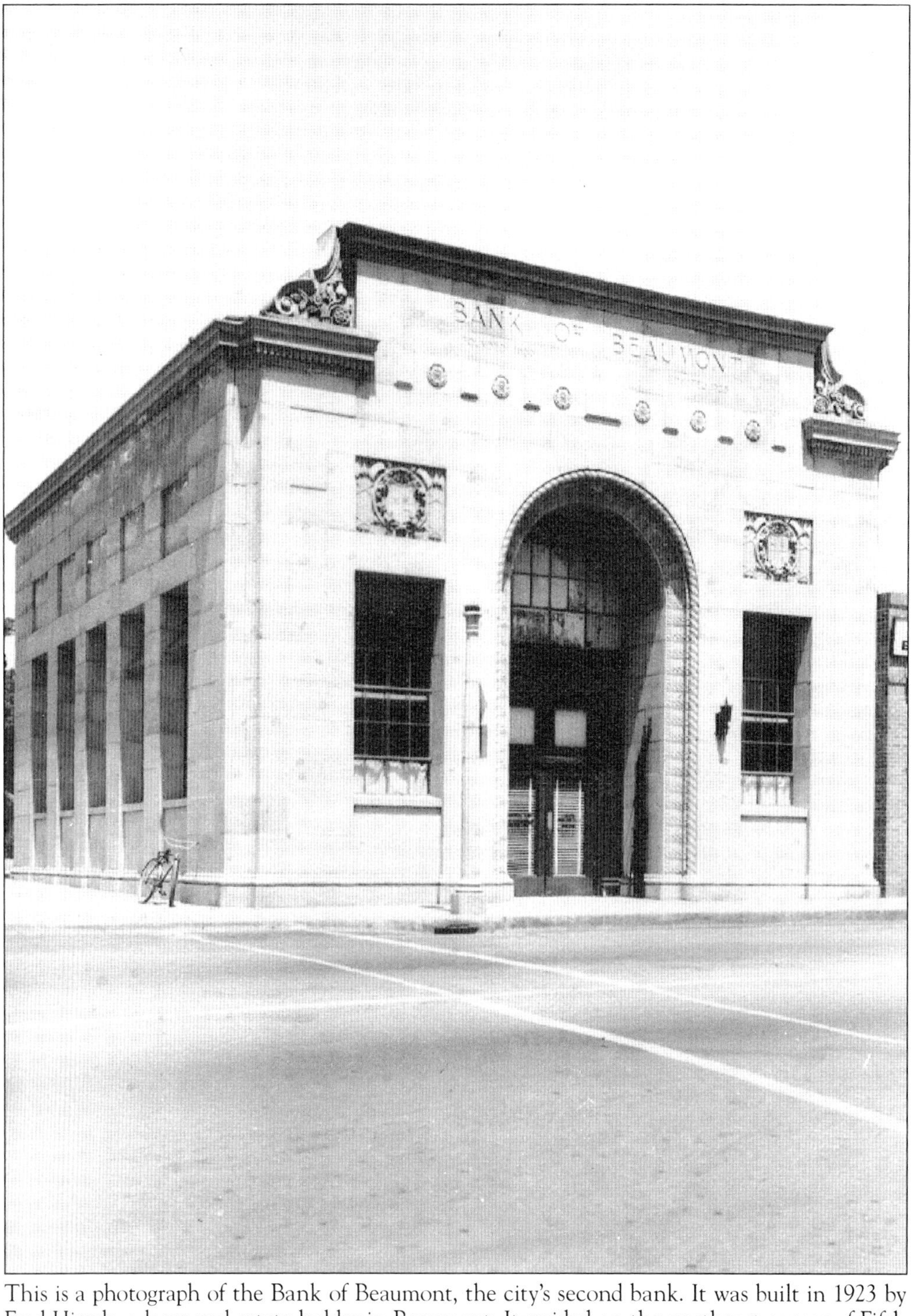

This is a photograph of the Bank of Beaumont, the city's second bank. It was built in 1923 by Fred Hirsch, a large real estate holder in Beaumont. It resided on the northeast corner of Fifth and Egan Streets and replaced the earlier bank, which had been built on the southeast corner of California Avenue and Fifth Street in 1909 and which eventually became too small to serve the growing populous. (Courtesy of Steve Lech.)

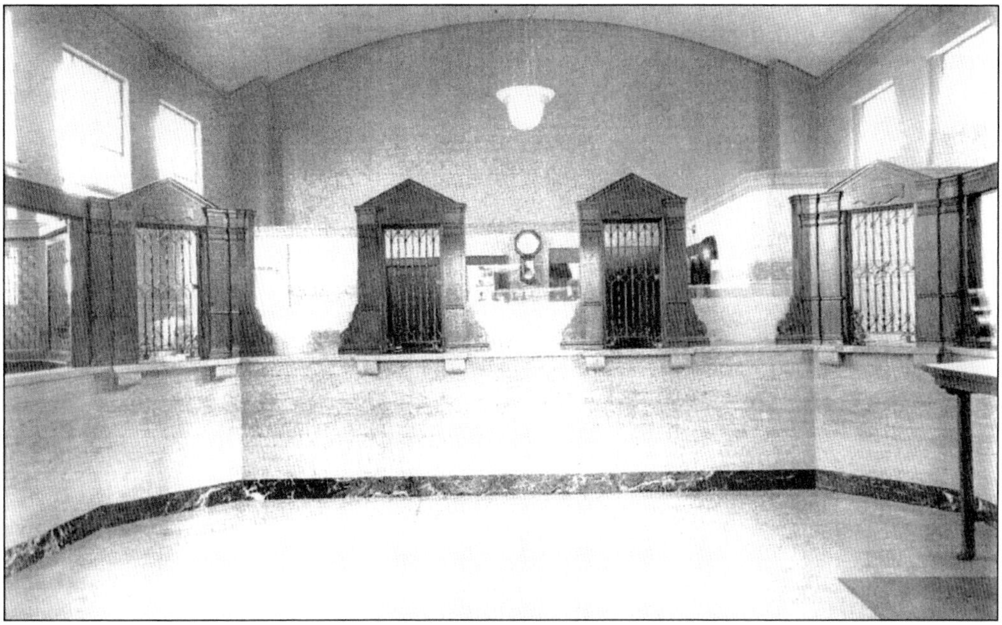

This scene depicts the interior of the second Bank of Beaumont sometime after its initial opening. By this time, the fruit industry had taken a firm hold on the area and agriculture was a boom to the city, which added much activity to the banking operation. Note the absence of a security shield here in contrast to many banks seen today. (Courtesy of Steve Morgan.)

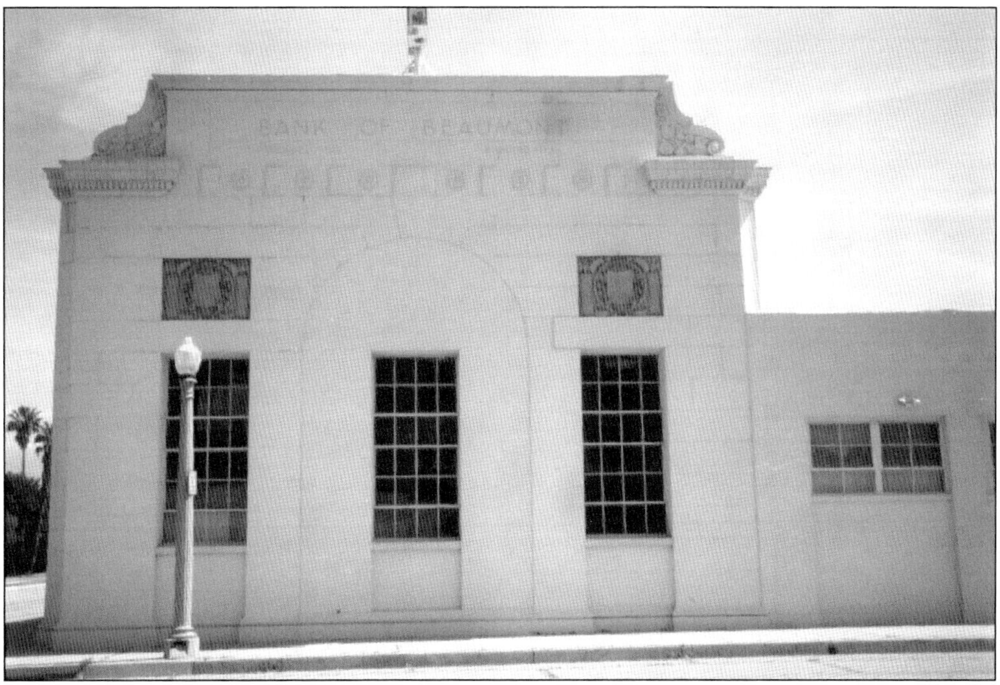

This scene of the old 1923 Bank of Beaumont Building can today be seen to the north when passing along Highway 10 through Beaumont. It is currently the home of Precision Stampings, Inc., a major, well-established machine-shop company in Beaumont. The company is currently expanding, with major construction being added to its north side. (Courtesy of authors.)

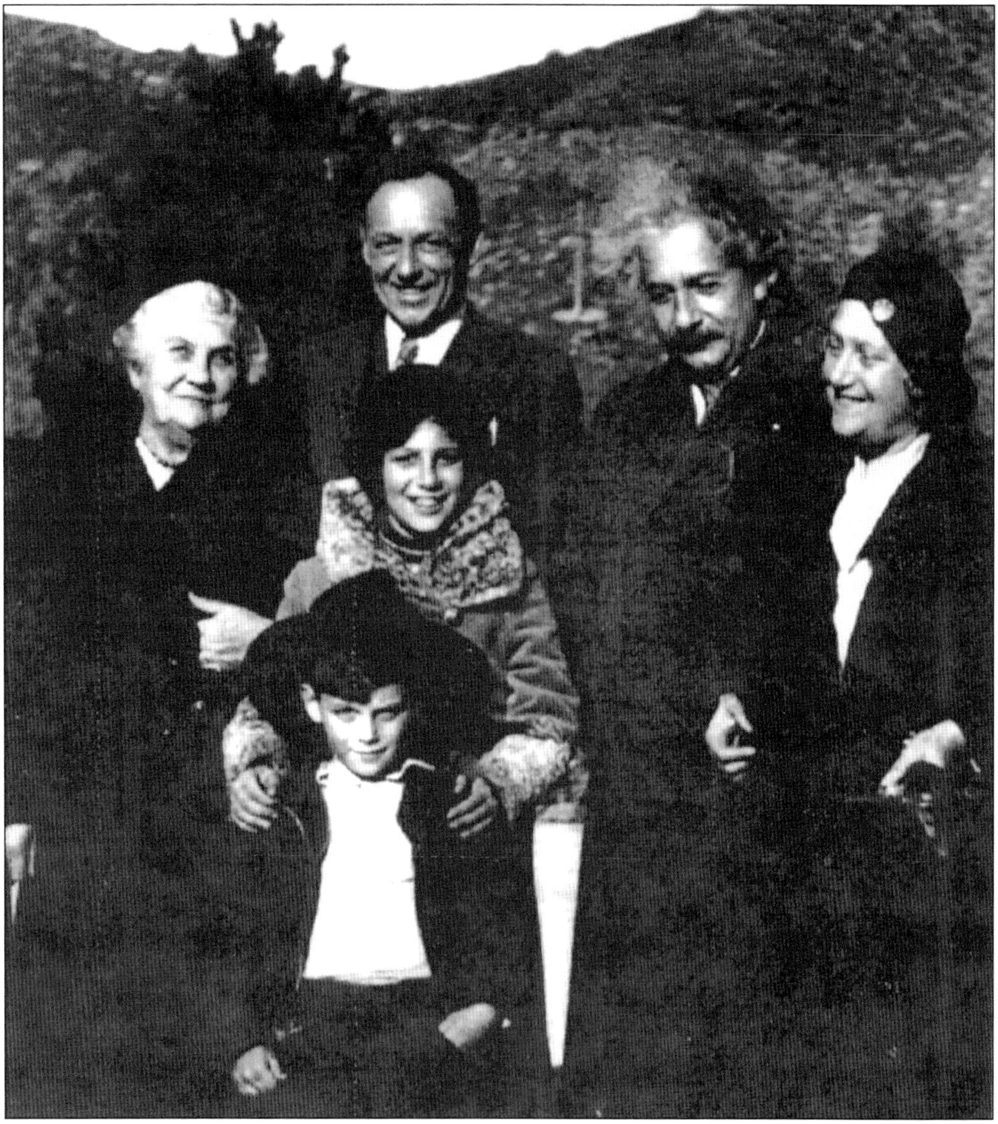

Professor Einstein is seen in this photograph with his wife at right. It was taken during a visit to Beaumont in 1933, when he came to visit his longtime friend Fred Hirsch (left), seen in the picture with his family. Hirsch owned a large real estate holding in Beaumont, including the bank he built in 1923 to its present stature. (Courtesy of Steven Morgan.)

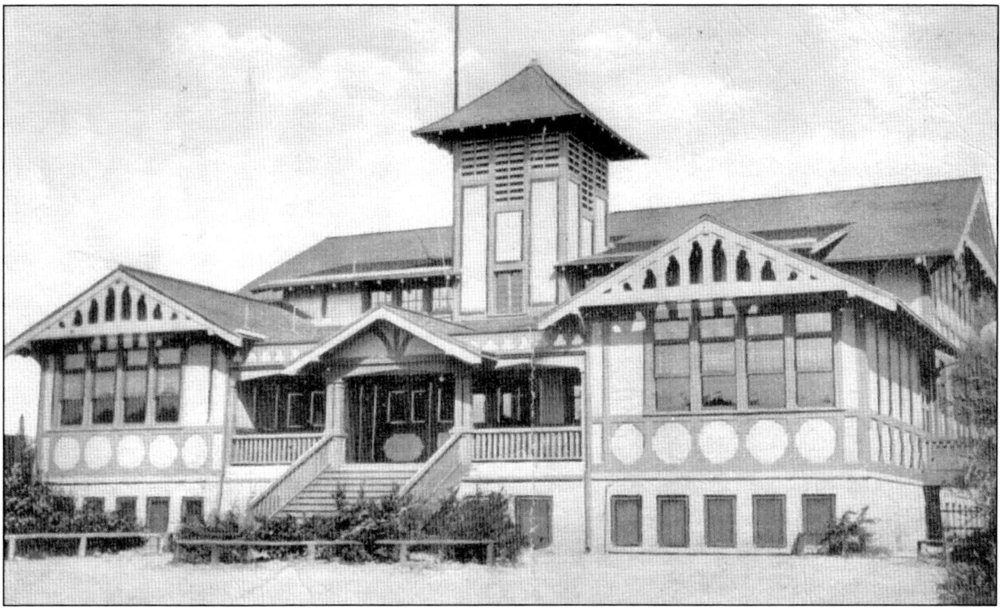

Beaumont High School was organized in September 1909 with 17 students enrolled the first year. D. S. Dodds and Miss Gall were the teachers. The school's meager start began in a 12-by-20-foot shack located on Egan Street. It moved to an abandoned store on Fifth Street, then to tents, and later to the newly constructed school seen here on Magnolia and Seventh Streets. (Courtesy of Steve Lech.)

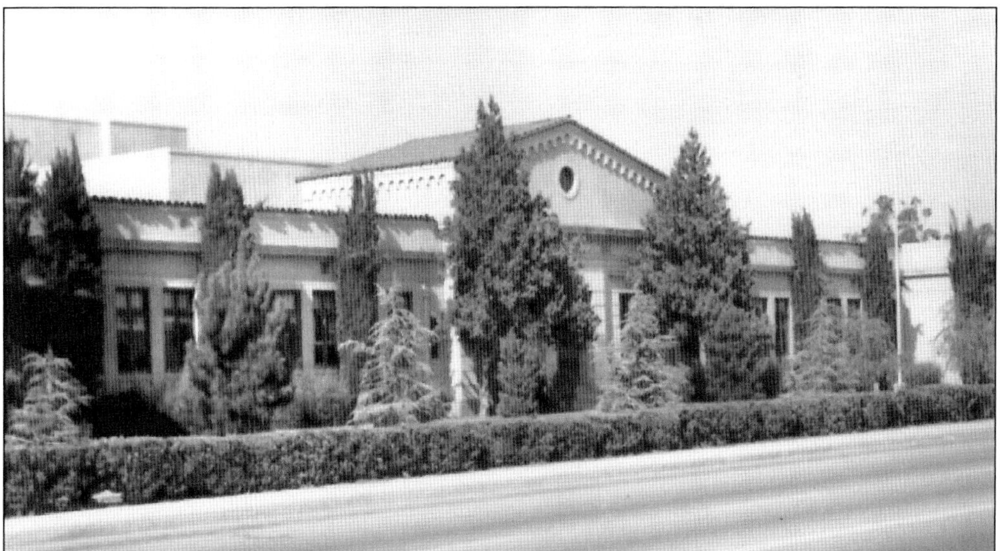

This photograph depicts the new high school constructed on Sixth Street in Beaumont after the demise of Magnolia High School. It served the community well until the high school was relocated again, at which time it became the home of a grammar school, which also moved elsewhere. It then became home of the civic center, housing all city offices. (Courtesy of Nara Haskell.)

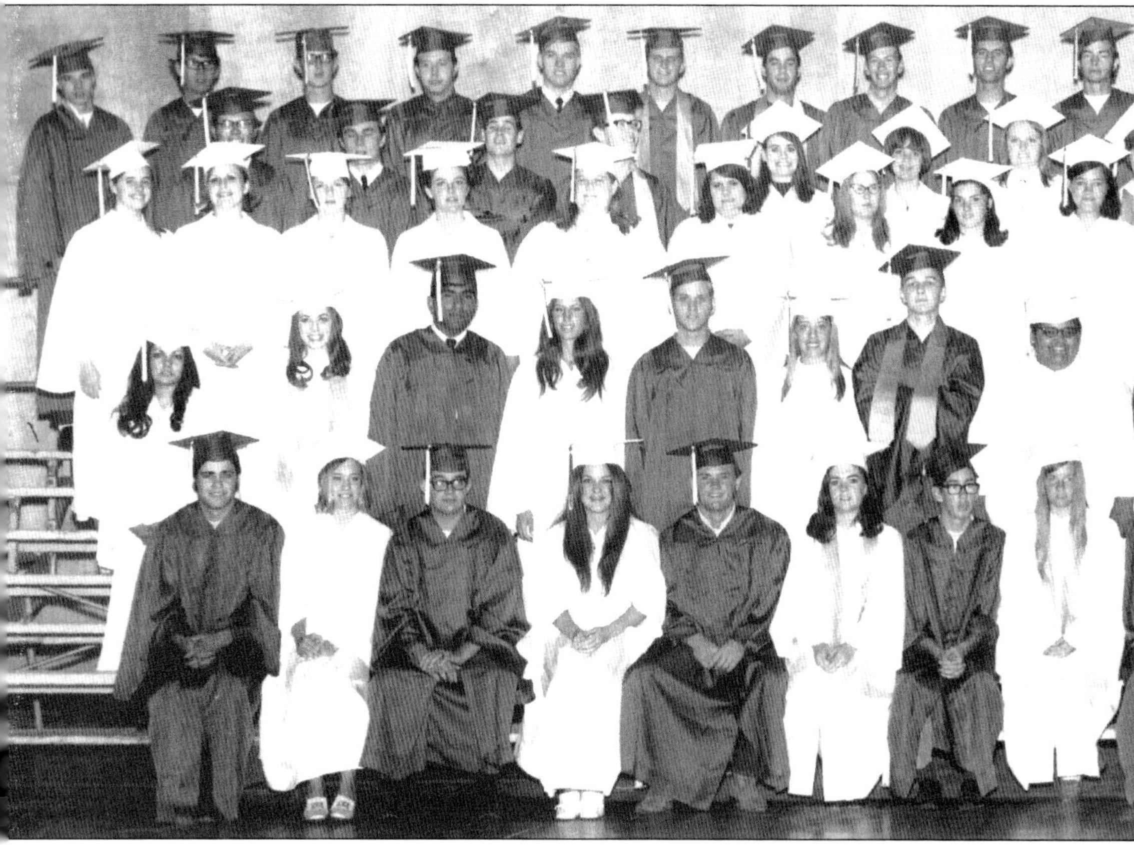

This is the graduating class of Beaumont High School in 1968, which included 97 graduates. Many of the class members would soon be enrolled in colleges and universities throughout the

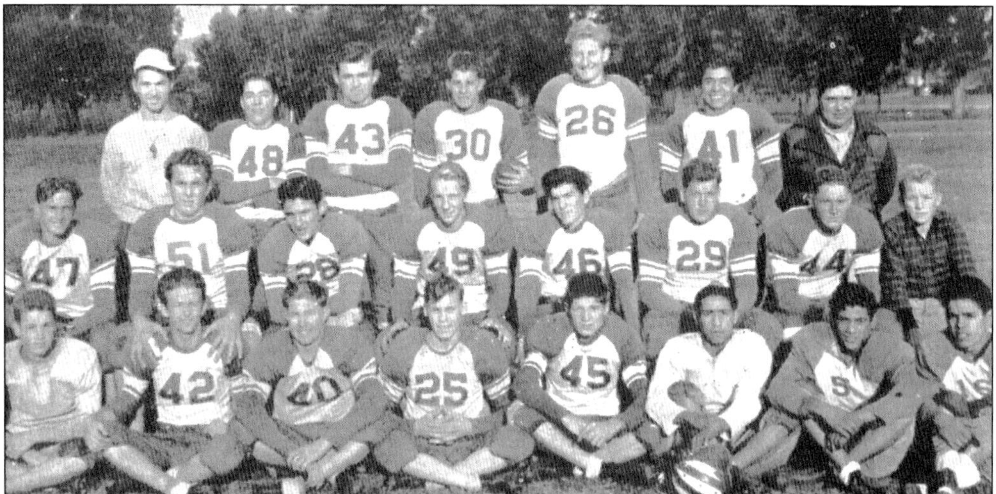

This is a photograph of Beaumont High's football team in 1943, when they had a great season. It was during the height of World War II, and some of the team's members had older siblings serving their country. These were patriotic years, and turnout for football games was high. (Courtesy of Bud Mathewson.)

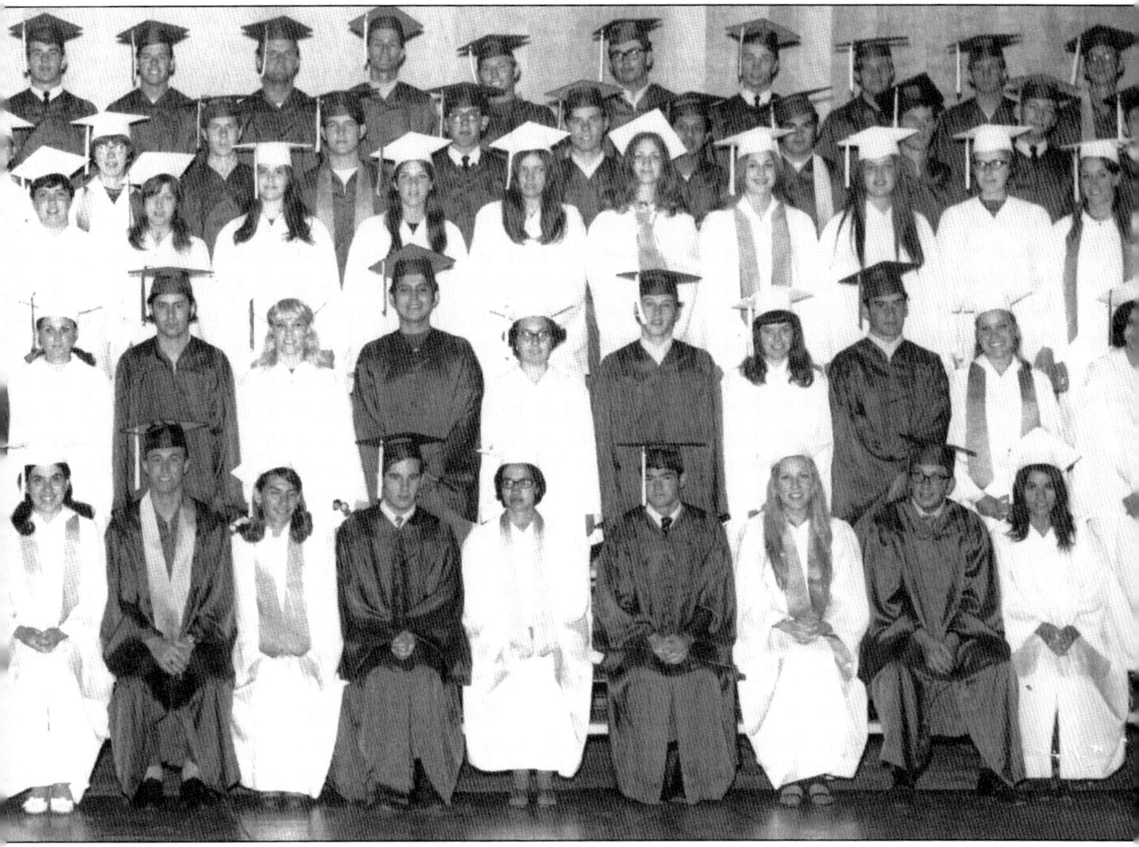

country. By this time, the population of Beaumont had grown significantly, and classes like this continued to increase in size. (Courtesy of Bud Mathewson.)

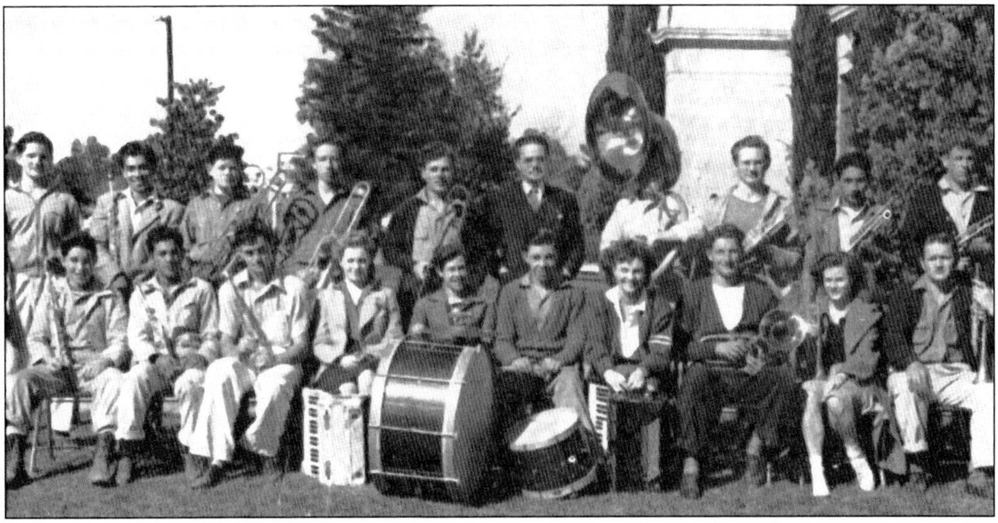

In 1943, Beaumont High also had a great school band. The war years brought many new patriotic war songs to the forefront, and some were added to their agenda when they played at special events, such as the Fourth of July parade. The band was also a standout at other events, and they especially enjoyed playing at their school's football games. (Courtesy of Bud Mathewson.)

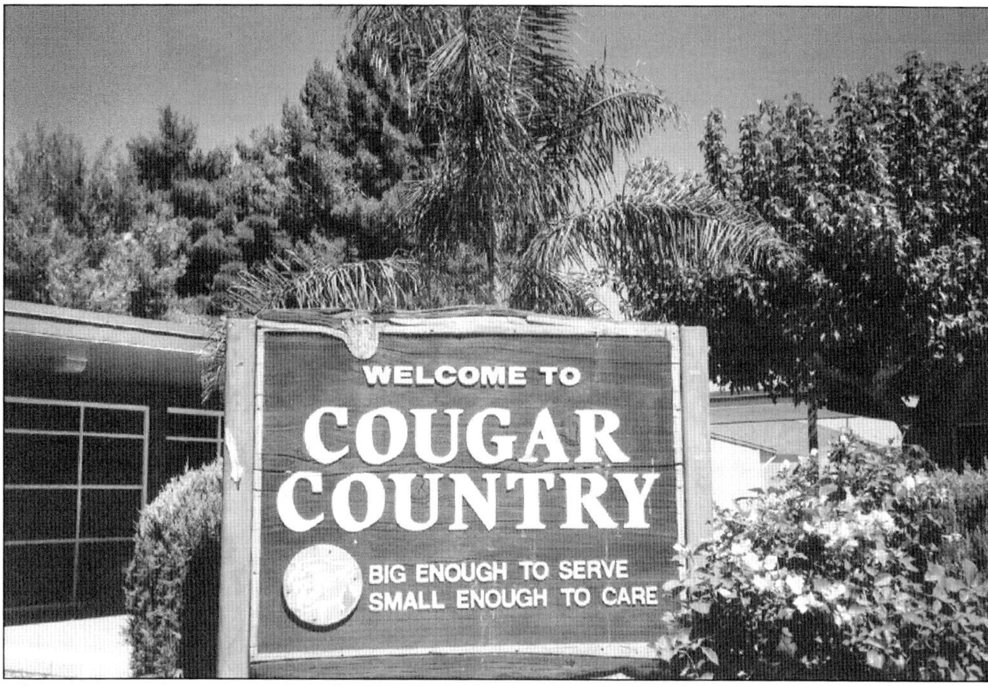

This photograph captures a small section of Beaumont High School, which was built on the west side of Cherry Avenue after the high school on Sixth Street was abandoned. It was moved here because a larger campus was required. This school had its own football field on its grounds and had an expansive campus. (Courtesy of authors.)

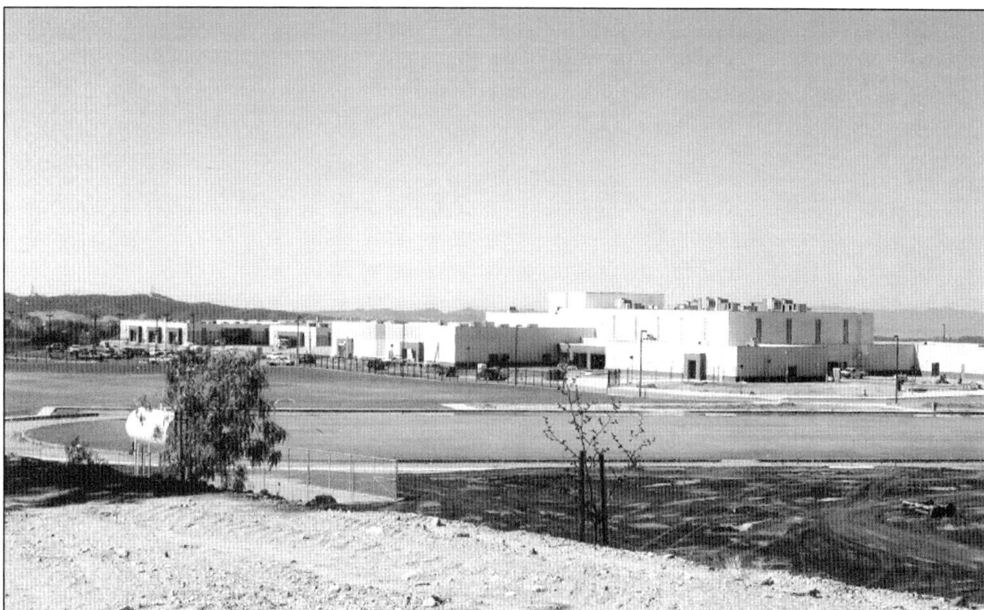
This new Beaumont High School on Beaumont Avenue borders Cherry Valley to the north. It became imperative to construct a large school like this with an adequate campus because of the large growth in the area leading to an unexpected influx of new students. Note the large football field in the foreground. (Courtesy of authors.)

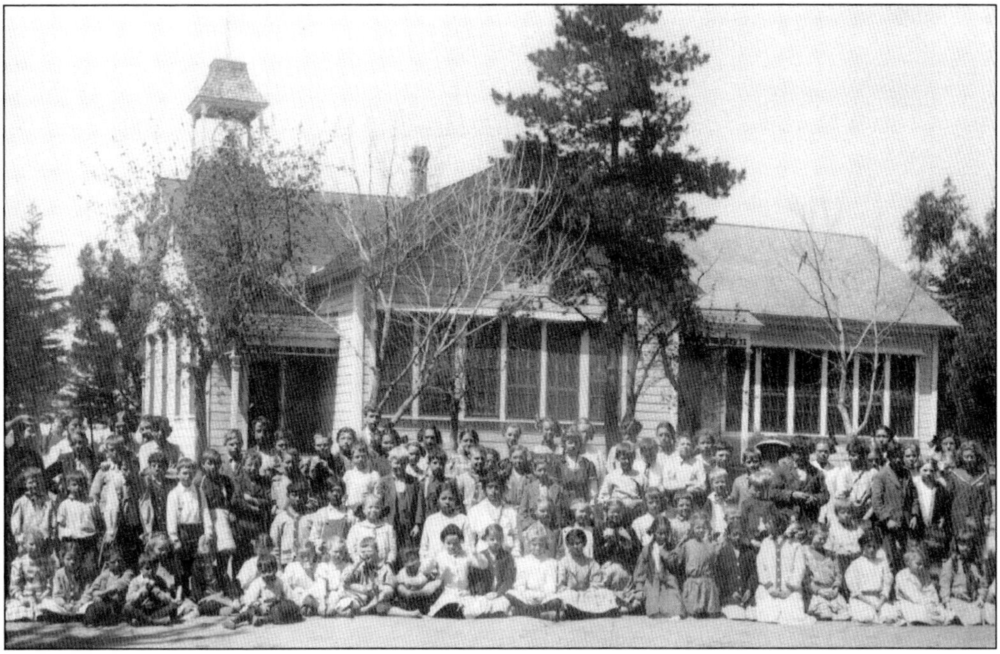

This photograph taken at the Wellwood School shows a group of around 100, including teachers. Class pictures were a highlight for both students and teachers. The year it was taken is unknown, but, based on the mature landscape and large class size, certainly it is some time after its construction in 1921. It was later demolished due to earthquake threat. (Courtesy of Nara Haskell.)

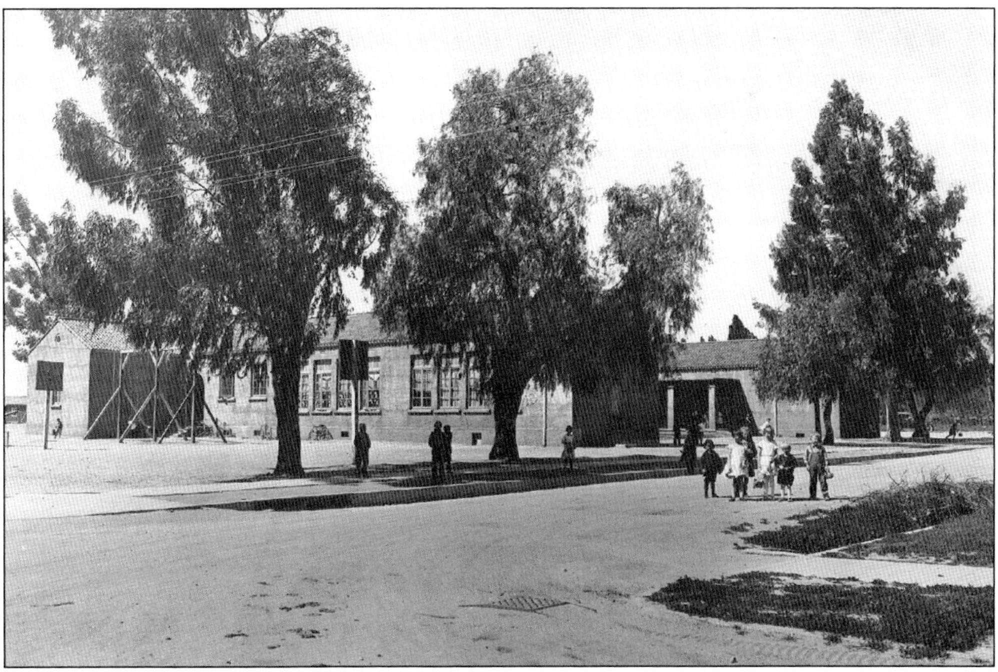

This is the more modern Wellwood School, which was built to replace the older structure in 1921. Notable are the children who all seem to have their eyes trained on the camera except the child at extreme right bounding the ball, who is totally oblivious to the activity. (Courtesy of SGPHS.)

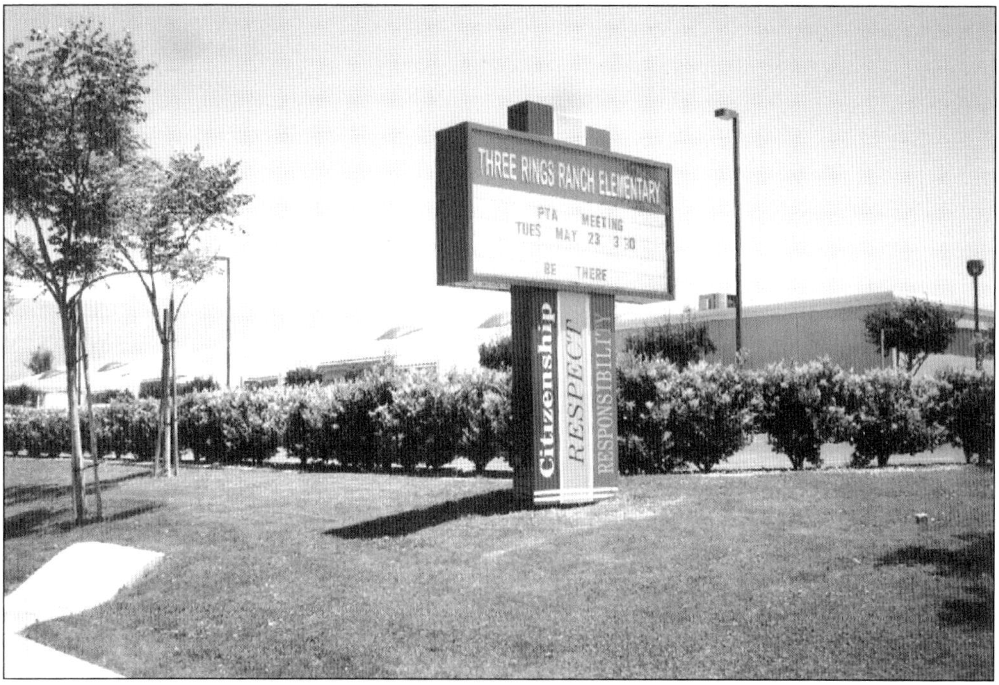

Population growth in Beaumont necessitated construction of additional elementary schools. This is Three Rings Ranch Elementary, built on the grounds of the Three Rings Ranch after it was sold to housing developers. It is among the list of four other elementary schools: Sundance, Palm, Chavez, and Brookside. In addition, Summit Middle School, now relocated on the old Beaumont High School grounds at the corner of Cougar and Cherry Streets, is among the group. (Courtesy of authors.)

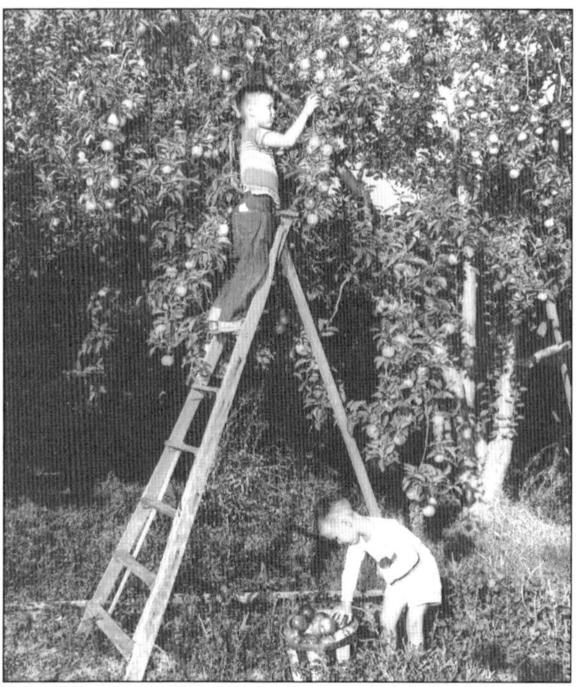

Apples were one of the major fruits produced in Beaumont in its early years. The climate and soil were ideal for good growth, and, with water plentiful, many farmers found it prudent to grow apples. Seen here are Eddie (on ladder) and Dick Davies of the nearby Davies Oak Glen Apple Ranch helping harvest a bumper crop. (Courtesy of SGPHS; Leonard McCulloh, photographer.)

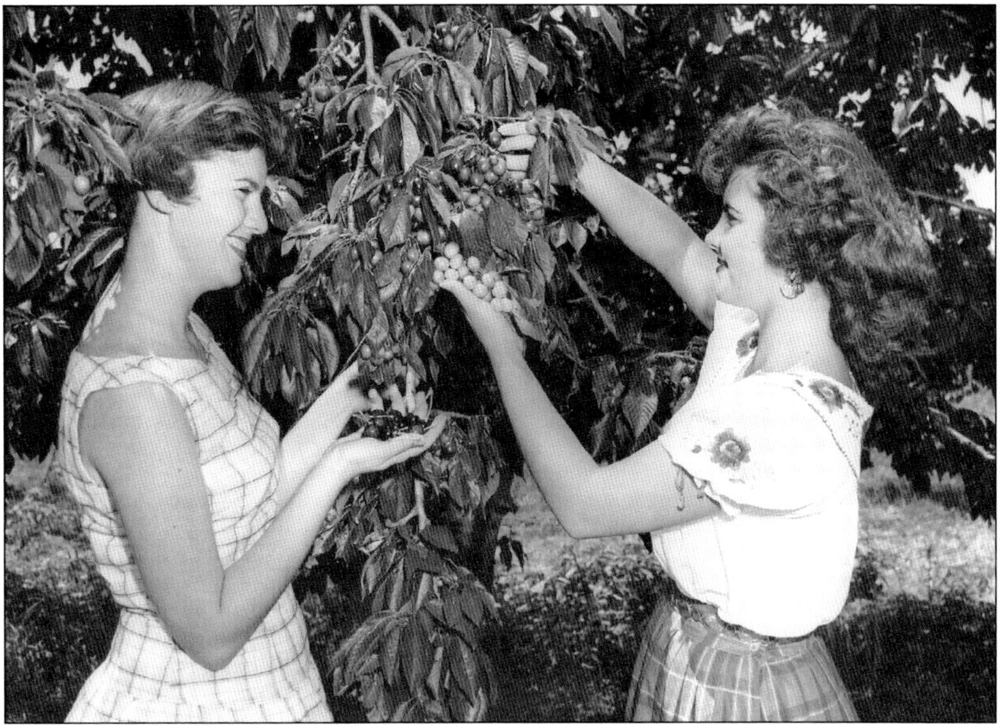

Cherries later replaced apples as the major fruit crop grown in Beaumont, but the first cherry trees were planted in an area north of Beaumont, which was resultantly named Cherry Valley. Here are two unidentified young ladies picking cherries, a legendary event that accompanied the cherry festival. (Courtesy of SGPHS; Leonard McCulloh, photographer.)

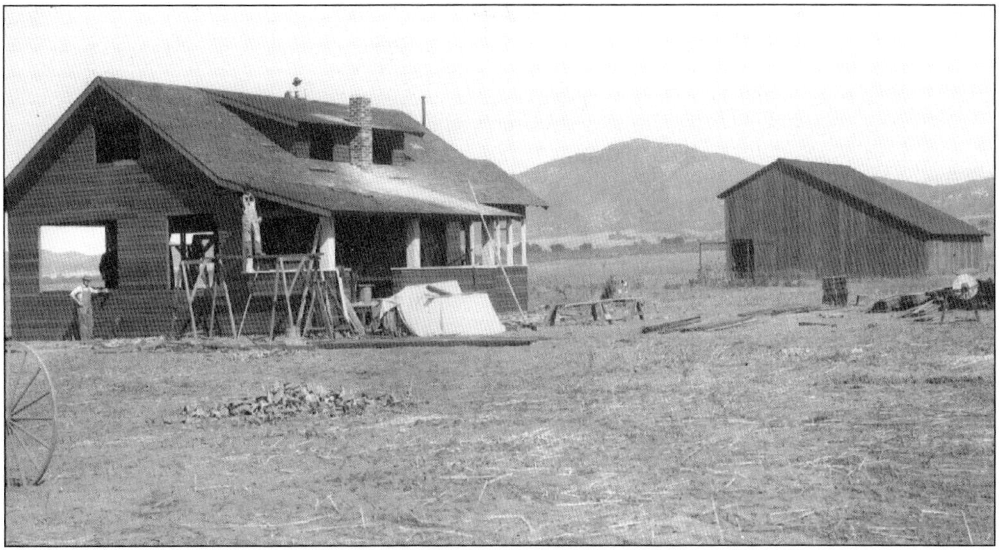

Houses like the Seiltz family home, being built in 1909 at Cougar Way and Cherry Street, began to dot open spaces around Beaumont as its population grew. This scene is north of Beaumont and comprises a small acreage where fruit trees were eventually planted. Note the barn and large implement grinding wheel near the barn at right. This was an important commodity of most small farms. The house was later occupied by Rae Edgar. (Courtesy of Nara Haskell.)

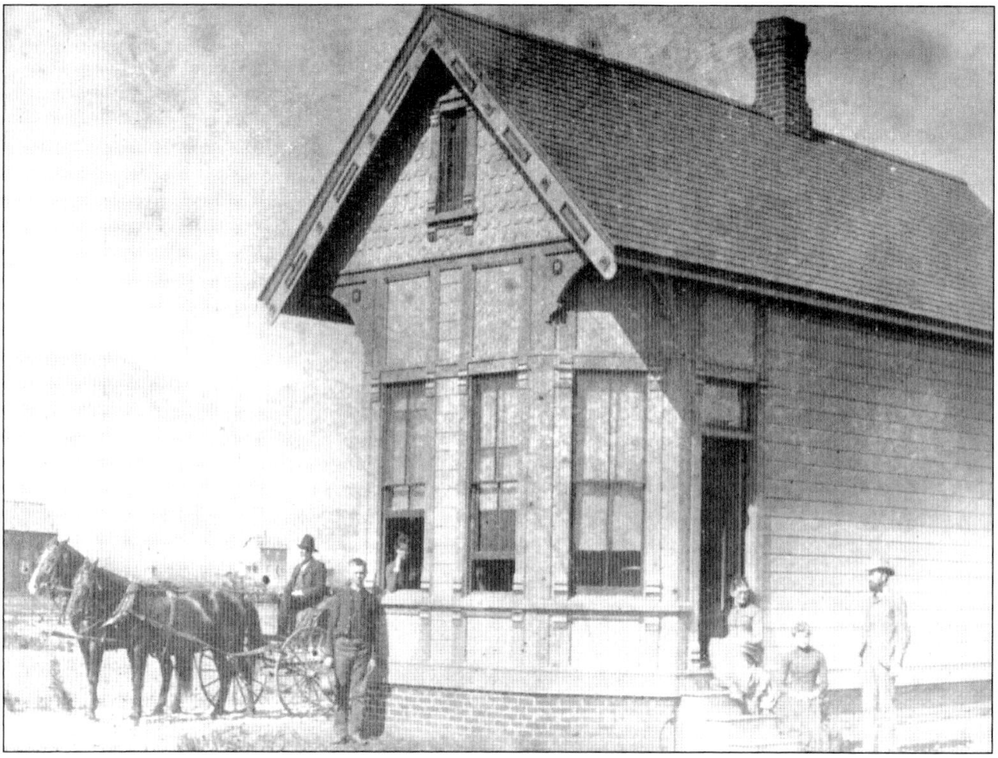

Pictured here is the original McCoy house, built in 1885 by John J. McCoy. McCoy's father and mother came to California from the East Coast and settled in Westminster, California. His father, Josiah, is in the carriage at left and John is standing at right. The home, with additions, today stands at 668 Egan Street. (Courtesy of Donald and Susan Echlin.)

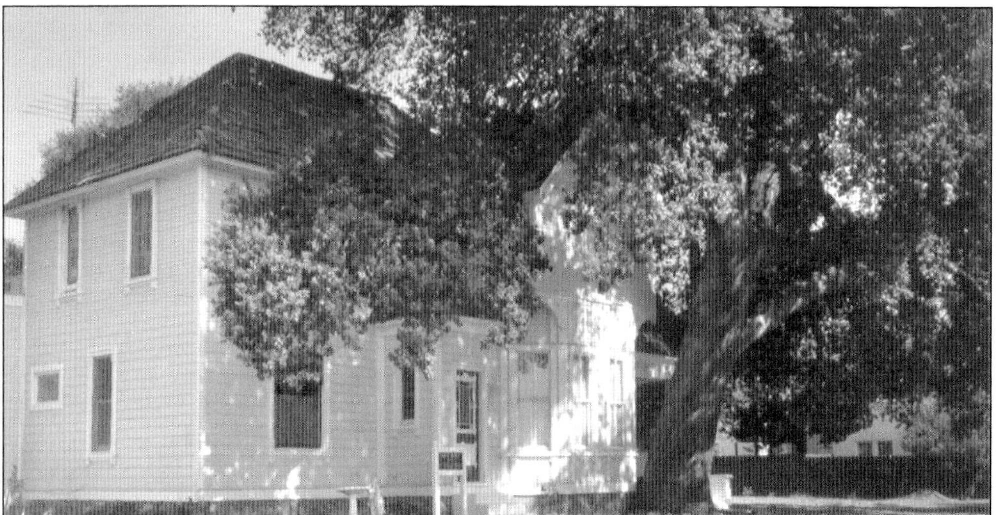

This is the McCoy house as seen today with its 100-year-old oak tree towering above. The house was dedicated in 2001 as a historical site by the Native Daughters of the Golden West. In 1976, it was bought by Donald Echlin and is home to him and his wife, Susan, and son Jeffery. Donald's mother, June Velma McCoy, once lived here as well. (Courtesy of Donald and Susan Echlin.)

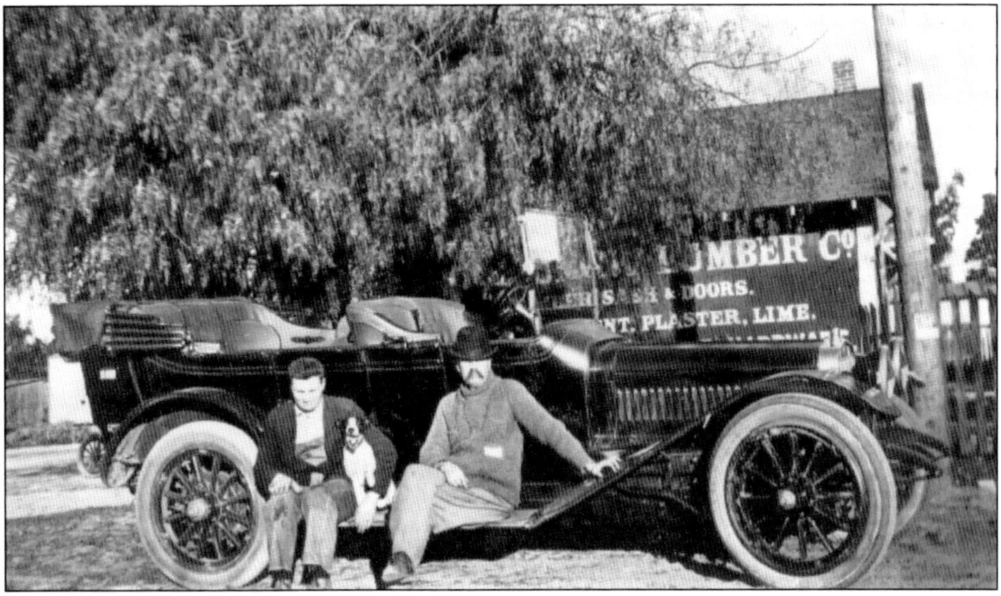

John J. McCoy is pictured here sitting on the running board of his prized automobile in front of his lumberyard with his son Horace and their dog. Cars during this era were status symbols, and proud owners were often photographed with their automobile as a backdrop. (Courtesy of Donald and Susan Echlin.)

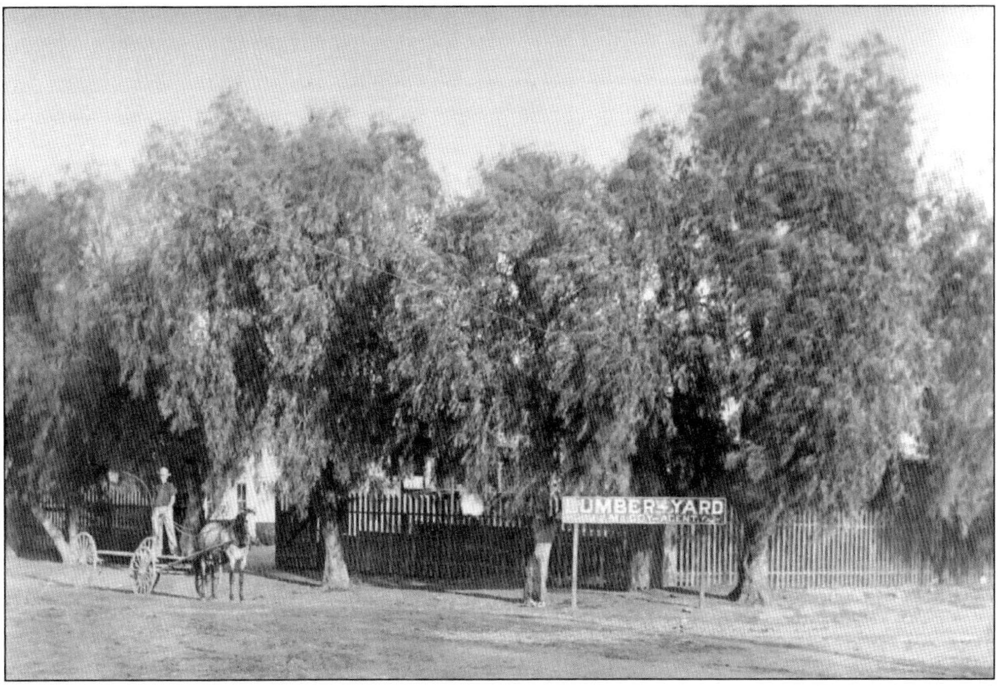

This is the entrance to the lumberyard owned by John J. McCoy. He was the first mayor of Beaumont and was active in many ventures. He was a builder, having constructed his own home in Beaumont, his brother's house in Cherry Valley, and the old stone Episcopal church on Egan and Seventh Streets. His son Horace built the historic Hilltop House in Banning. (Courtesy of Donald and Susan Echlin.)

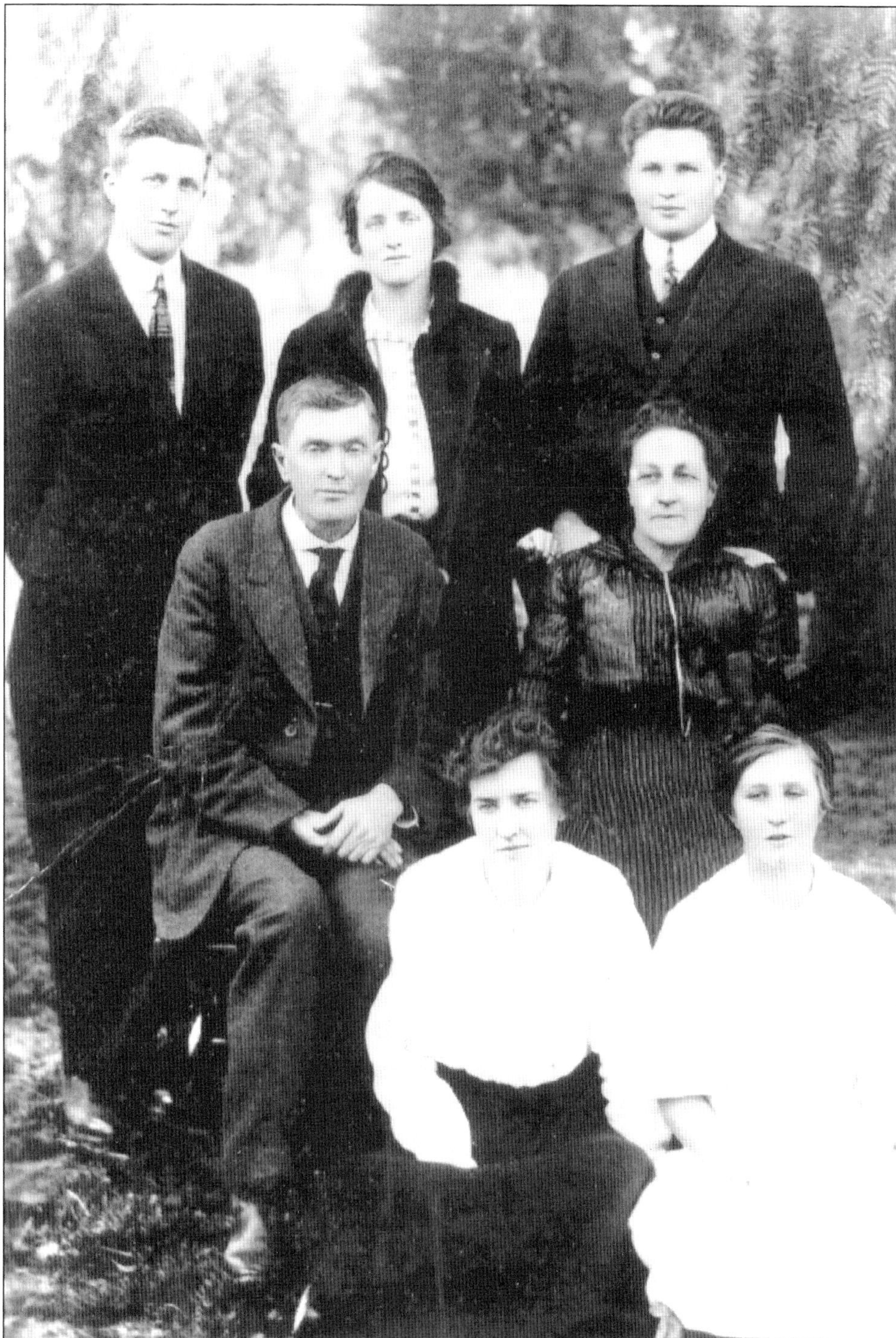

This is a photograph of the John J. McCoy family years after he came to Beaumont and built his home there. John is pictured sitting in the center with his wife, Mary, beside him. One of John's sons, Horace, an orthopedic surgeon, built the historic Hilltop House in Banning. (Courtesy of Donald and Susan Echlin.)

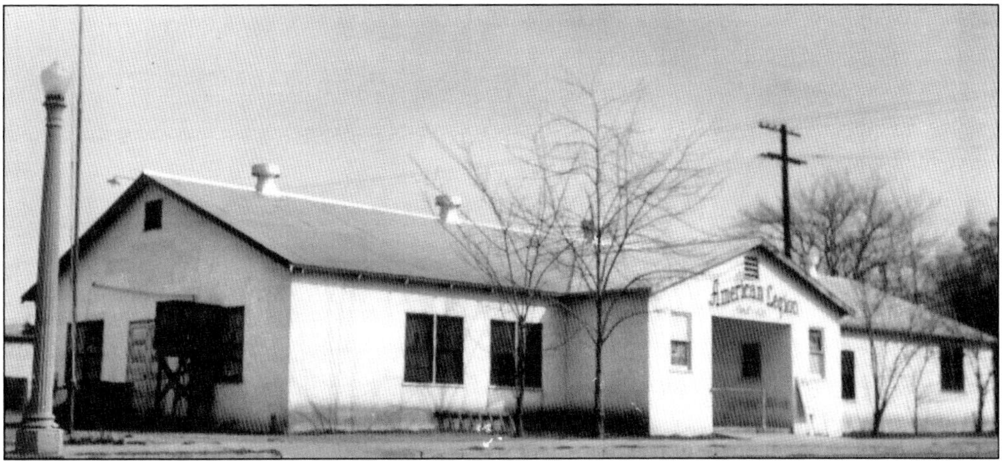

American Legion Post 428 was instituted in Beaumont in August 1931 and was located at Fifth Street and Elm Avenue, as pictured here. The building was razed due to being in the path of Interstate 10 when it came through. Around 10 years ago, Post 428 took up headquarters in Banning and meets regularly at 70 South Street. The American Legion is the world's largest veteran's organization, and there are many loyal veterans in town to support this post. (Courtesy of Steve Lech.)

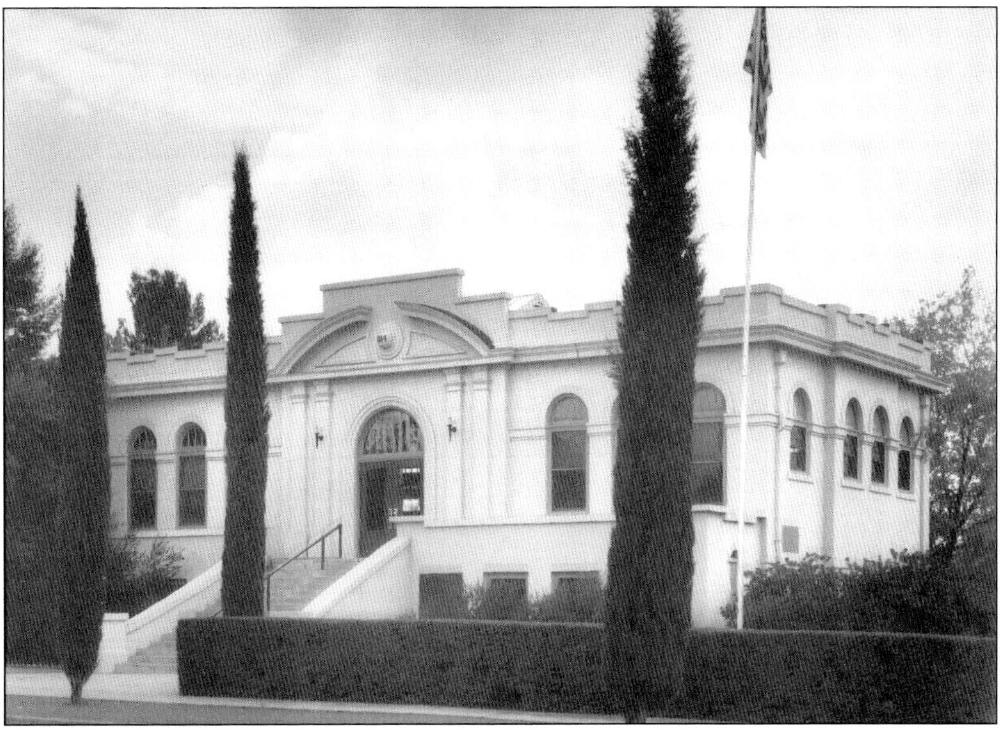

The *Gateway Gazette* of Beaumont, founded by Arthur J. Burdick in 1908, stated in its August 17, 1911, issue that the Beaumont Township a library district was established. This was done to promote a library, which was subsequently built in 1914 on the southwest corner of Eighth Street and California Avenue and was named the Beaumont Library District. It was funded by Carnegie and was independent of city or county. It is pictured here around 1939. (Courtesy of Clara DiFelice.)

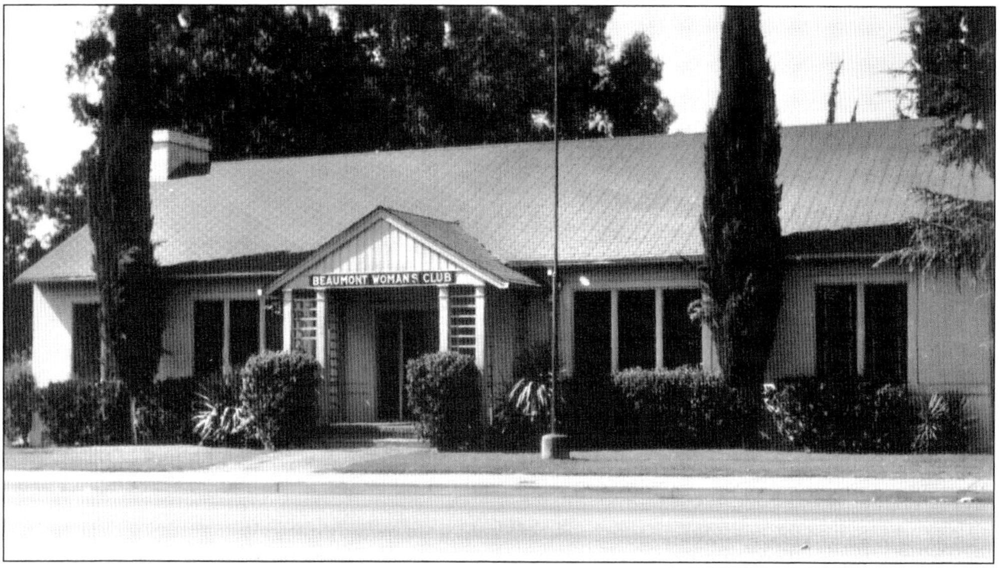

This early photograph is of the Woman's Club in Beaumont on Sixth Street in Beaumont. The structure still remains relatively the same on its original site. It was founded in 1916—four years before the town of Beaumont—in the home of Mrs. J. W. Elder, and meetings were held there for some time. The club has a long history of effective service to the community. (Courtesy of Steve Lech.)

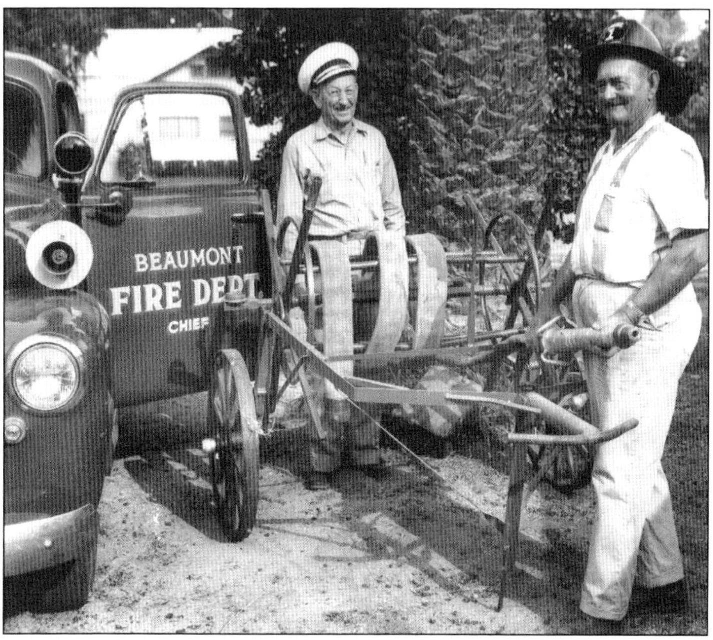

Chief Clarence Lewis and fireman Ray Samson stand beside this 1949 Chevrolet fire truck with a spotlight and fender-mounted horn. The contrast between this antiquated firefighting equipment is interesting to compare with today's large trucks and elaborate hose system in Beaumont's new fire department, which has improved in the 50 years or so since this photograph was taken. (Courtesy of SGPHS.)

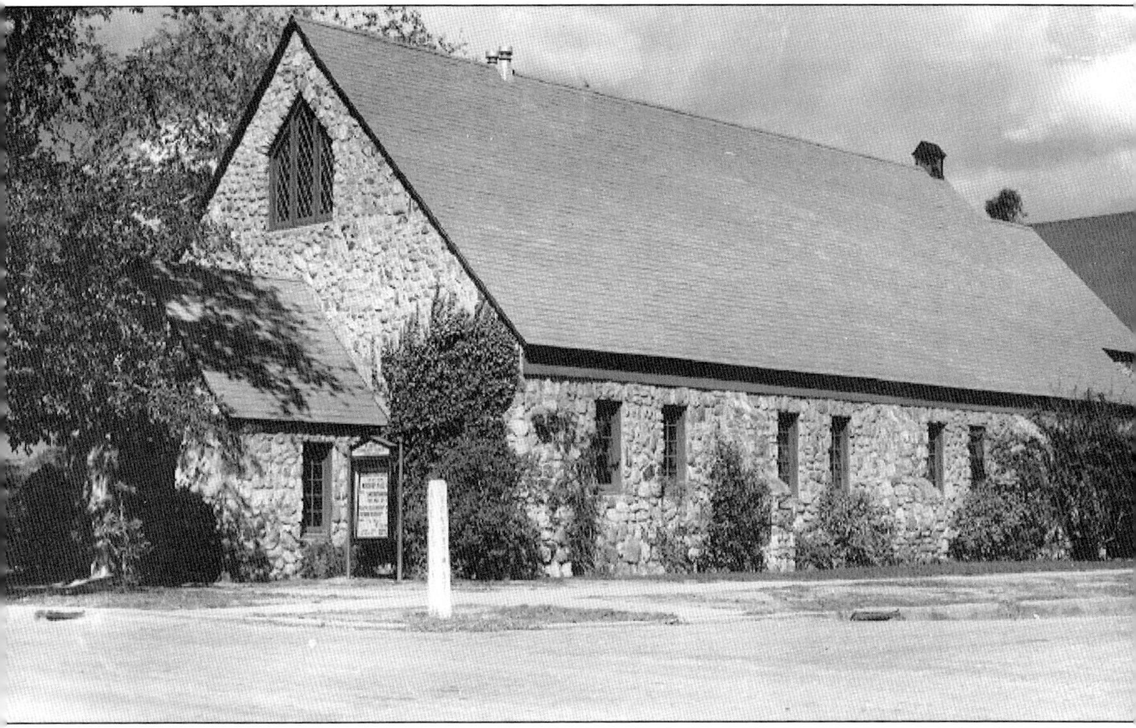

This is Beaumont's 70-year-old Presbyterian rock church, dedicated in 1934. It is a city landmark due in part to its beautiful rock construction, its portals, and its unique design. Nara Haskell, a longtime resident of Beaumont, indicated to the authors that she helped bring rocks from the desert to build the church. (Courtesy of Bud Mathewson.)

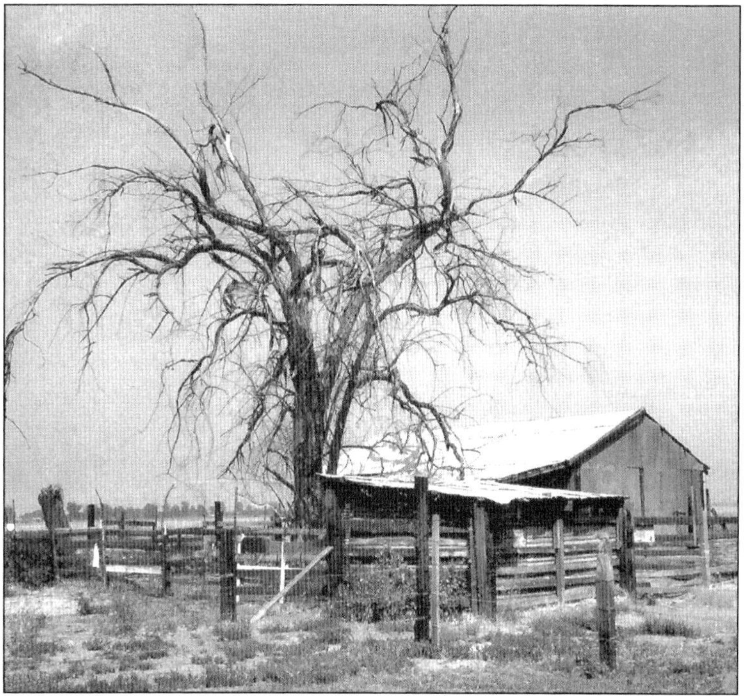

This photograph was taken of a portion of the land holdings of the Dysart family on the northwest corner of Highland Avenue and Wilson Street in Beaumont. Around 80 years ago, A. C. Dysart owned about 1,800 acres in the area. A park in Banning carries his name on land donated by him. Today descendants David A. Dysart Jr. and others watch over his agricultural paradise. (Courtesy of Norman McGary.)

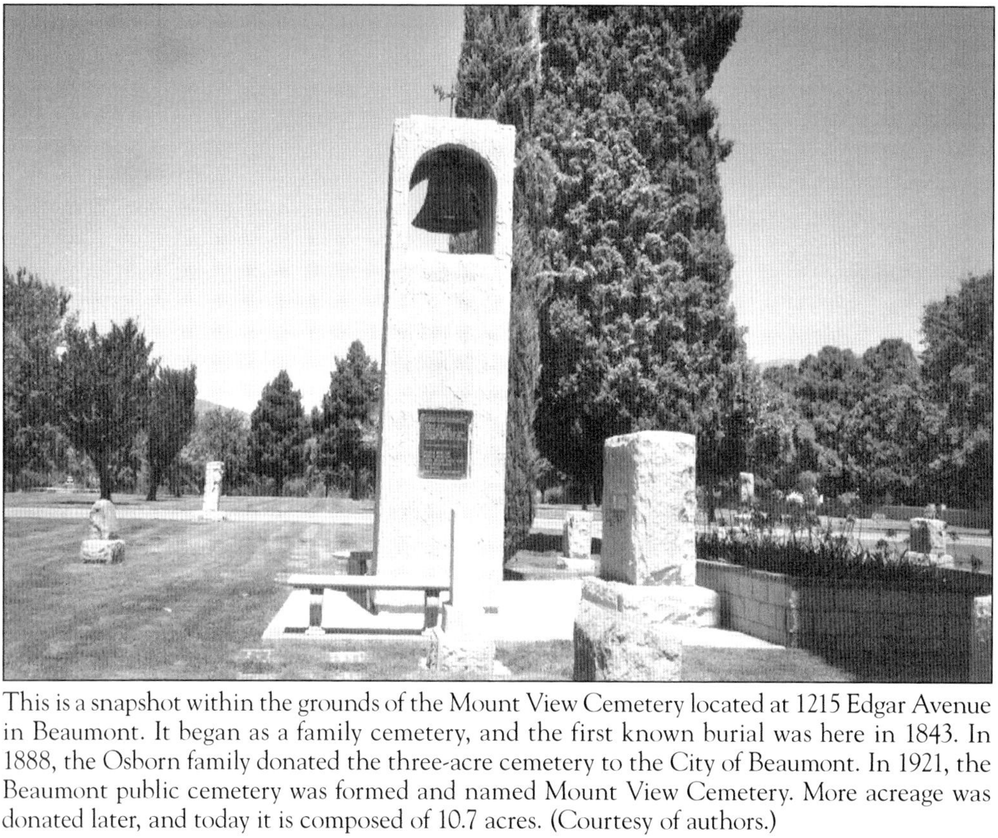

This is a snapshot within the grounds of the Mount View Cemetery located at 1215 Edgar Avenue in Beaumont. It began as a family cemetery, and the first known burial was here in 1843. In 1888, the Osborn family donated the three-acre cemetery to the City of Beaumont. In 1921, the Beaumont public cemetery was formed and named Mount View Cemetery. More acreage was donated later, and today it is composed of 10.7 acres. (Courtesy of authors.)

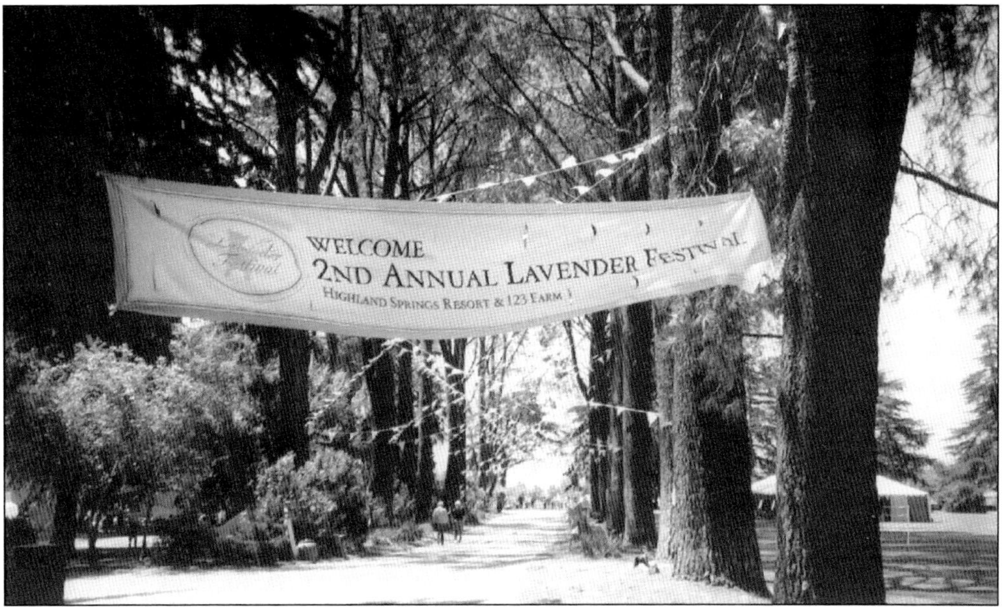

This is the welcome banner leading to the second annual Lavender Festival at Highland Springs Resort and Convention Center in Beaumont. During this event, visitors were invited to walk through a sea of blue-lavender beauty and observe the numerous varieties that are grown on the farm. (Courtesy of authors.)

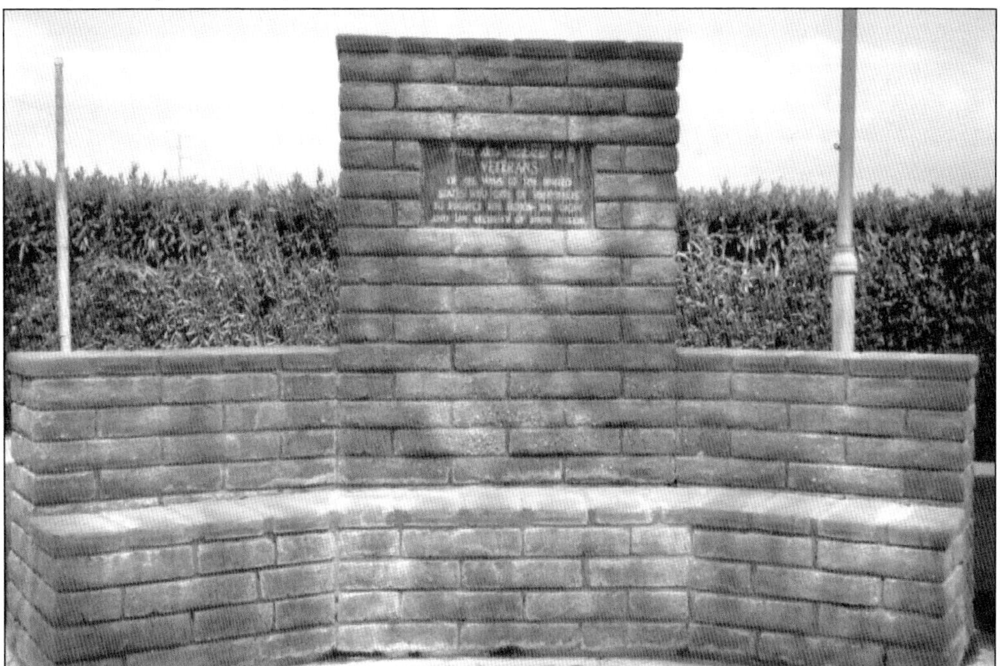

This memorial at Stewart Sunny Slope Cemetery in Beaumont on Pennsylvania Avenue dedicates this area to veterans of all wars of the United States who gave of themselves to protect the honor, the glory, and the security of their nation. American Legion Post 428 and the Laura Stewart Trust Fund donated funds for the project. (Courtesy of authors.)

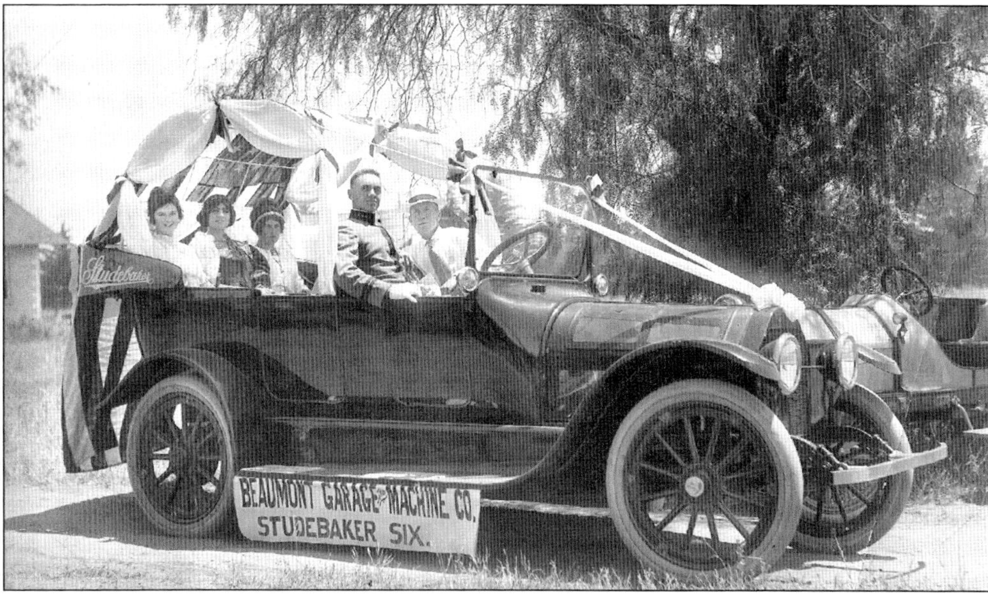

The first Cherry Festival began in 1913 and, along with the following year's festival, was a great success. This Studebaker was brought out from Los Angeles to carry the festival's first queen during the 1919 parade. Laura Mae Stewart is seen in the center rear seat of the Studebaker. Princesses Lois Behu (right) and Clara Dietrich (left) flank her. Lawrence Rulier, in uniform, is the queen's escort, and E. O. Jones is the driver. (Courtesy of Marilyn Vonderheide and LMSF.)

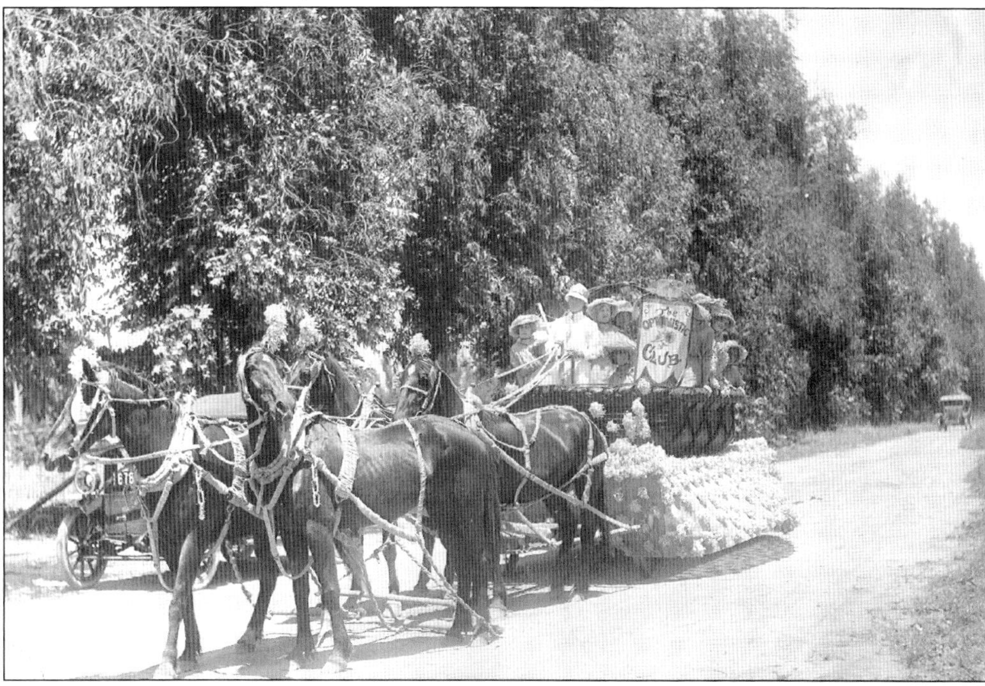

This is the Optimistic Club of Beaumont's impressive float that entered the second Cherry Festival in 1914. The scene is probably set along Beaumont Boulevard. It is interesting to observe that the road had not at yet been paved. This route would be followed for Cherry Festival parades for years to come. (Courtesy of Marilyn Vonderheide and LMSF.)

Two

BEAUMONT STREET SCENES

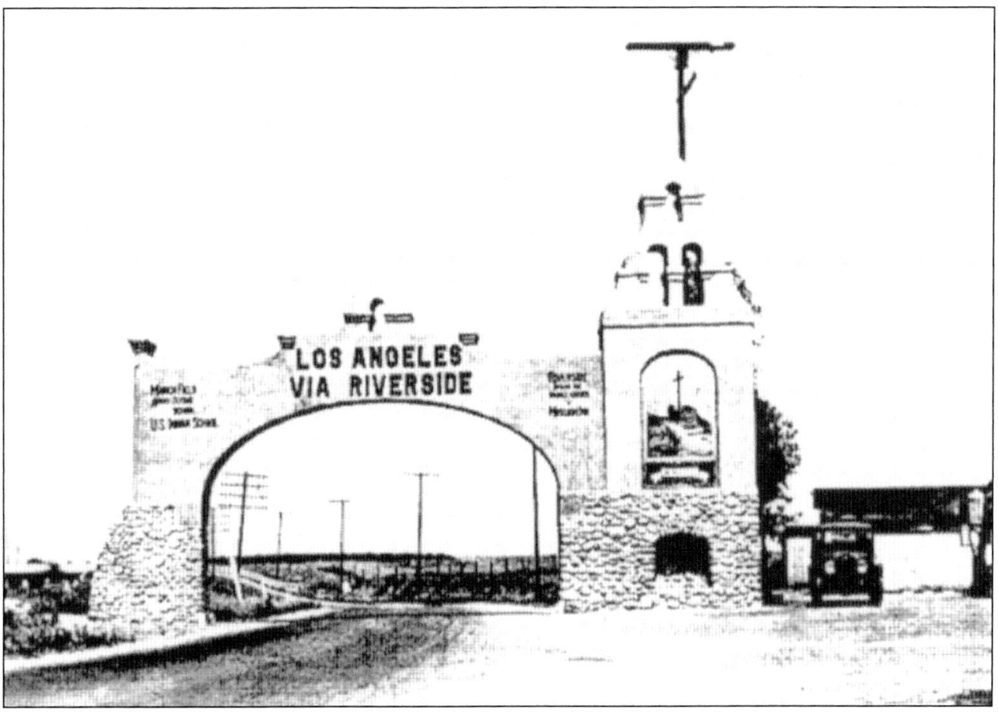

The arch seen here once spanned and adorned the entrance to the city of Beaumont at its west entrance. As one left Beaumont heading west, it was evident that Los Angeles could only be accessed through the city of Riverside because Interstate 10 had not yet been constructed and travel via the city of Redlands was not an option. The archway was razed to make way for the construction of Interstate 10. (Courtesy of Bill Bell.)

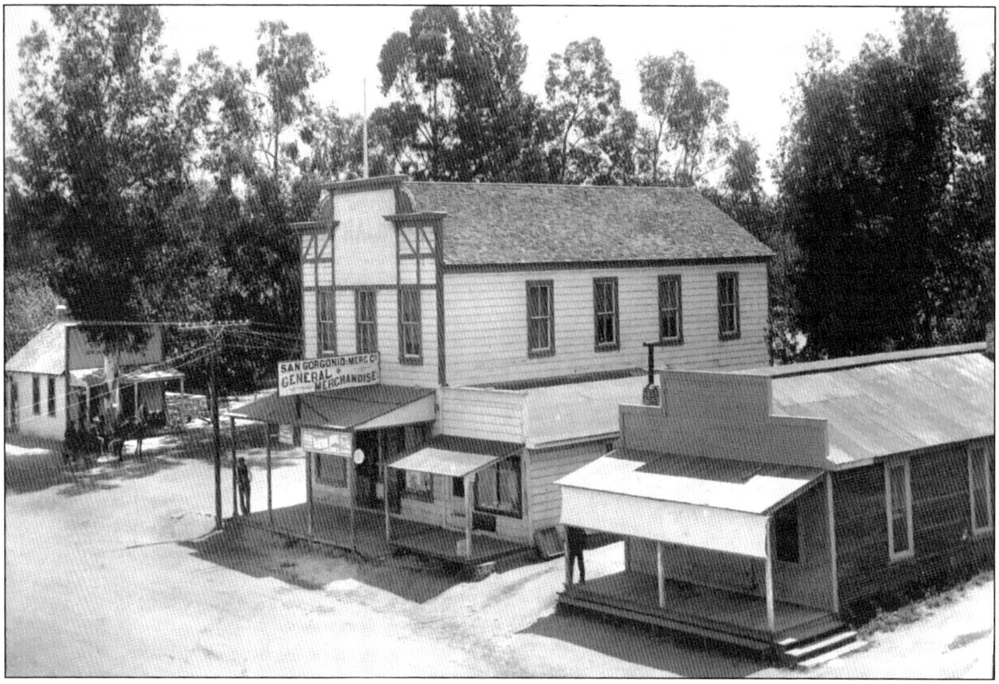

This is the intersection of Fifth Street and Egan Avenue as it looked in the 1890s. The view depicts Egan Avenue looking south with the old Beaumont Post Office, at the extreme left on the southwest corner of Fifth Street and Egan Avenue and diagonally across from the northeast corner, where the second Bank of Beaumont building currently stands. The San Gorgonio Mercantile Company and a pool hall are the other two buildings, both fronting east. This was main business section in town for many years, which stood near the railroad depot. (Courtesy of Marilyn Vonderheide and LMSF.)

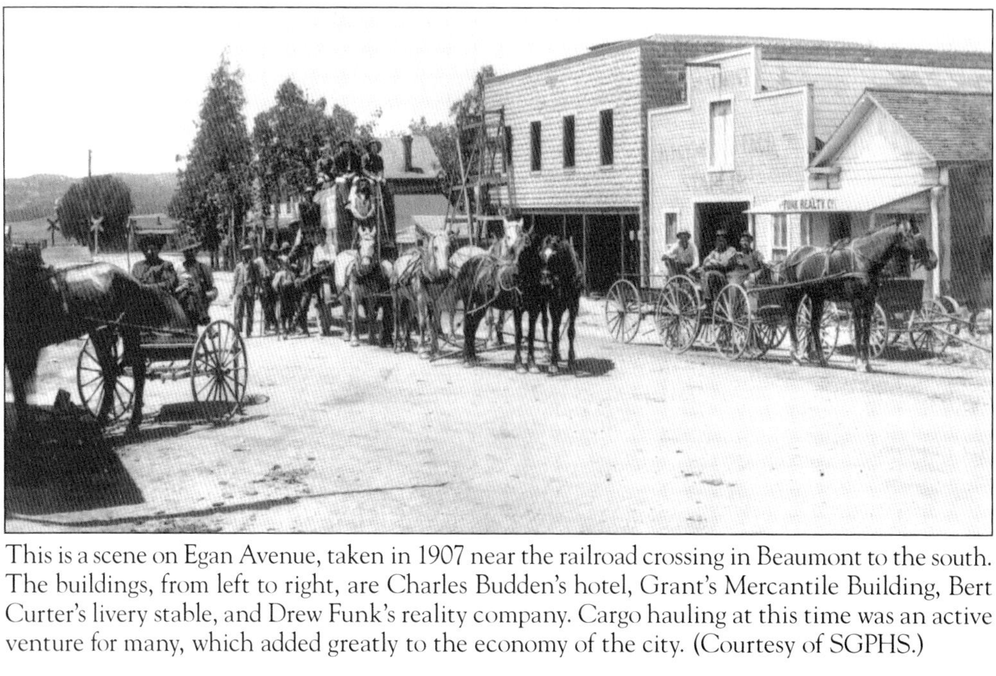

This is a scene on Egan Avenue, taken in 1907 near the railroad crossing in Beaumont to the south. The buildings, from left to right, are Charles Budden's hotel, Grant's Mercantile Building, Bert Curter's livery stable, and Drew Funk's reality company. Cargo hauling at this time was an active venture for many, which added greatly to the economy of the city. (Courtesy of SGPHS.)

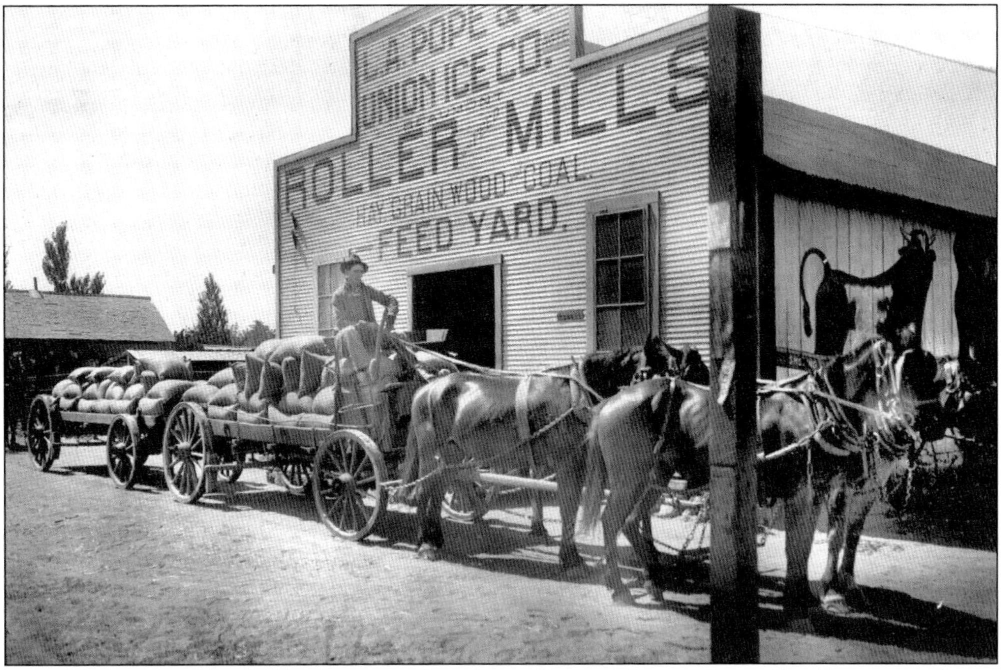

A freshly harvested load of barley is seen here being deposited to a roller mill in Beaumont. Street scenes like this were not uncommon during the era, because grains were extensively grown and were required to be transported by cart-and-horse team. The establishment revealed dealt in grains, wood, coal, and ice. (Courtesy of Marilyn Vonderheide and LMSF.)

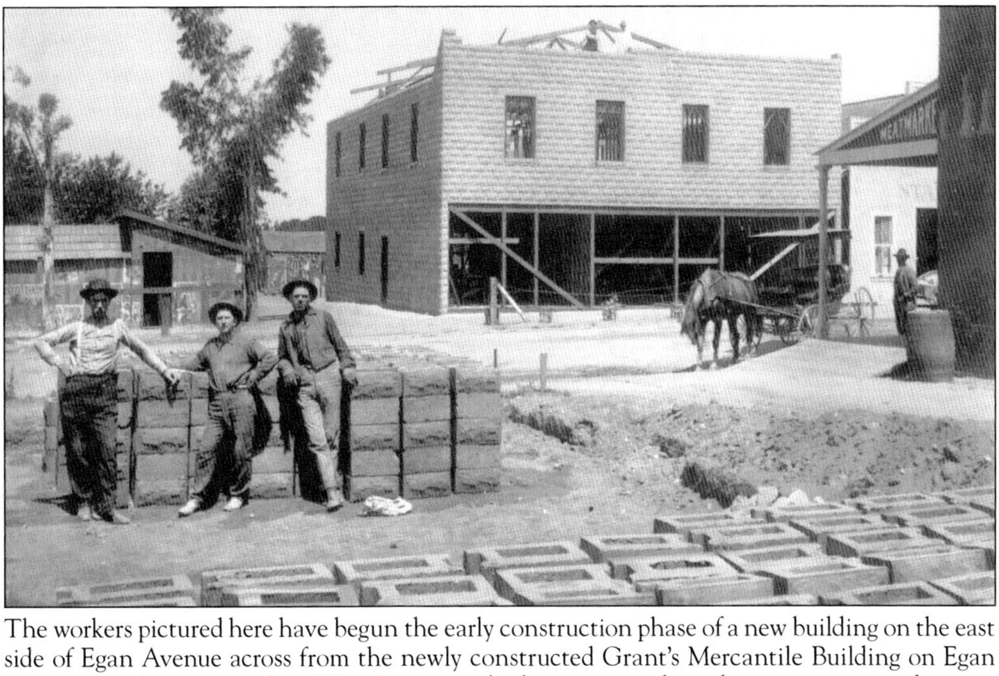

The workers pictured here have begun the early construction phase of a new building on the east side of Egan Avenue across from the newly constructed Grant's Mercantile Building on Egan Avenue. By this time in the 1900s, Beaumont had incorporated sturdy construction techniques to erect new buildings, as can be evidenced by the heavy cement blocks in the foreground of the picture and the block building across the street. (Courtesy of SGPHS.)

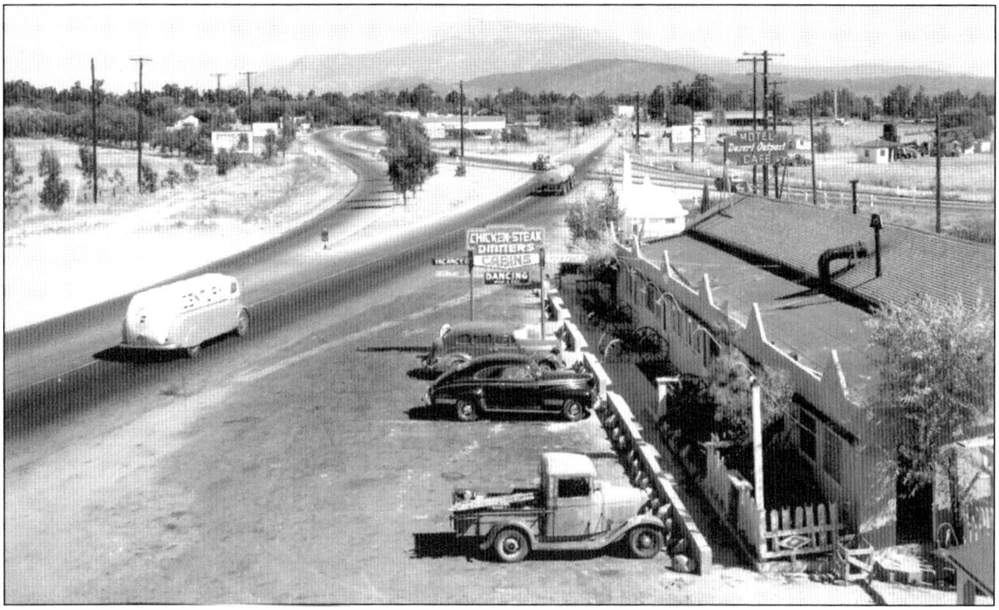

Seen here is the Desert Outpost Motel and Café as it appeared on the outskirts of Beaumont in its early years of development. The view is looking to the east at the intersection of U.S. Highways 99 and 60 with Mount Jacinto in the background. Note the light traffic on the highways encompassing the general area around the café. (Courtesy of Steve Lech.)

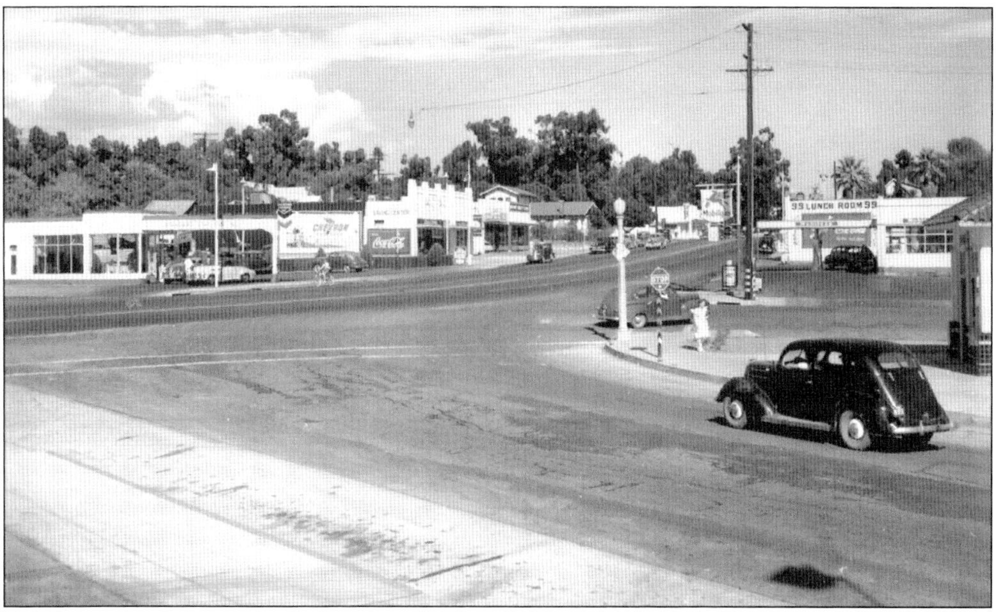

This photograph was taken on Sixth Street, where it is intersected at the right by Grace Street and also at upper right of California Avenue, slightly farther east. Note the Mobil gas station on the corner of Sixth and Grace Streets, across from the Chevron station on the opposite side of Sixth. The edge of the small building that appears at the extreme right of the photograph today serves as a dry-cleaning business. (Courtesy of Steve Lech.)

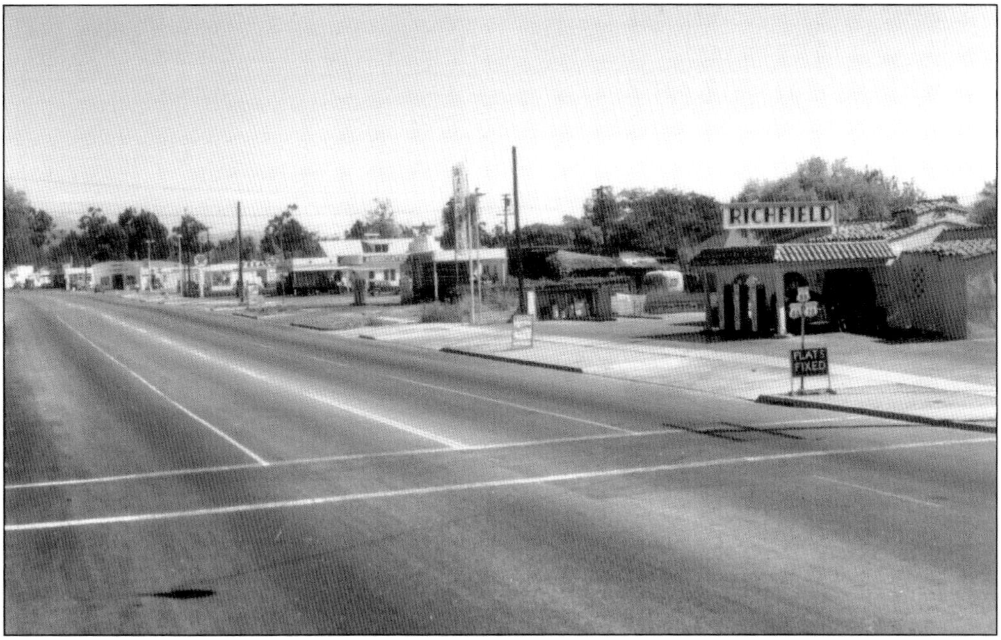

The view of Sixth Street depicted in this photograph along Highways 99, 60, and 70, as noted on the street sign at the roadside near the Richfield station, indicates the extent of gas stations in Beaumont during this era. In this block alone, Richfield, Associated, and Texaco are seen nearly side by side, and others were nearby. (Courtesy of Steve Lech.)

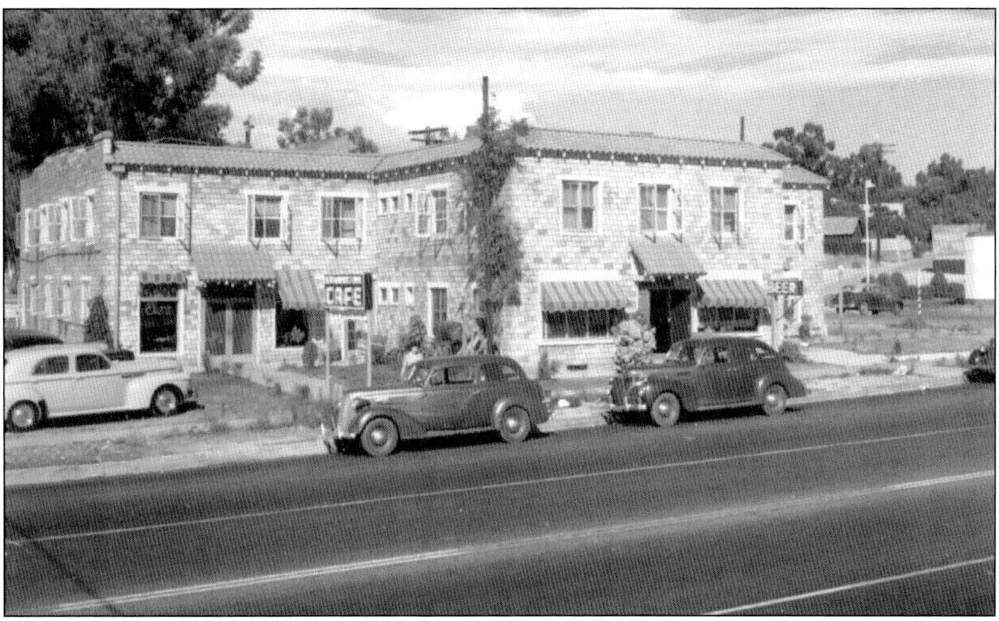

By 1946, California Hotel had changed its name to Beaumont Inn and Café. It is pictured here at the time when it operated as an inn and café. It was located on the corner of California Avenue and Sixth Street, and the structure can still be seen there today, as it houses a shelter for battered women and children. (Courtesy of Steve Lech.)

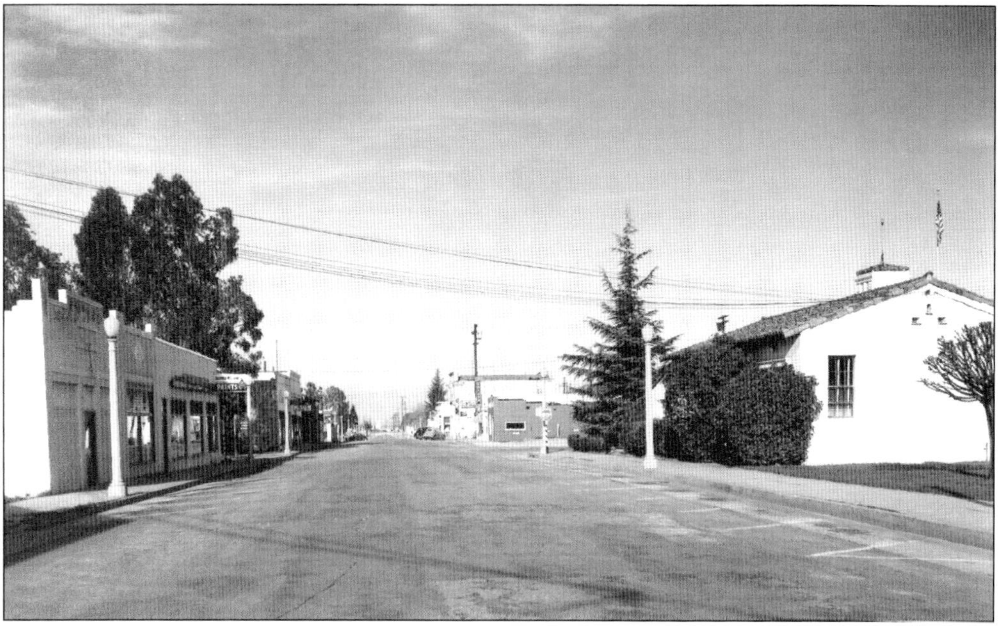

This is a view of Fifth Street just east of the intersection of Grace Street, which passes in front of the civic center. The photograph was taken sometime after 1923, because the new Bank of Beaumont is seen in the center, just behind the tall electric pole, and it was built in 1923. (Courtesy of Steve Lech.)

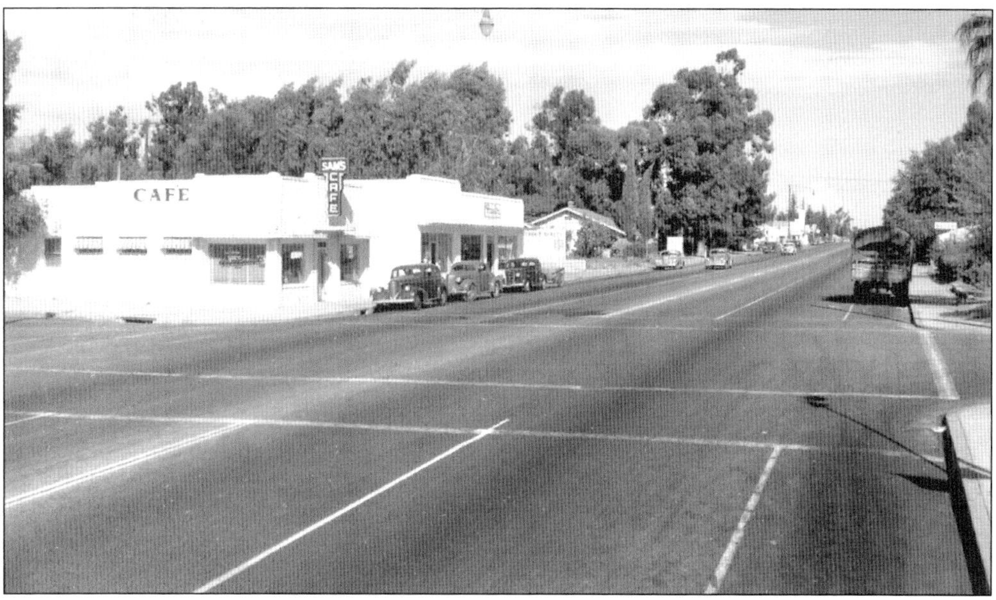

Pictured here is a scene along Sixth Street in Beaumont looking east during the late 1930s. Sam's Café, at left, was a popular stop for many of Beaumont locals. Note the 1936 Ford that is supporting a trailer at the curb beside Sam's. During this time, Beaumont appears to be a quiet and serene town. (Courtesy of Steve Lech.)

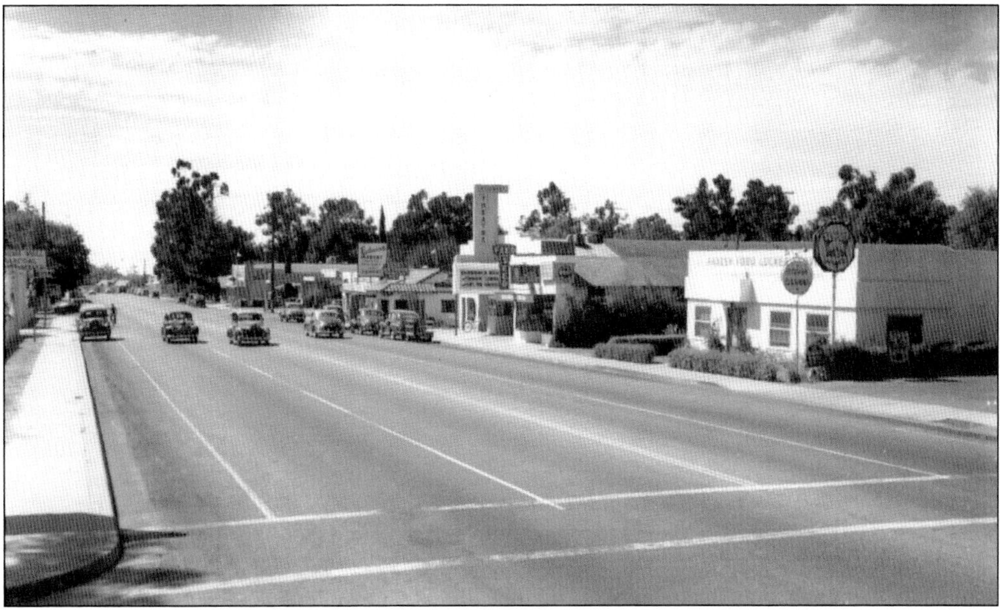

This photograph was taken on Sixth Street looking west. Note the Beaumont Theater, at center, which today houses an antique shop, one of many in Beaumont. Also note the line of cars across the highway, which helps date the photograph to the mid-1940s. (Courtesy of Steve Lech.)

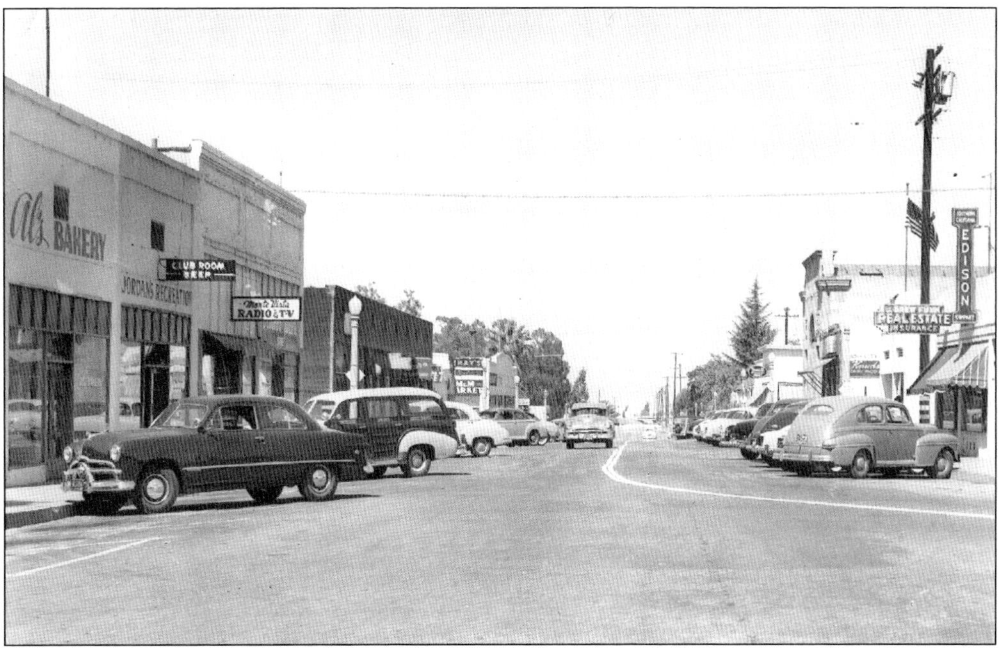

This post-1923 street scene was taken looking west on Fifth Street at the Grace Street intersection in the heart of Beaumont. The facade of the second bank of Beaumont, which was built in 1923 by land developer Fred Hirsch, stands out prominently at the right of the photograph. The late 1940s and early 1950s cars somewhat date the scene. (Courtesy of Steve Lech.)

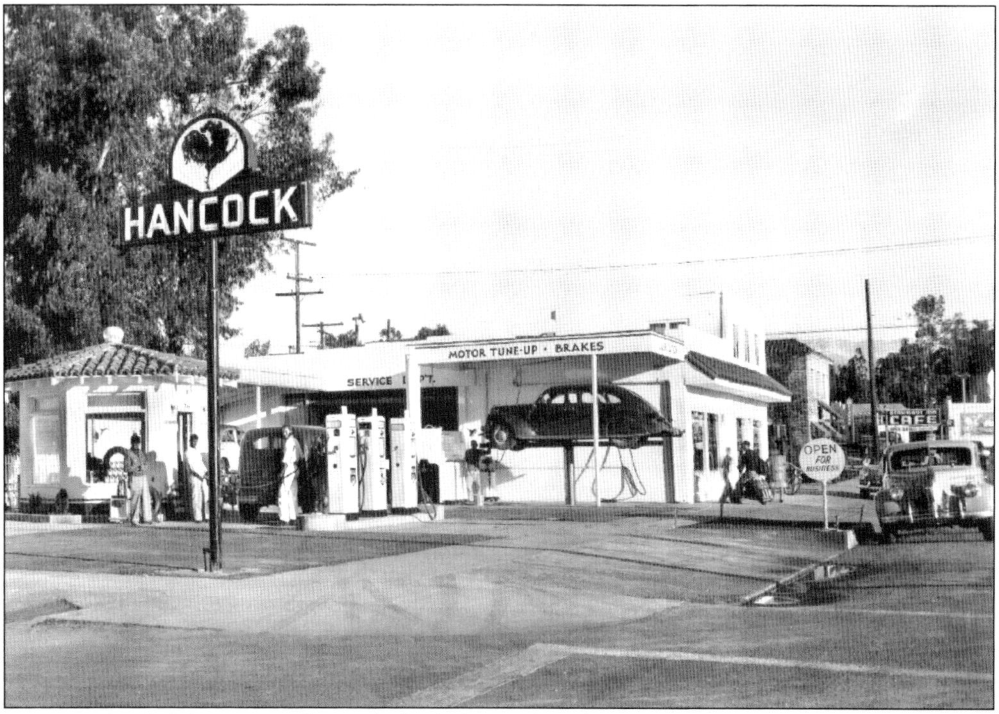

By 1946, the California Hotel at right had changed to the Beaumont Inn and Café. To its west is the Hancock Station, which bought the old Chevron station and updated it with a hydraulic car lift and an automobile-parts store. The property was leased and operated by Clarence Lewis, who is pictured servicing a car on the lift. (Courtesy of Beverly Lewis.)

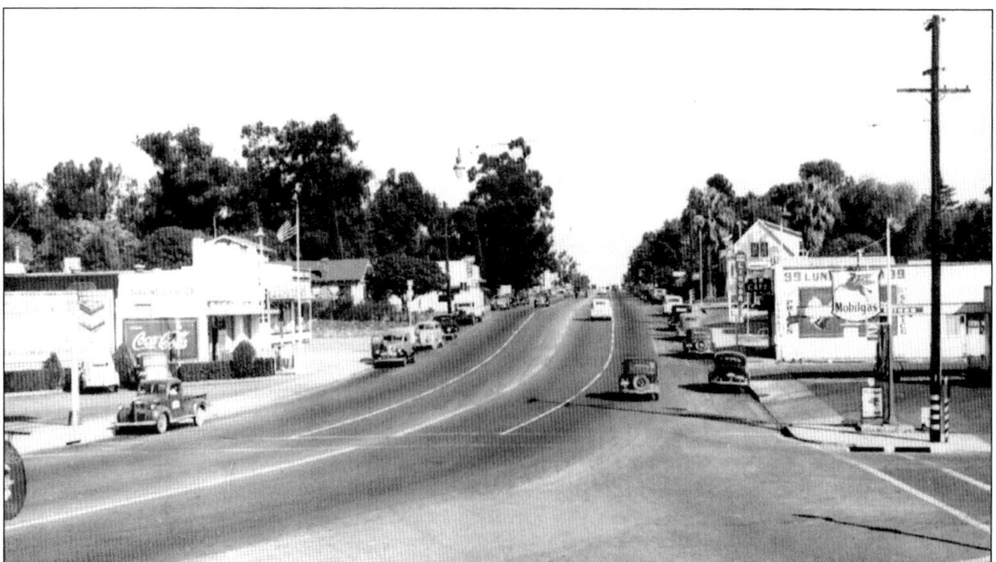

This is an early scene in Beaumont looking east down Sixth Street. The street is populated with old cars, which indicates the activity in Beaumont during this time. The cross street, at right entering the curve, is California Avenue, which leads to Fifth Street a block to the south. Fifth Street was once considered the center artery of town. (Courtesy of Steve Lech.)

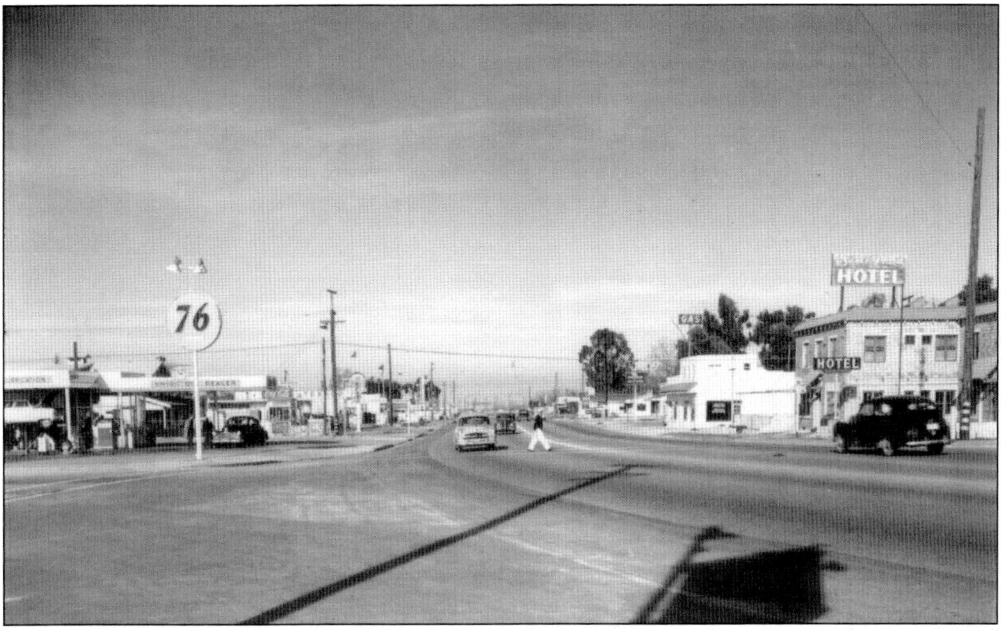

Pictured here in an early scene on Sixth Street looking west at the curve at the crossing of California Avenue. To the right is a popular establishment along the street called the California Hotel. Throughout the years, it went by several different names, usually changing with new ownership. The Chevron Station to its west later became the Hancock Station. (Courtesy of Steve Lech.)

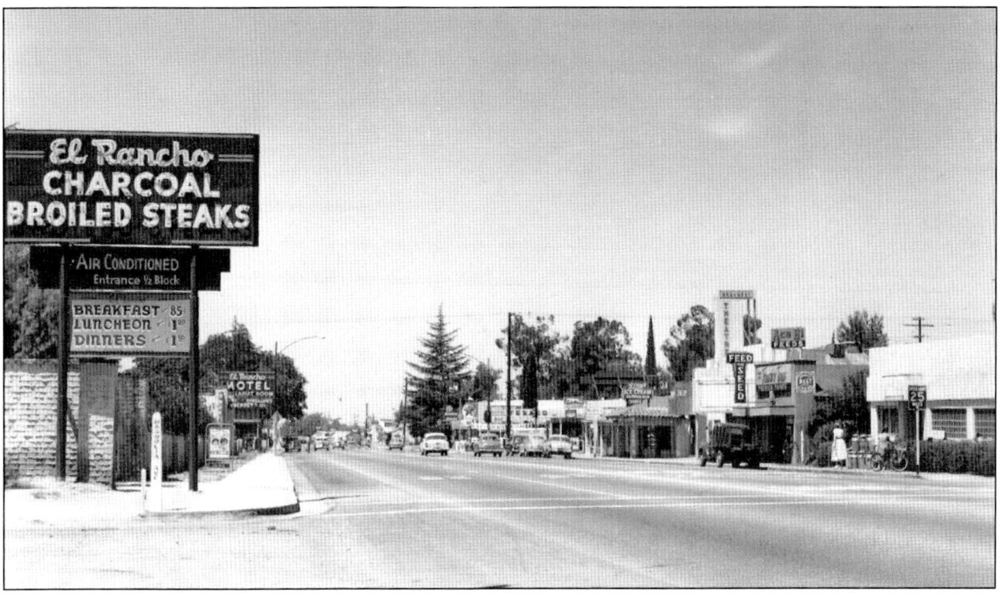

This photograph depicts Sixth Street looking west from Magnolia Avenue in the center of Beaumont. Notable is the marquee of the Beaumont Theater on the right and the El Rancho Motel sign on the left advertising its lariat room, thusly denoting its western viewpoint. The location where the El Rancho sign then stood is now occupied by Wells Fargo Bank. (Courtesy of Steve Lech.)

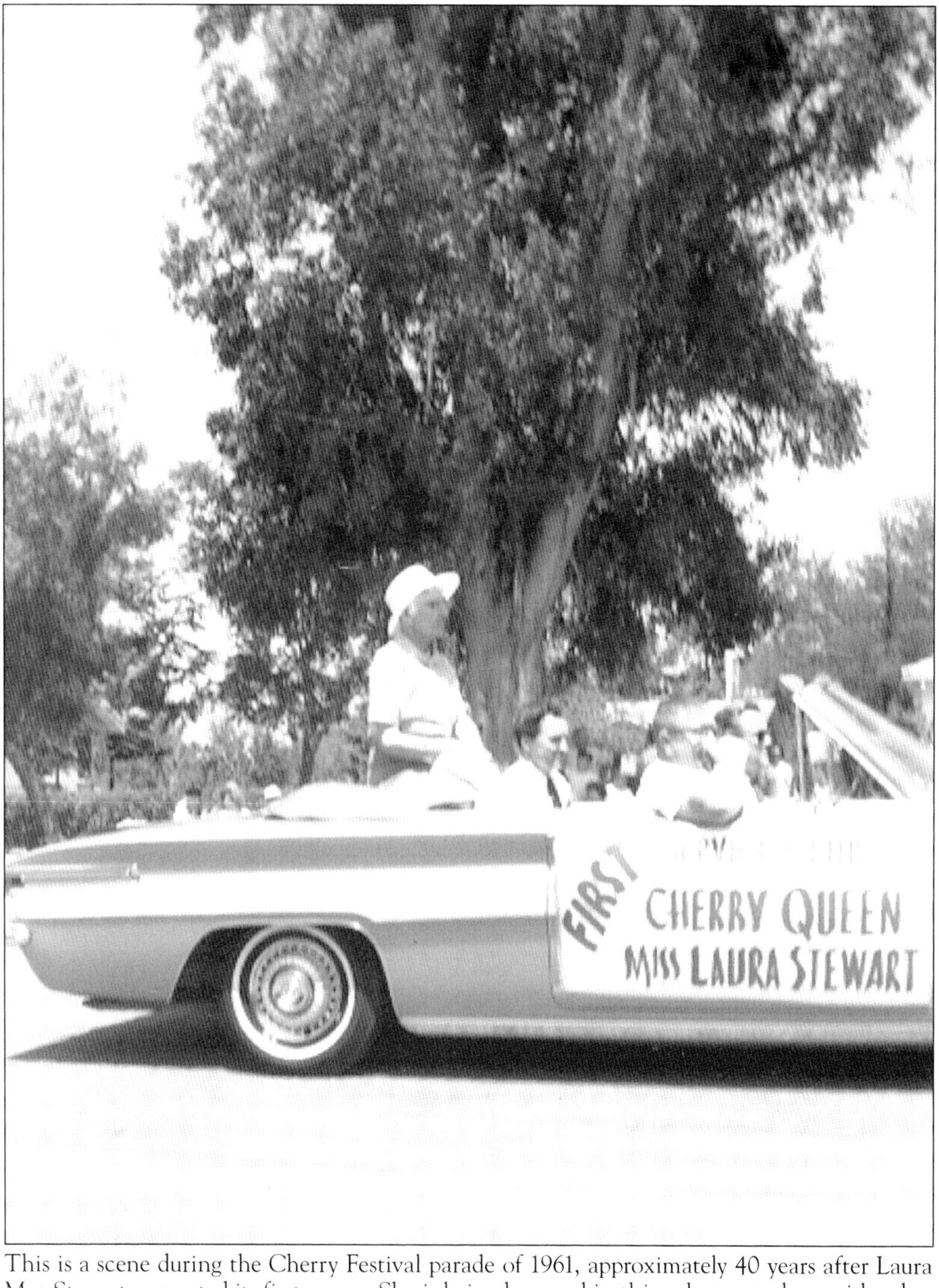

This is a scene during the Cherry Festival parade of 1961, approximately 40 years after Laura Mae Stewart was voted its first queen. She is being honored in this gala event along with other Beaumont prominent citizens. The parade by now had changed in many respects. It was around this time that a local roller-skating rink in Beaumont entered Pinky, a donkey painted pink who would skate on roller skates for the length of the parade course. (Courtesy of Marilyn Vonderheide and LMSF.)

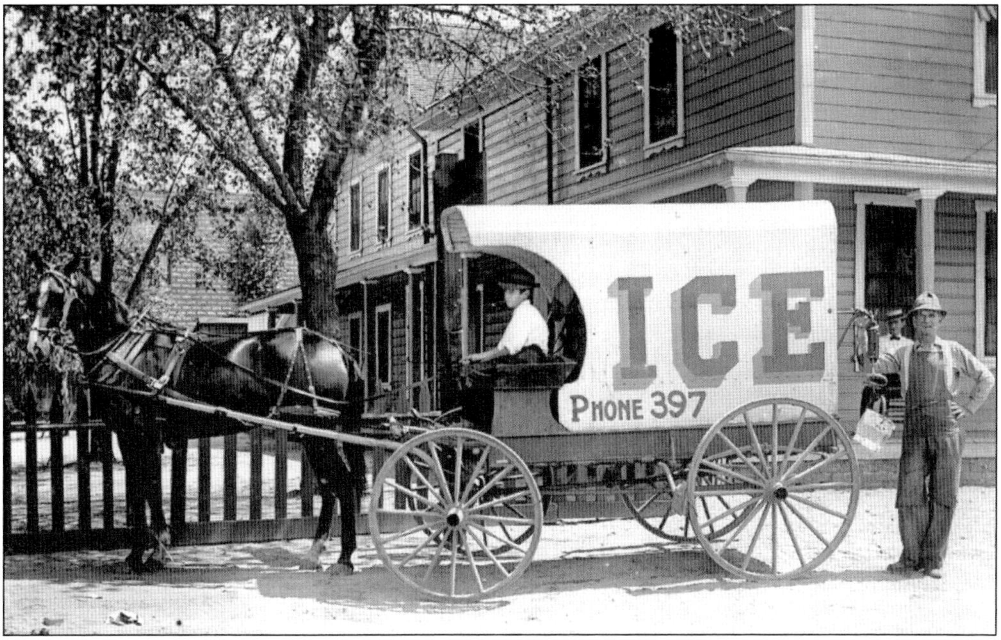

When ice became available in the San Gorgonio Pass, ice business proved a lucrative venture. It was hauled from San Bernardino and delivered to Beaumont, Banning, and Palm Springs in large 300-pound slabs, often used in that form for cooling cabinets. This Beaumont ice-delivery wagon is pictured here with a cake of ice being weighed at the rear of the wagon. (Courtesy of Marilyn Vonderheide, LMSF.)

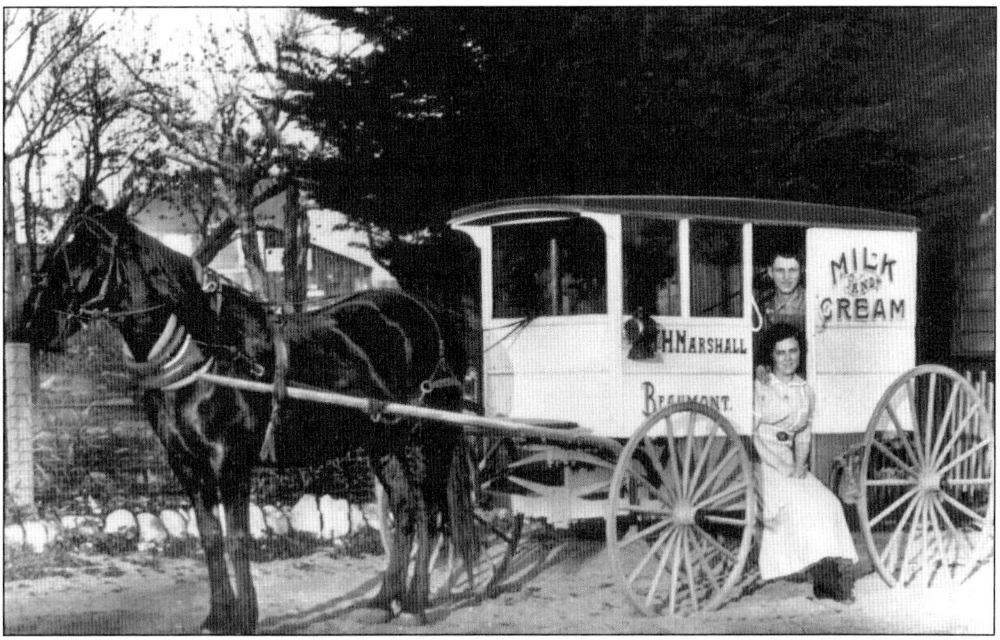

This one-horse carriage of the Marshall Company of Beaumont was often seen delivering milk and cream around the streets of Beaumont. Delivery services such as this were quite prevalent for both milk and ice during the town's early years. The horse appears to be waiting patiently while the driver and delivery lady stop to pose for the photograph. (Courtesy of SGPHS.)

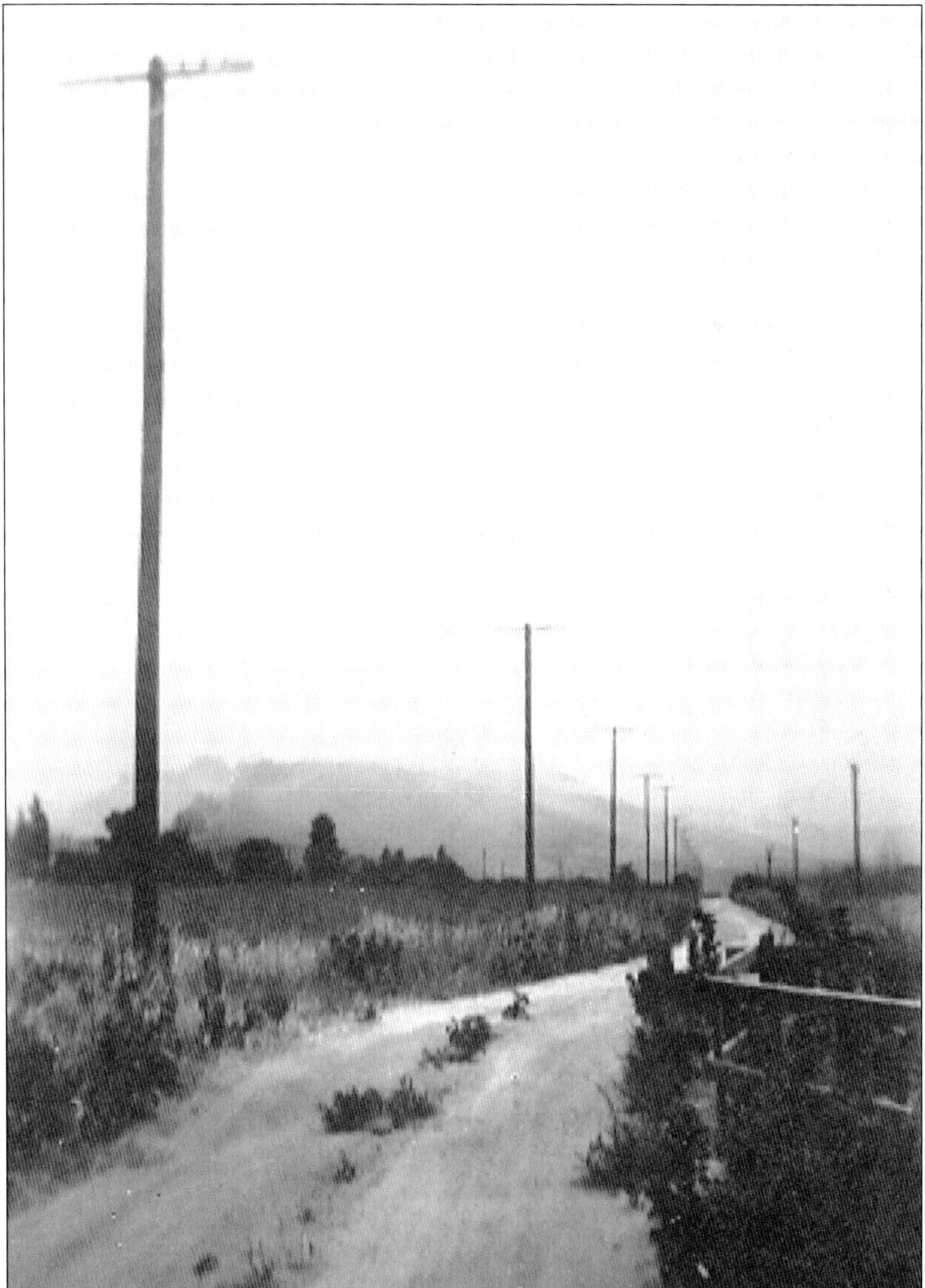

This photograph, taken July 15, 1929, depicts Highland Springs Boulevard looking south before it was improved and paved. It has changed drastically since that time, although today it still essentially follows the same path. Notice the overgrown weeds and shrubs in and along the road, denoting infrequent use. (Courtesy of SGPHS.)

Three

CIRCLE C RANCH

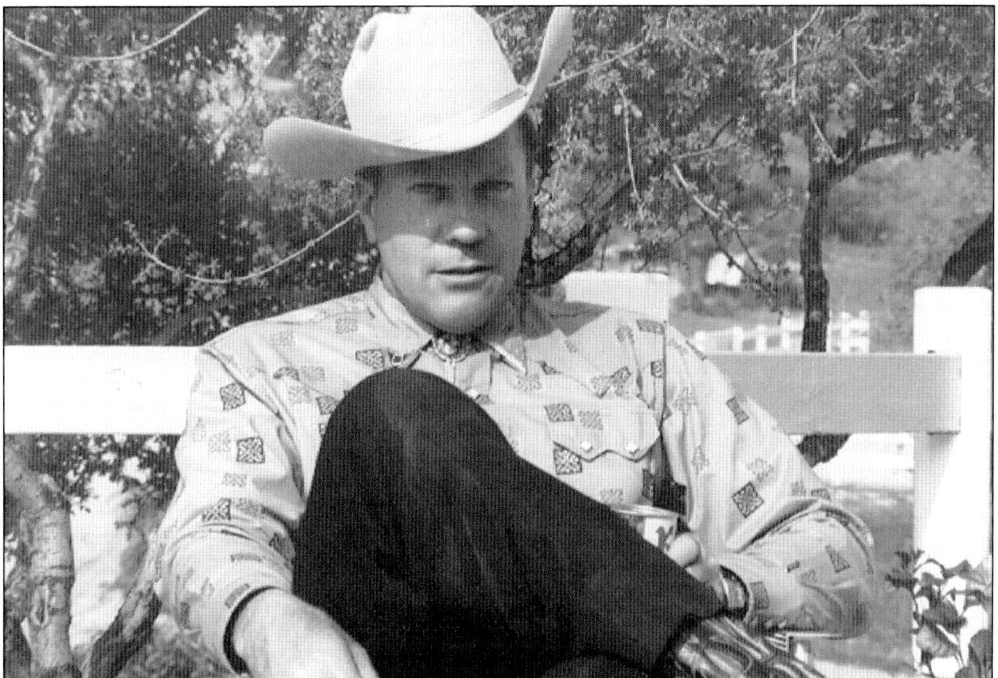

This photograph has been dubbed "Founding Father" because it portrays Phil Smith, the man who extended much of his energy toward founding one of the great ranches in the Beaumont area, an abode he shared with many others. Visitors who often came here were housed in appealing cottages on the ranch. (Courtesy of Sue Smith.)

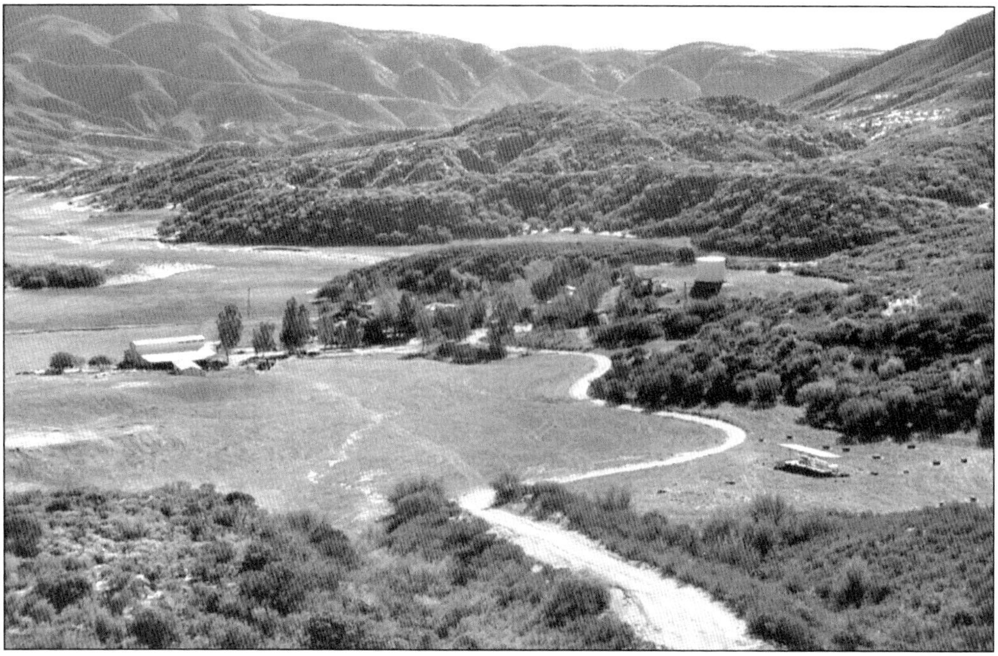

This photograph is of the Circle C Ranch after it had undergone extensive modernization after being bought by Phil and Sue Smith in 1957 from Bob Cardwell. It was located in Beaumont's southern area and faced and bordered the portreo area to the south known as the Wolfskill Ranch, which was later bought by Lockheed Propulsion. (Courtesy of Circle C Ranch.)

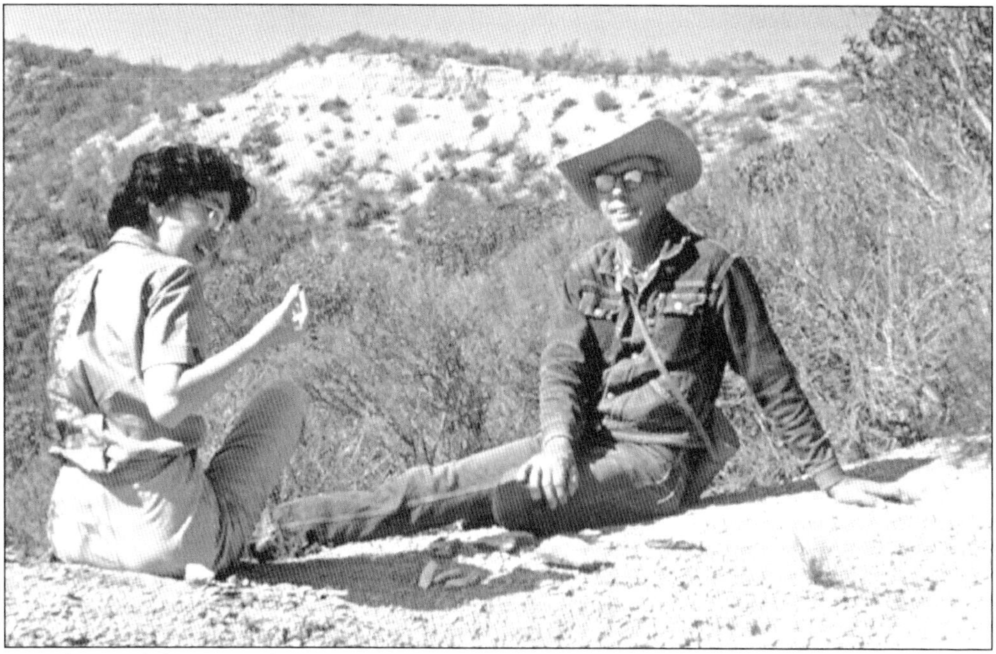

Seen here at left is a Circle C Ranch visitor of Bob Cardwell, a previous owner of the Circle C Ranch in the late 1950s. Bob has a few artifacts before him on the ground, which he is describing to an interested visitor. She appears to be quite engrossed in the small object she is holding and inspecting. (Courtesy of Sue Smith.)

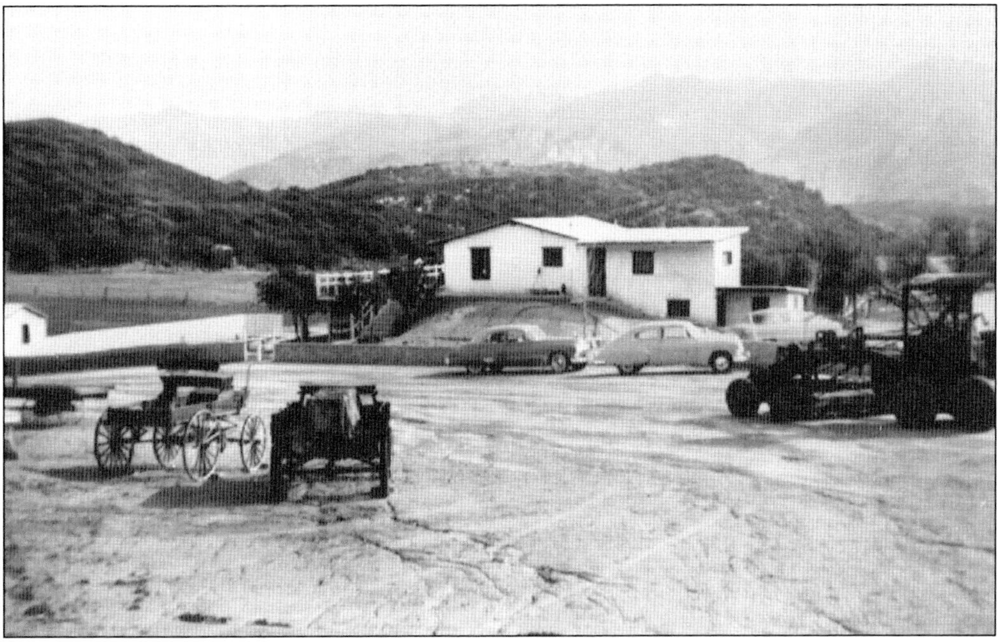

The Circle C Ranch of Bob Cardwell, in the early years of his ownership, is pictured here. Art Leth owned the ranch prior to Cardwell. Leth had a business of making cement blocks and consequently used them for various projects on the ranch, such as watering troughs for his animals and construction of a reservoir. (Courtesy of Circle C Ranch.)

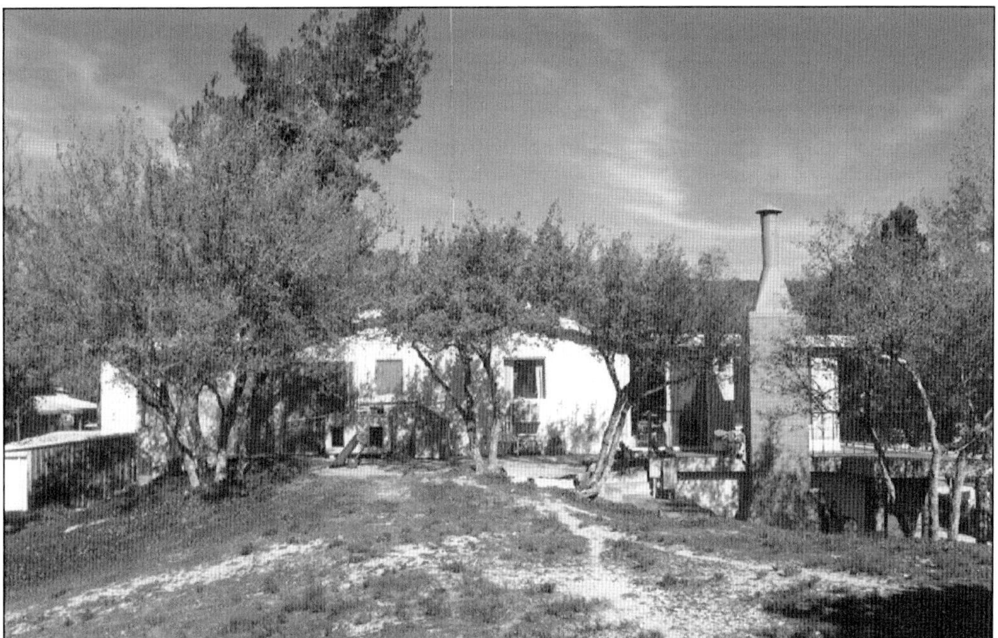

This is the southern view of the renovated Circle C Ranch house. One of the major revisions to the old homestead was the addition of the "Coyote Room," seen here with its fireplace chimney at right. It derived this name because nearby coyotes could be heard howling through the plate-glass wall in the evenings. (Courtesy of Sue Smith.)

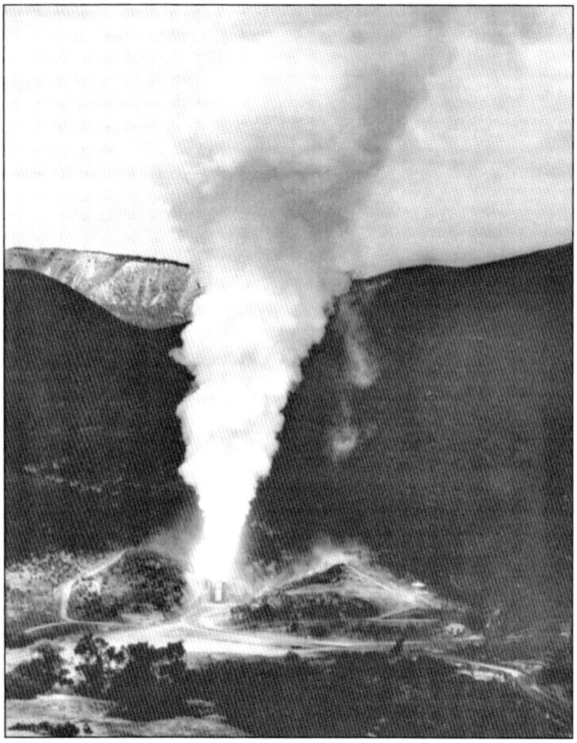

In the 1960s, the Wolfskill Ranch bordering the Circle C Ranch to the south was owned by Lockheed Propulsion in Mentone, California. It was to be used primarily as a site to test fire Lockheed's solid-state propellant motors in development for the Apollo space project. This photograph depicts a test firing in progress. (Courtesy of Banning Library.)

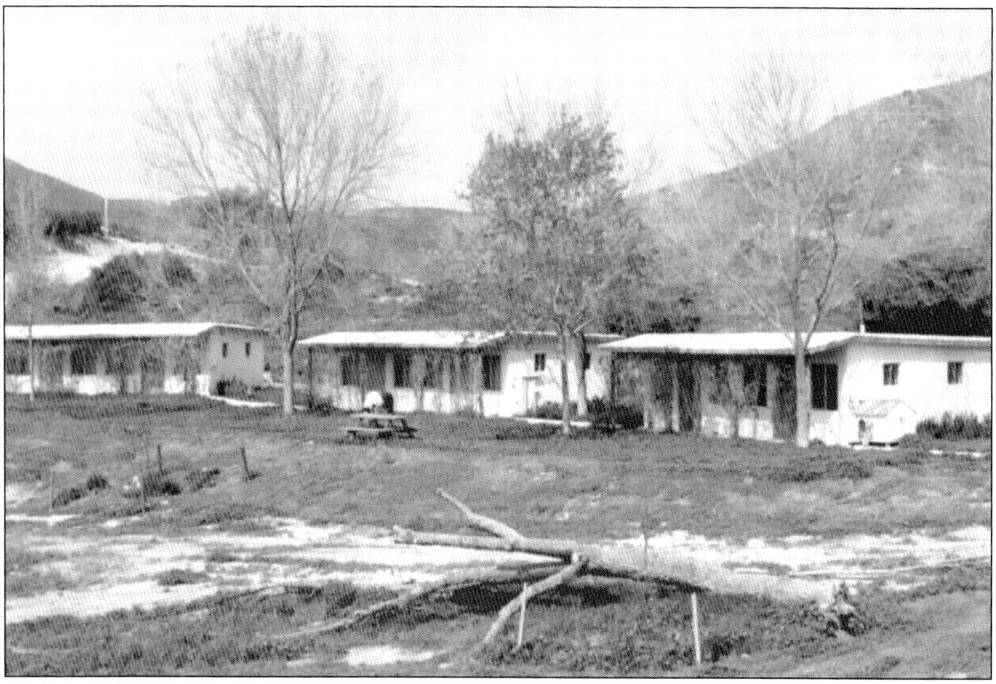

Although the large barn, tack room, and shooting range were important additions to the Circle C Ranch constructed by the Smiths, they considered a string of cottages they built to be important as well, because they often had visitors at the ranch who lodged there. This photograph depicts three duplex cottages on the ranch they named Sleepy Hollow. (Courtesy of Circle C Ranch.)

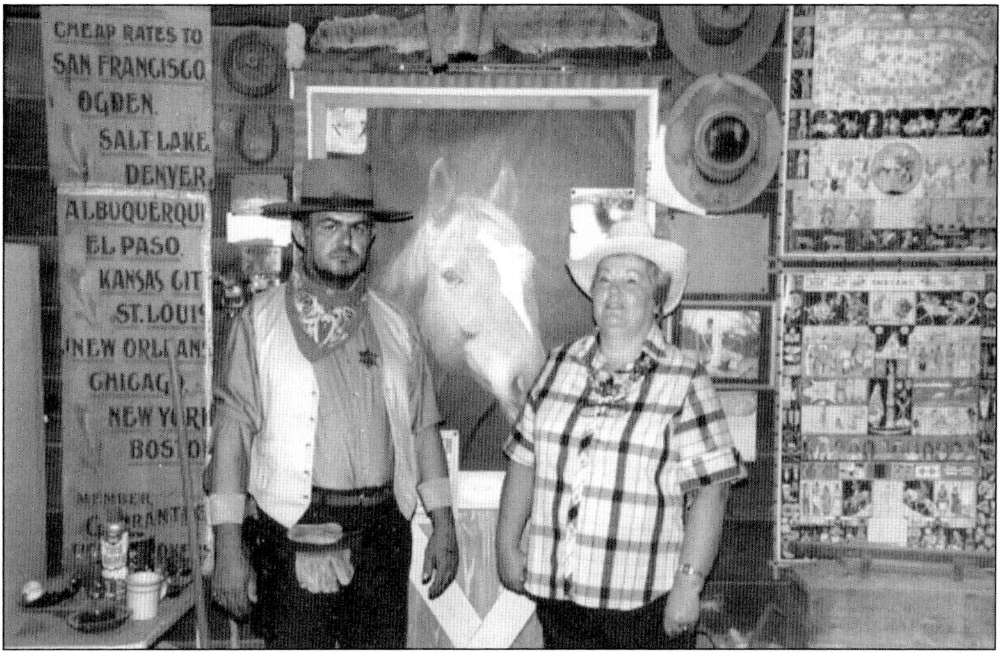

Pictured here are two of the several caretakers of the Circle C Ranch over the years. At left is an actual sign used by a local stagecoach line to advertise its cheap rates and available destinations. It was obscured on an old dresser top for years until Sue Smith discovered it when restoring the dresser, which had been given to the Smiths by Marian Gilman Hunt. The sign can be seen today at the Gilman Historic Ranch and Wagon Museum in Banning where the Smiths donated it. (Courtesy of Sue Smith.)

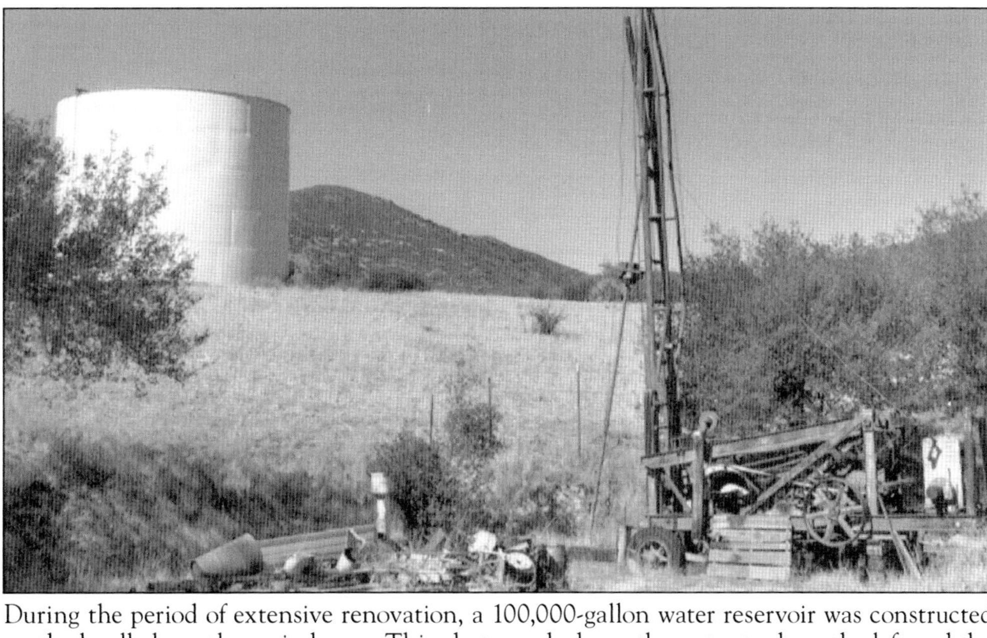

During the period of extensive renovation, a 100,000-gallon water reservoir was constructed on the knoll above the main house. This photograph shows the water tank on the left and the drilling rig in the bottom foreground. The drill rig was a part of the Circle C equipment and was named "Phyllis Driller" by Phil Smith. (Courtesy of Circle C Ranch.)

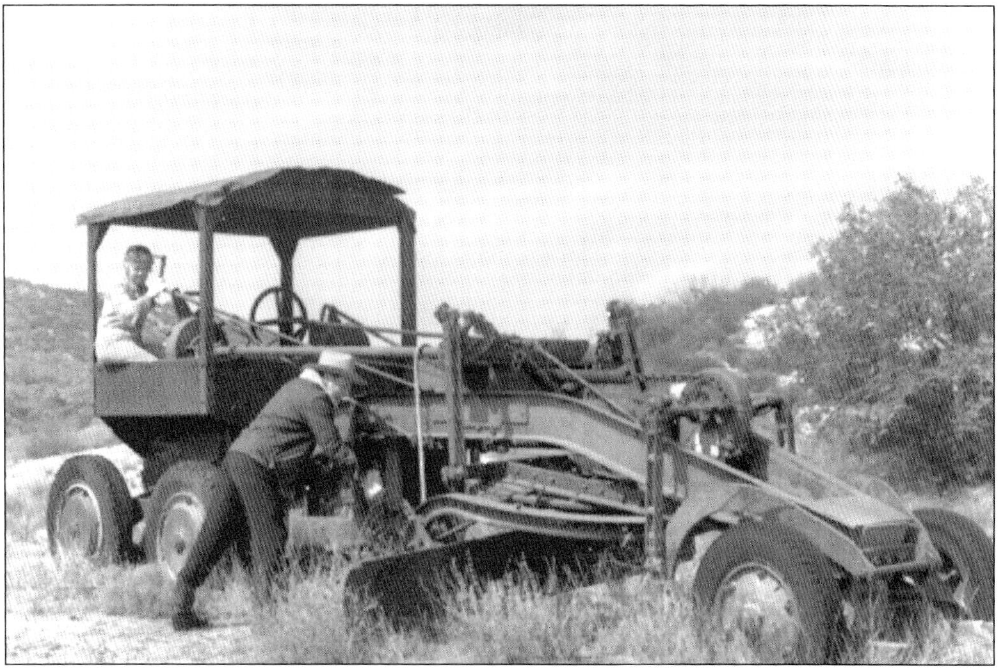

This photograph depicts the Smiths checking out the 1934 grader. It was used in the Pacific Islands during World War II to build landing strips and was purchased by Cardwell, the previous owner of the ranch. Sue is seen sitting behind the blade-control lever, and Phil is checking the engine. It was used to maintain the road to the ranch and was dubbed "Sweet Rosie O'Grader" by Phil. (Courtesy of Sue Smith.)

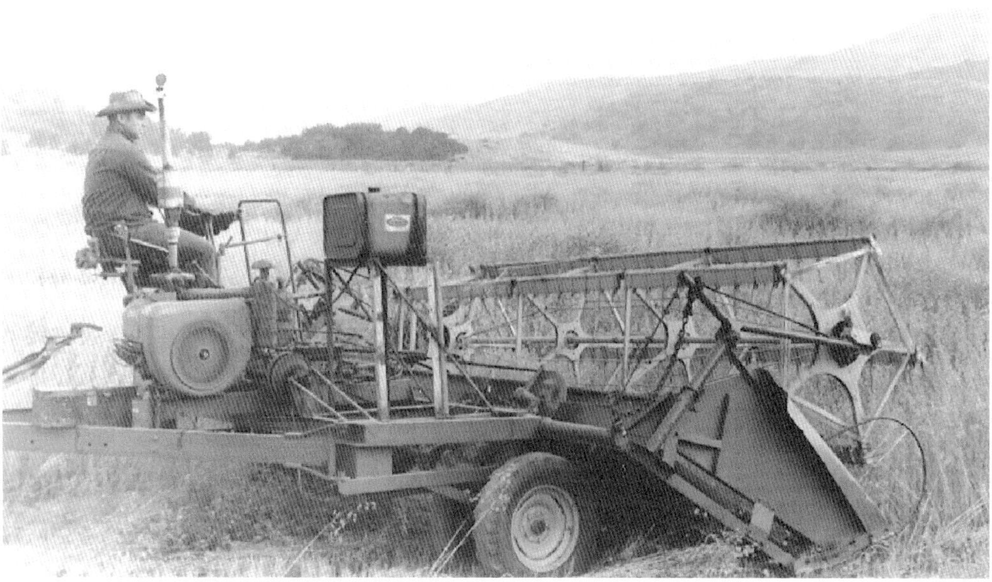

Although the Dysart's Ranch was in Banning, east of Beaumont, it also farmed on leased acreage on the Circle C Ranch. Dave Dysart is seen here cutting the oats on the Circle C Ranch that had been dry farmed. Barley and oats were lucrative crops for livestock feed during this era, and they appealed to many farmers in the area because they dry farmed well. (Courtesy of Sue Smith.)

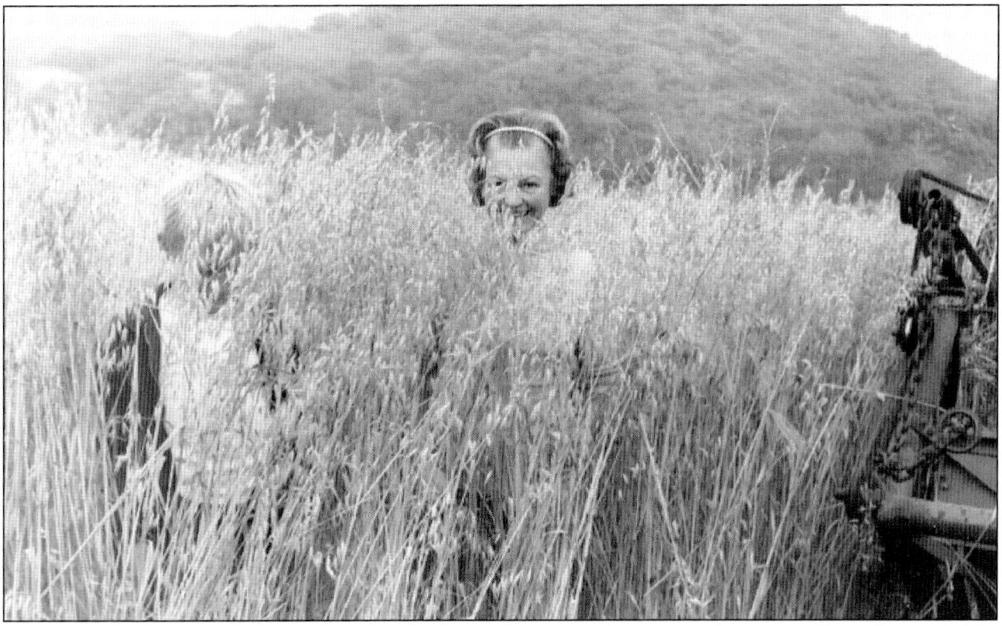

Dave Dysart's son Dennis stands in a crop of tall barley with Sue Smith in one of Circle C's fields. Dennis is almost totally obscured by the barley, and for Sue it reached head high. Barley was the major crop grown on the 160-acre ranch that the Smiths operated. (Courtesy of Sue Smith.)

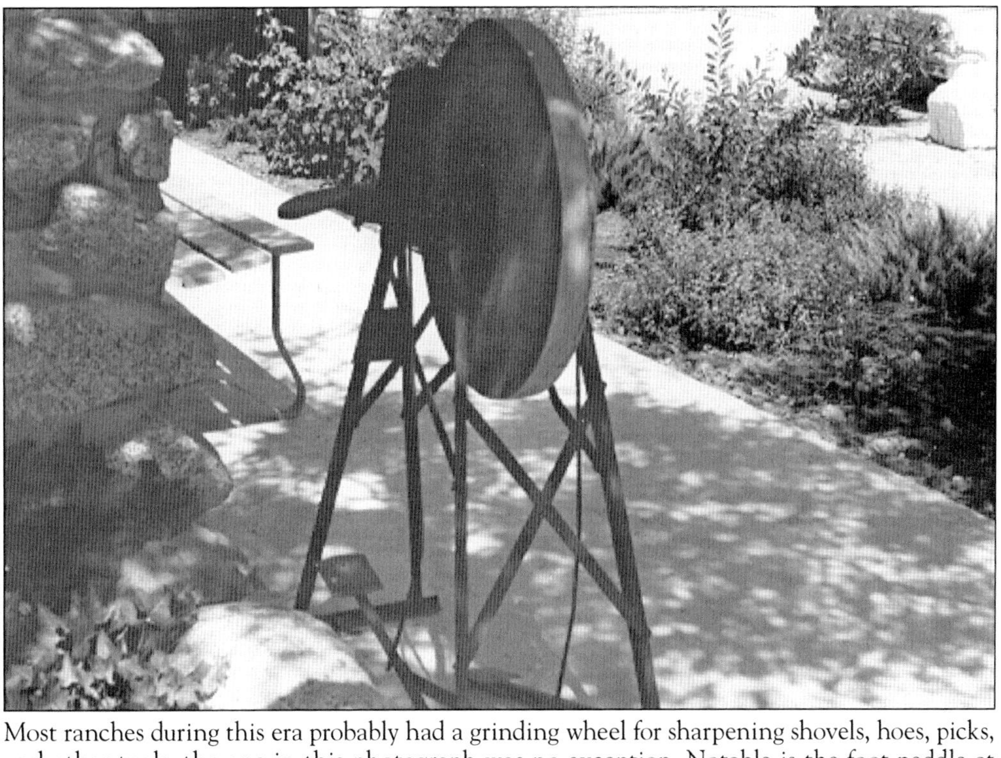

Most ranches during this era probably had a grinding wheel for sharpening shovels, hoes, picks, and other tools; the one in this photograph was no exception. Notable is the foot peddle at the bottom of the large stone grinding wheel that was used to turn the wheel while grinding. (Courtesy of Circle C Ranch.)

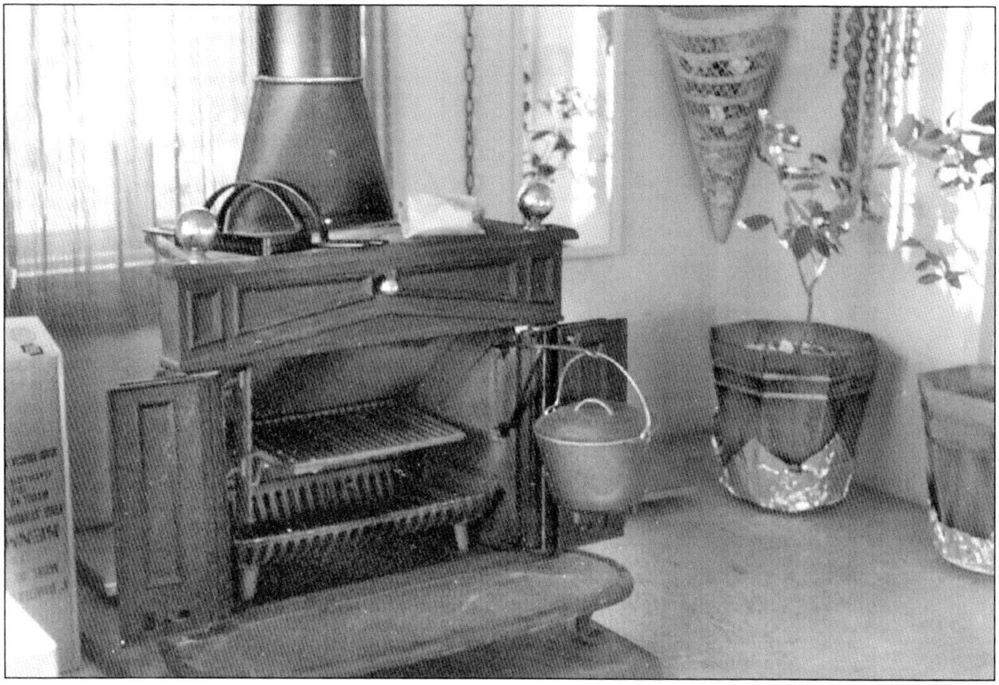

This large Franklin stove replica served the ranch house well for heating the homestead at the Circle C Ranch. It had an alternative use as well; note the large cooking pot hanging on the arm at the right side of the stove that could be swung into the interior and placed over the coals for cooking. (Courtesy of Circle C Ranch.)

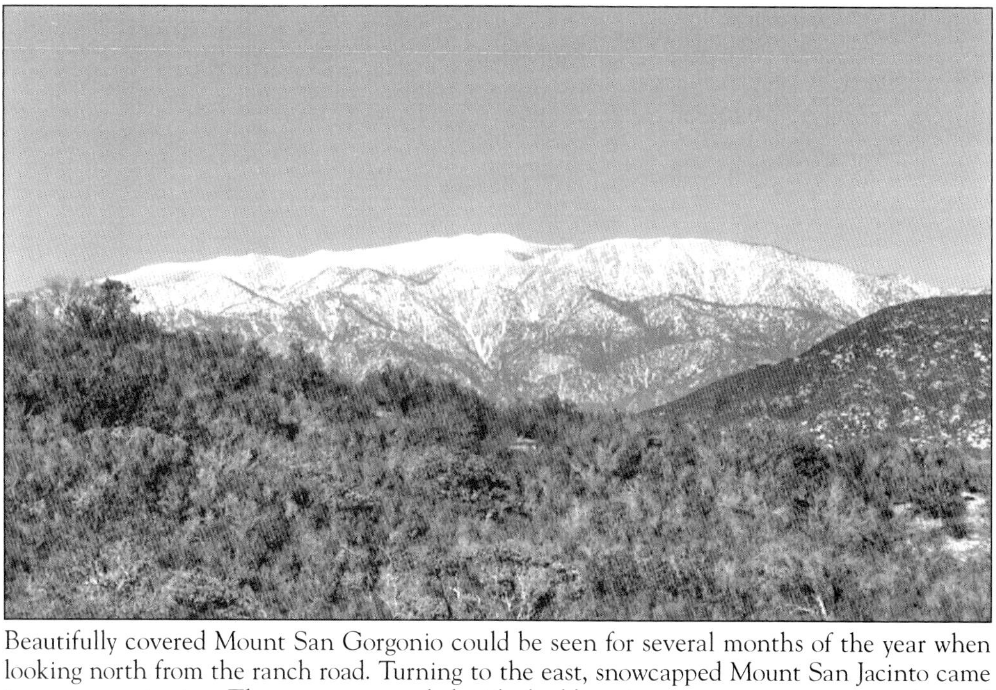

Beautifully covered Mount San Gorgonio could be seen for several months of the year when looking north from the ranch road. Turning to the east, snowcapped Mount San Jacinto came into panoramic view. These scenes, coupled with the blooming sage, rosemary, manzanita, and wildflowers, composed the abounding beauty found in the area. (Courtesy of Sue Smith.)

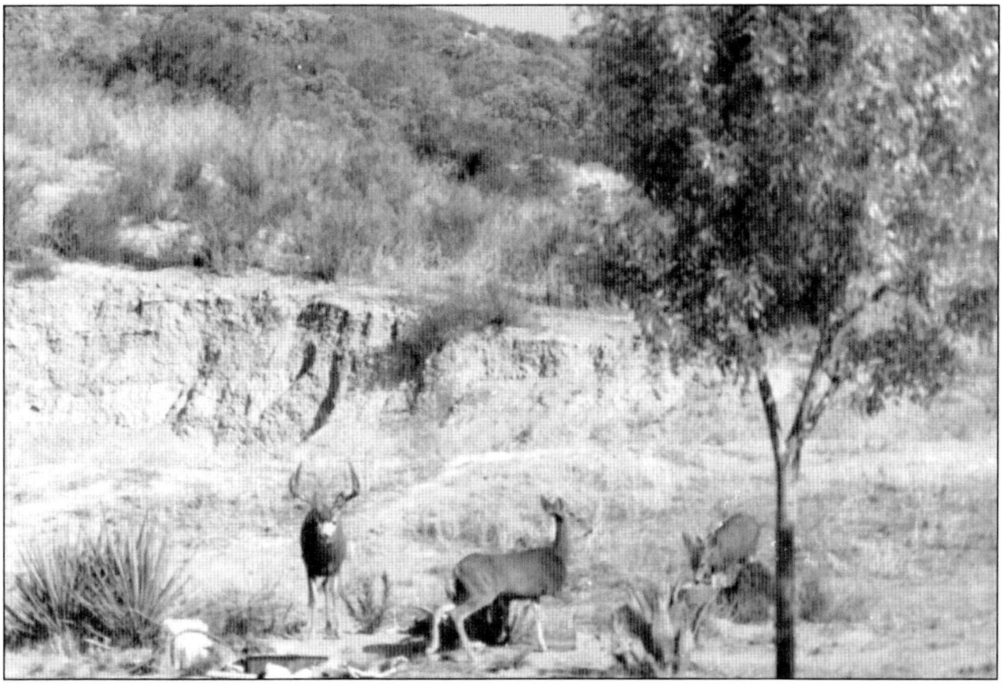

Seen here are deer that frequented the landscape around the Circle C Ranch. They added much to the scenic aura of the grounds. Visitors would often seek them out to photograph them so they could return home with an enlightening picture. The deer were welcomed guests of the Smiths, who provided them with drinking water and a salt block. The tall fence around a nearby garden was an obvious required addition. (Courtesy of Sue Smith.)

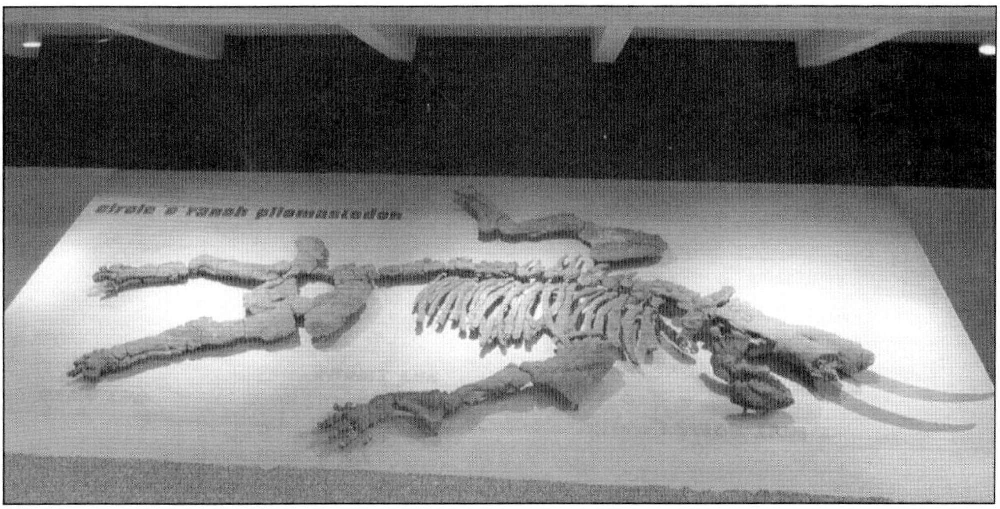

When Sue Smith discovered the initial bones of a mastodon on the Circle C Ranch, she realized the importance of her find, because she had earlier learned the history of the fossil beds in the area from Bob Cardwell. When the Los Angeles County Museum was notified of this fact, the museum paleontologists wasted no time in sending a crew to the ranch to excavate the mid-Pliocene specimen. The mastodon's nearly completely fossilized remains became one of the museum's exhibits, as seen here. The tusks are drawn in because they were too fragile to excavate. (Courtesy of Los Angeles County Museum.)

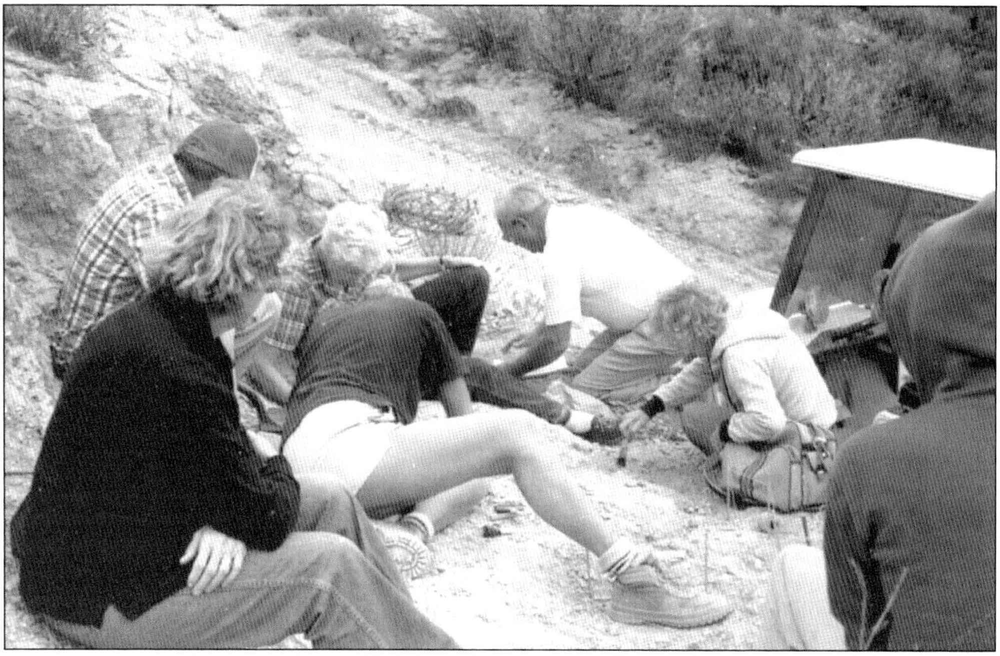

This is a group from the Los Angeles County Museum headed by paleontologist Dr. Reed McDonald. They are hard at work uncovering the mastodon so it can be prepared for transport to the museum laboratory for assembly. Sue Smith is on the right, assisting with the tedious soil removal. (Courtesy of Sue Smith.)

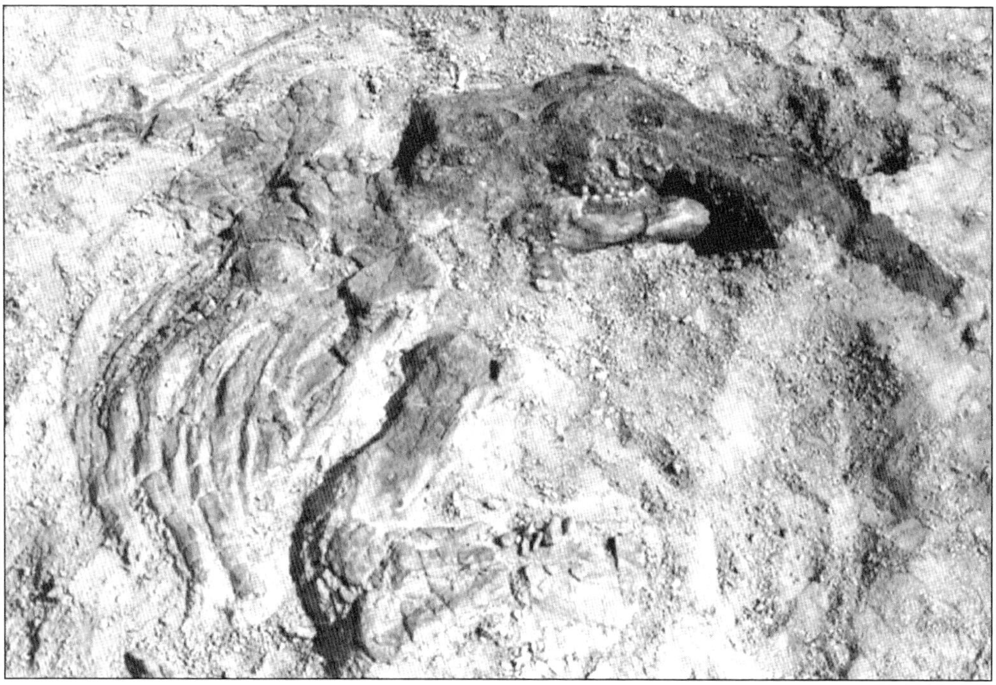

The head and rib section of the mastodon found on the Circle C Ranch is plainly seen here. The large jawbone and teeth are clearly seen below the head section. Careful excavation almost removed the entire fossilized skeleton. (Courtesy of Sue Smith.)

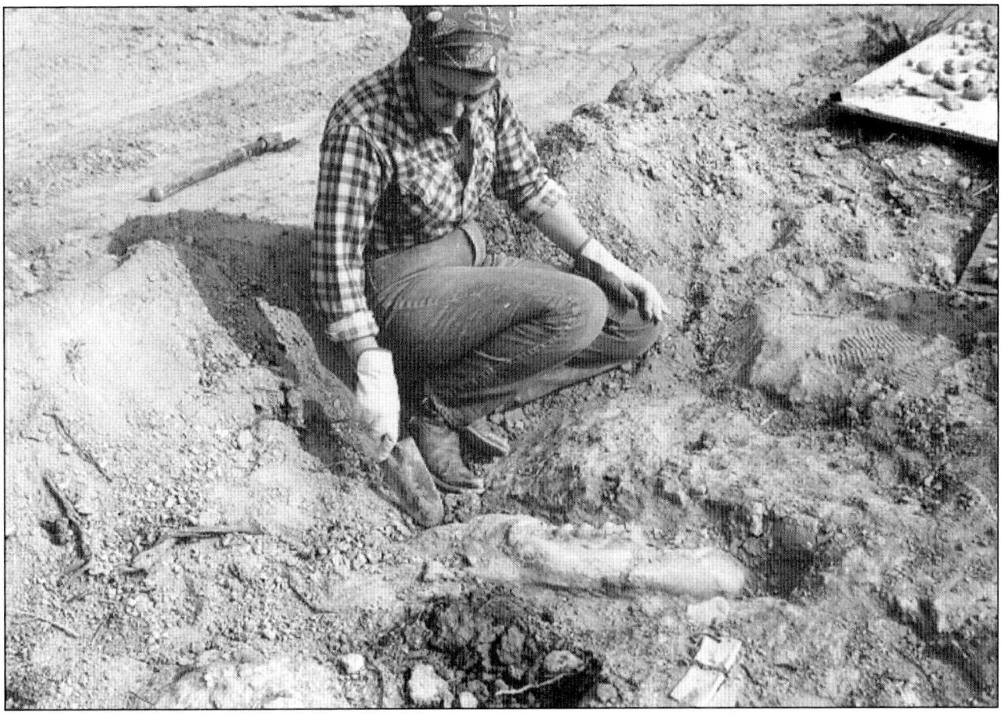

Sue Smith is seen here on a dig uncovering the jawbone of the mastodon she discovered. It took many hours of strenuous work to loosen the fragile jawbone from its encrusted site and free it from the soil environment where it had laid dormant for millions of years. The magnitude of the jawbone perhaps portrays its overall massiveness—around 8 to 10 feet tall and approximately 2,000 pounds. (Courtesy of Sue Smith.)

The lower jawbone section is seen here after it had been essentially excavated from its environment. The large teeth of the mastodon exemplify how large this mid-Pliocene beast must have been. Observing this particular segmented section, it must have been difficult to put the pieces together, although the large bones were extremely well preserved. (Courtesy of Sue Smith.)

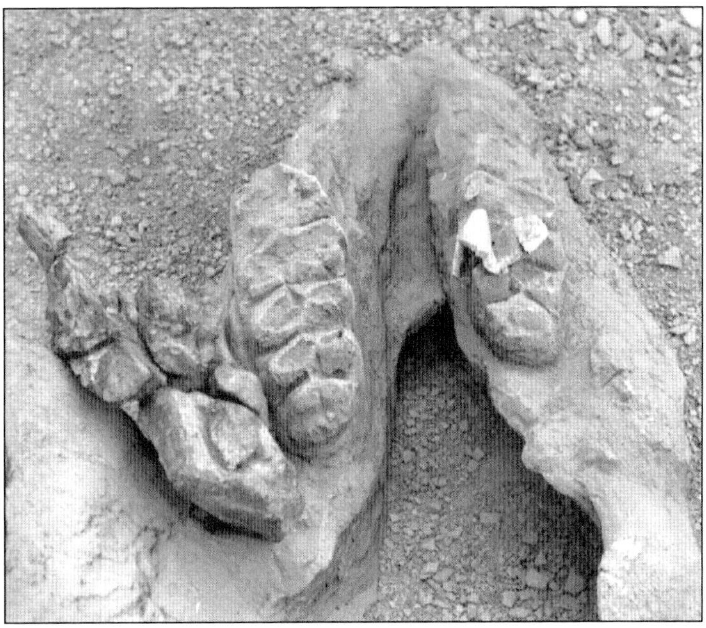

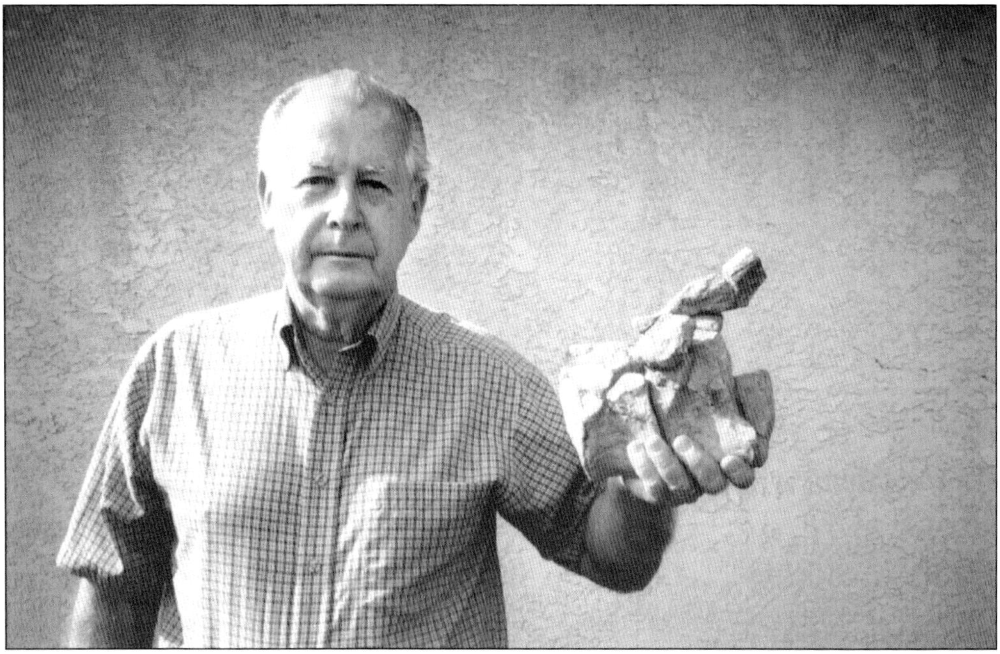

Author Ken Holtzclaw is seen here holding a complete vertebrae section with an attached rib section. It is an actual fossilized bone segment of the mid-Pliocene mastodon found on the Circle C Ranch and is approximately 10 million years old. Sue Smith excavated it after the museum dig site was abandoned, and it is now part of her private collection. (Courtesy of Sue Smith.)

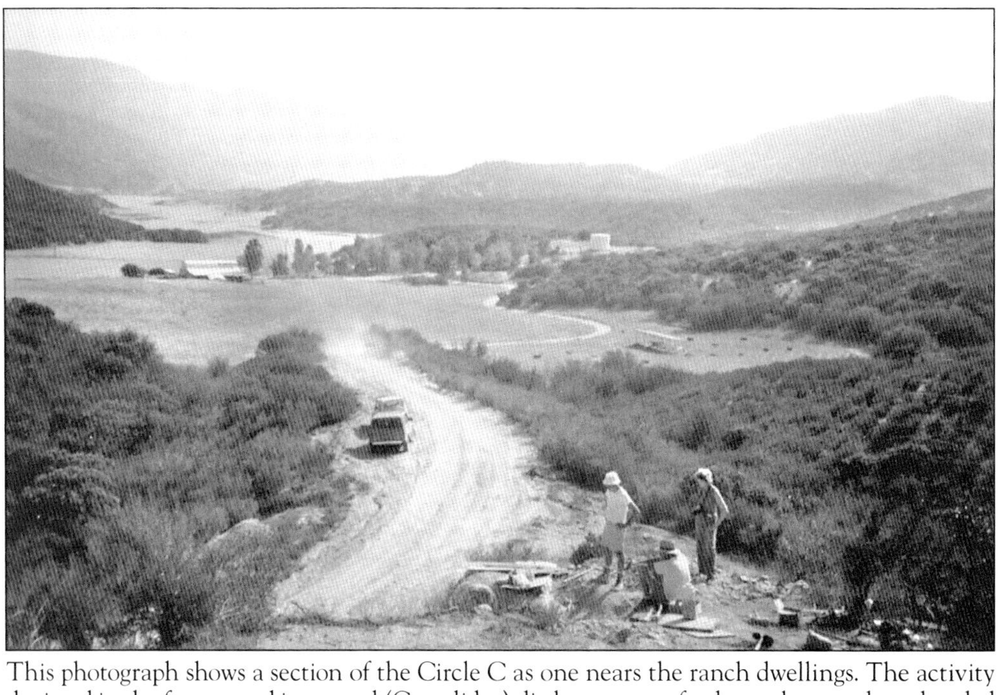

This photograph shows a section of the Circle C as one nears the ranch dwellings. The activity depicted in the foreground is a camel (Camelidae) dig by a group of paleontology students headed by Dr. George Miller of Imperial Valley College. The bones were discovered by Sue Smith during one of her evening hikes. (Courtesy of Circle C Ranch.)

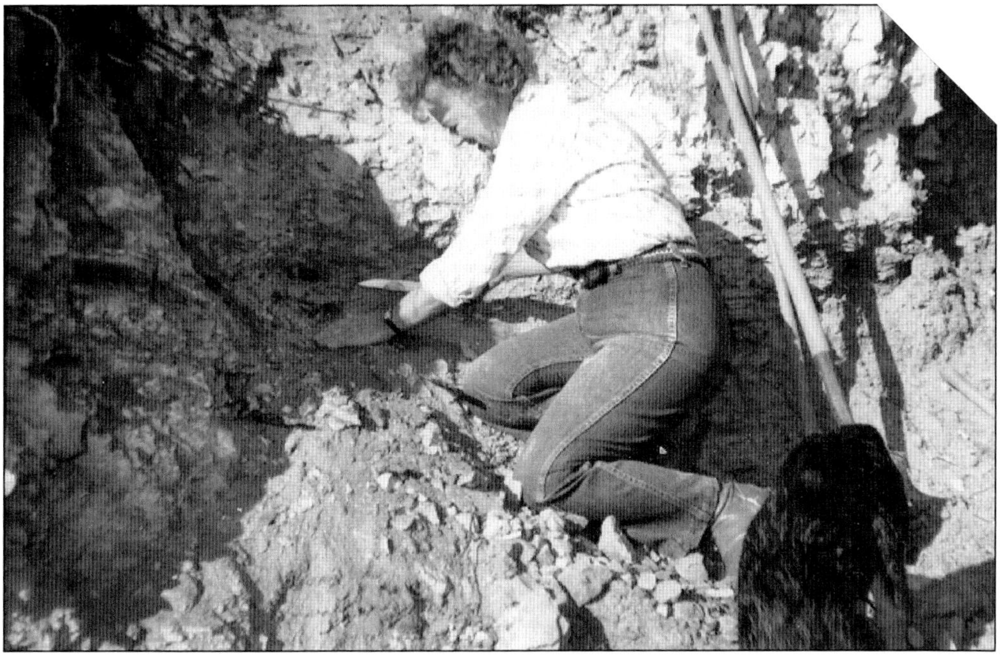

This is Sue Smith on one of the mid-Pliocene camel sites on the ranch. It was hard, tedious work but was quite rewarding. The Smiths became extremely interested in the fossilization found on their ranch, and this is why they soon began to develop a museum in one of the rooms of their large barn. (Courtesy of Sue Smith.)

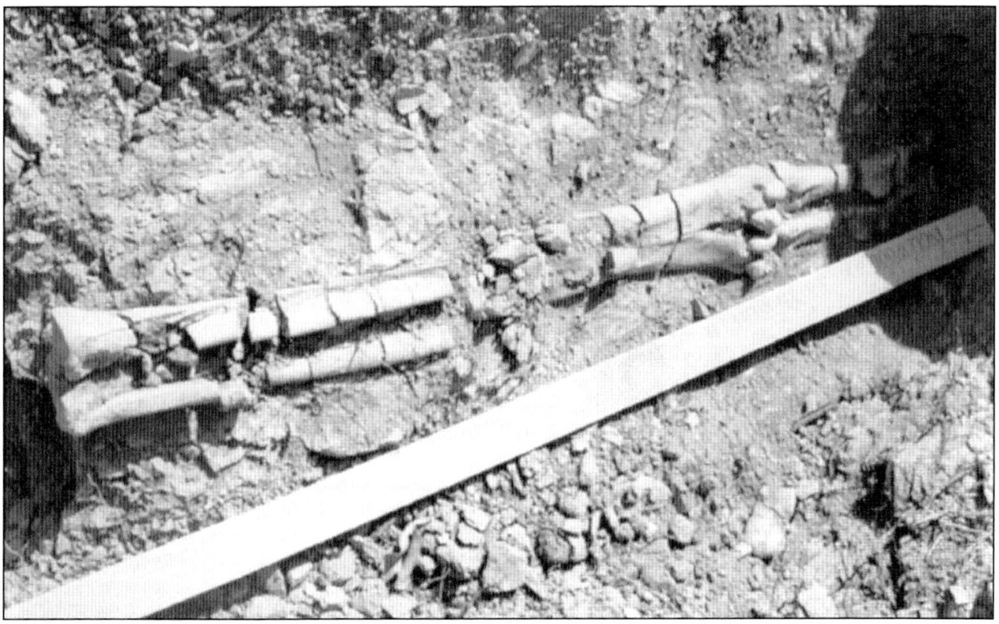

Seen here is a camel leg and foot section that was uncovered during one of the digs. There were several excavation sites of the camels millions of years old, and each was usually named after someone on the dig or a nearby event. When one was named George on George Washington Day, it was later discerned that it was of female gender. A correction was made—it was renamed Georgia. (Courtesy of Sue Smith.)

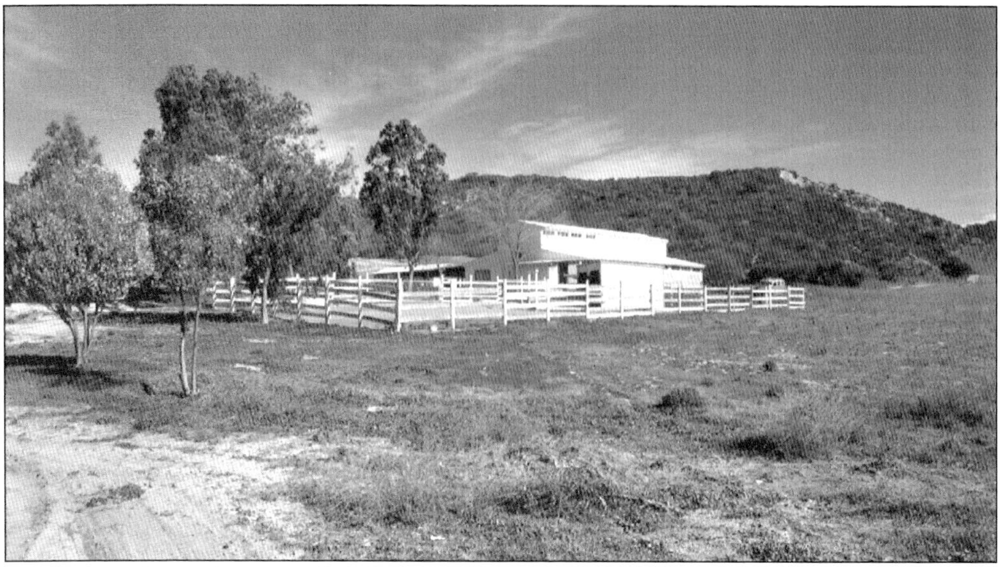

The barn and corral seen in this photograph was a special entity of the Circle C Ranch. The barn housed the Smiths' museum, which contained many of the artifacts found in the area as well as a memorabilia museum and library. A cover spanning the length of the barn housed a collection of antique automobiles. The stable and corral contained the horses and goats. (Courtesy of Circle C Ranch.)

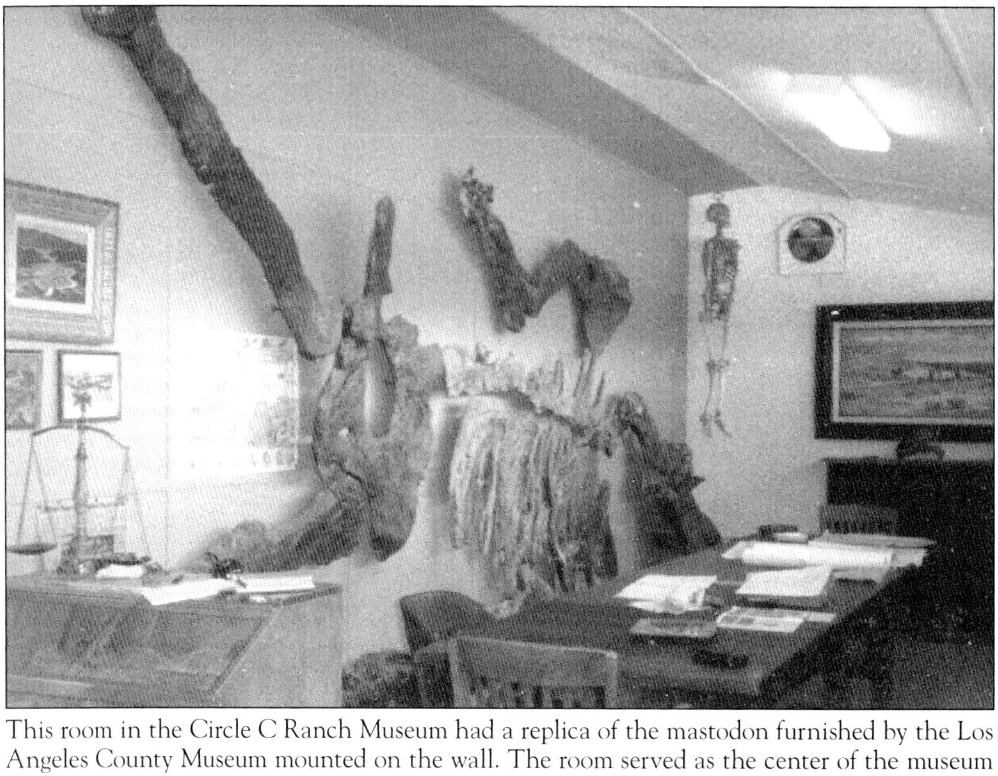

This room in the Circle C Ranch Museum had a replica of the mastodon furnished by the Los Angeles County Museum mounted on the wall. The room served as the center of the museum and was where fossils were brought in, catalogued, and added to the appropriate segment of the museum collection. (Courtesy of Circle C Ranch.)

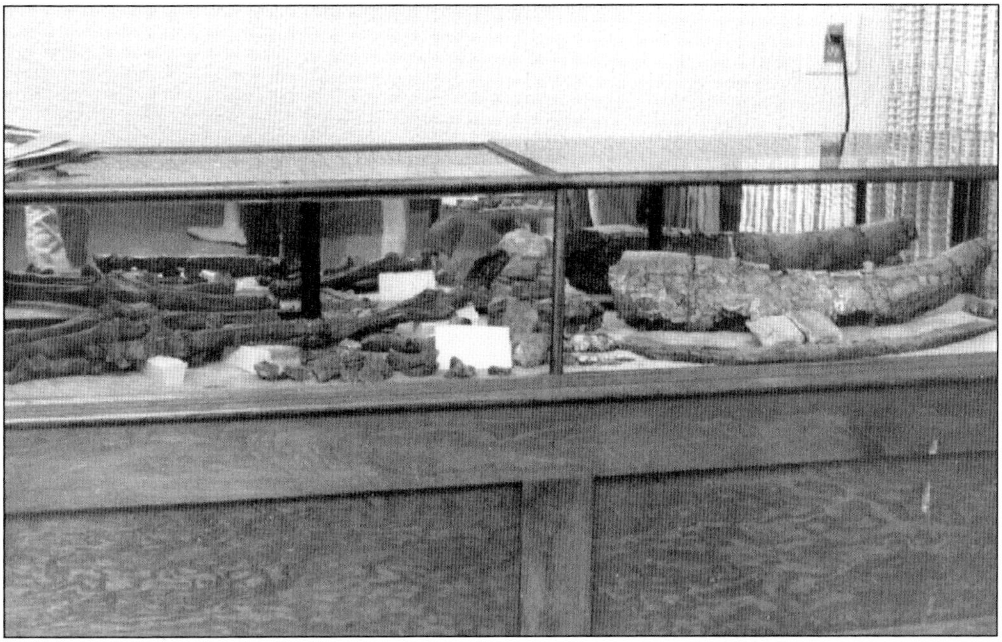

This is a photograph of a display that was in the Smiths' museum. In the left front of the case is fossilized legs of a Pliohippus (little horse), in the left rear is a Camelidae (camel) leg, and in the front right is a tusk left behind by the museum, because it was too fragile to excavate. However, Phil and Sue Smith later exhumed it after applying preservatives. It is in the exhibit case at right and appears to be two tusks because there is a mirror in back. (Courtesy of Sue Smith.)

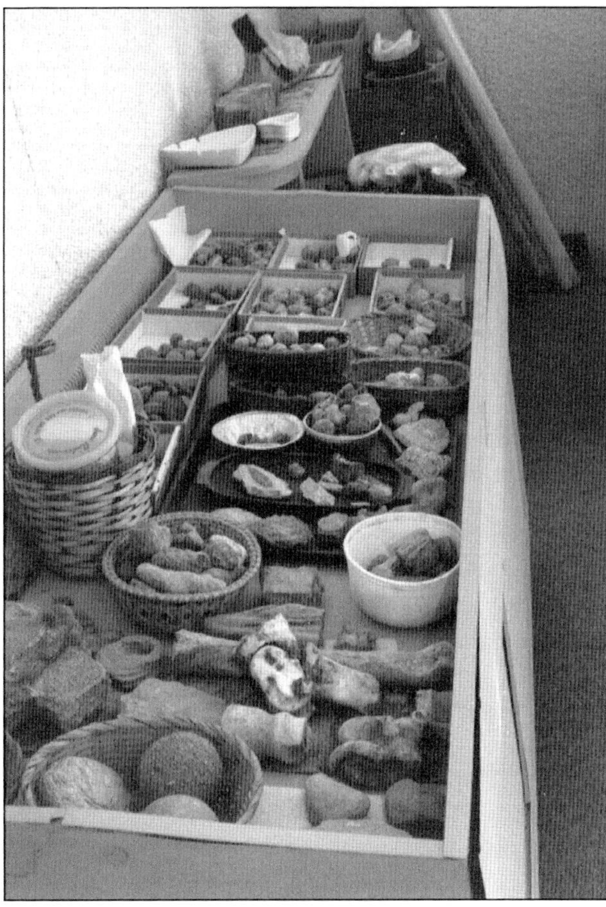

In addition to the mastodon, small horse, and the camels found on the Smiths' ranch, there were numerous other fossilized artifacts. In this display rack are treasures that were discovered on the ranch and added to the museum room in the barn. Notable in the center basket next to the tall basket are the petrified pinecones, which still look realistic. (Courtesy of Sue Smith.)

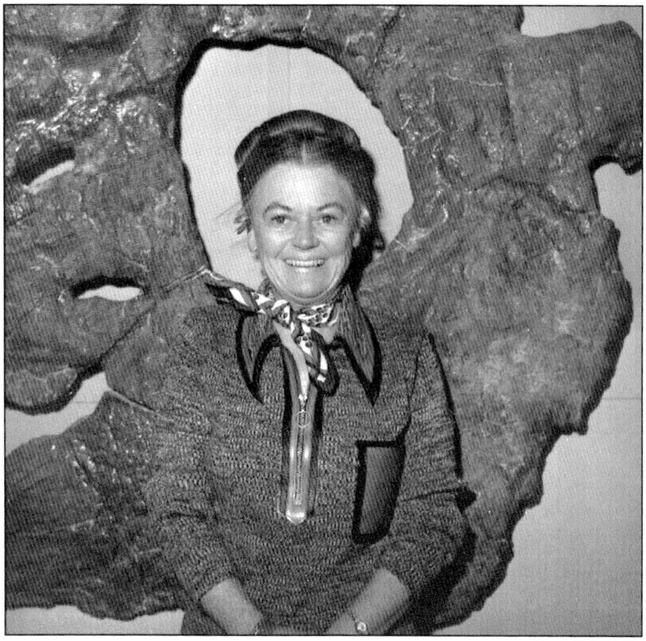

In this photograph, Sue Smith poses, framed by a replica of a large pelvic section of a mastodon that was uncovered on the Circle C Ranch. After Sue discovered the mastodon on their ranch, there followed a furry of activity that included a number of other digs in addition to the one for the mastodon. (Courtesy of Sue Smith.)

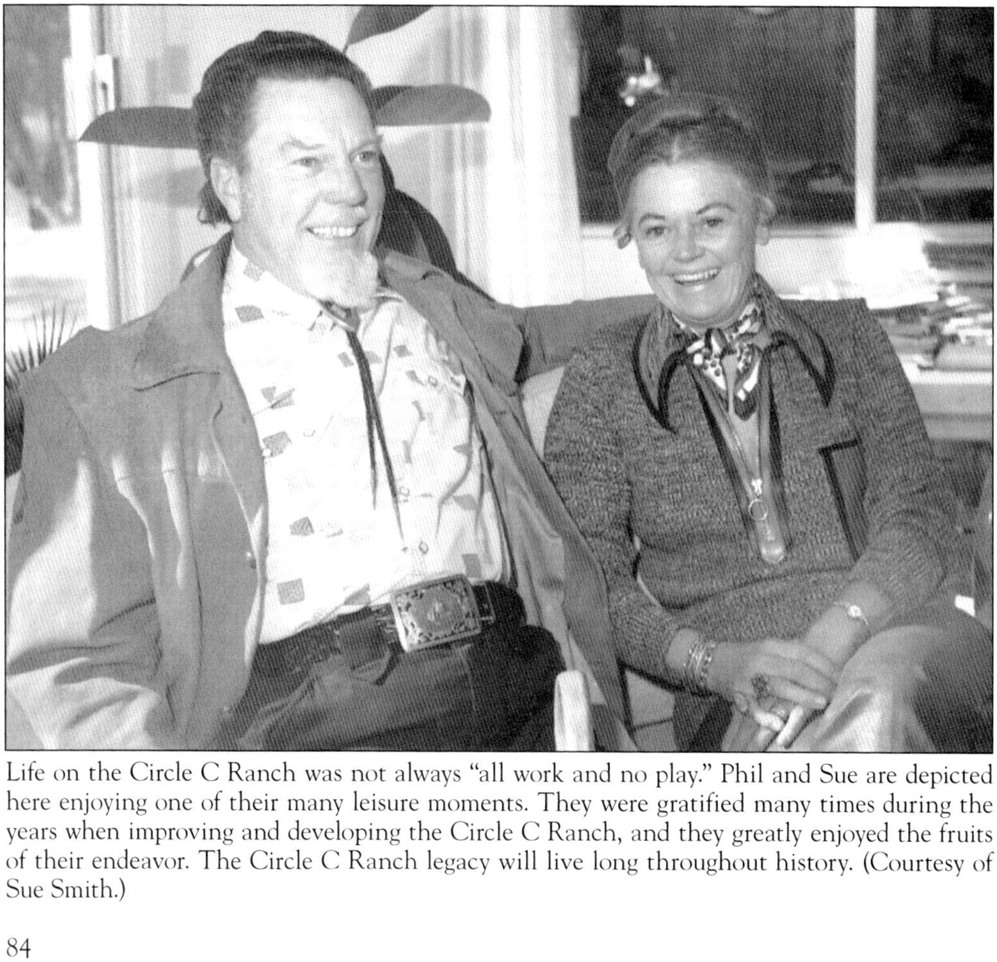

Life on the Circle C Ranch was not always "all work and no play." Phil and Sue are depicted here enjoying one of their many leisure moments. They were gratified many times during the years when improving and developing the Circle C Ranch, and they greatly enjoyed the fruits of their endeavor. The Circle C Ranch legacy will live long throughout history. (Courtesy of Sue Smith.)

Four

Beaumont Endeavors

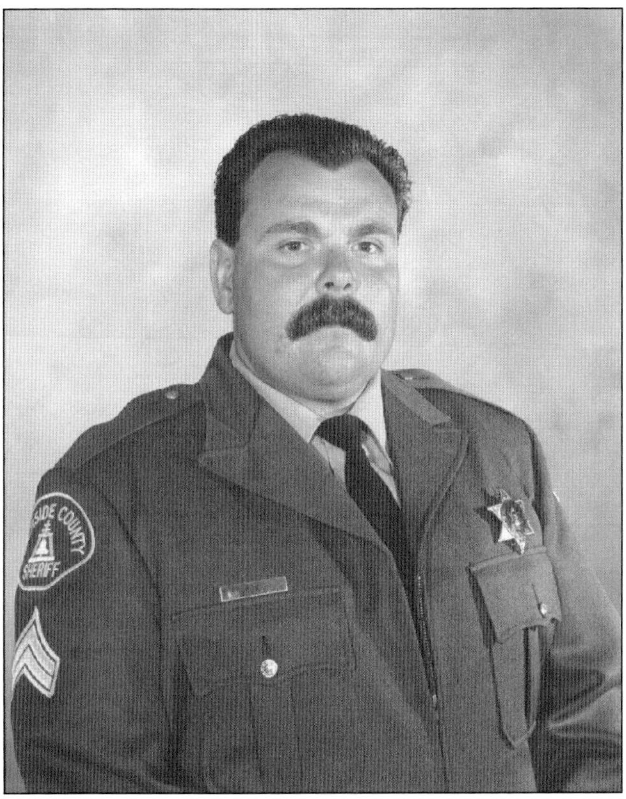

This is Jeff Fox when he served as a Riverside County Sheriff at the level of senior corporal, but he is now retired. Born July 5, 1962, he is a lifelong resident of Beaumont. He and his wife, Lori, have been married 22 years and have three sons. Jeff is a U.S. Army veteran, served on the Beaumont Chamber of Commerce from 2000 to 2006, and is currently Beaumont's mayor. (Courtesy of Mayor Jeff Fox.)

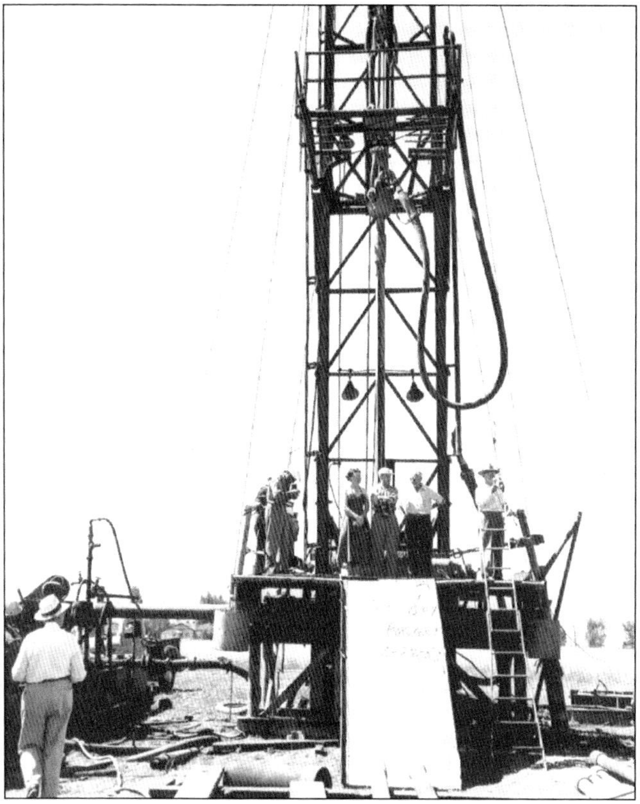

Seen here is an oil-drilling endeavor that once took place in the San Gorgonio Pass near the town of Beaumont. Successful oil wells in other parts of the state were an inducement to explore numerous other places, and this area was no exception. Guy Bogart, Beaumont's civil-minded citizen, is on the rig second from right with hands on his hips. (Courtesy of SGPHS; Leonard McCulloh, photographer.)

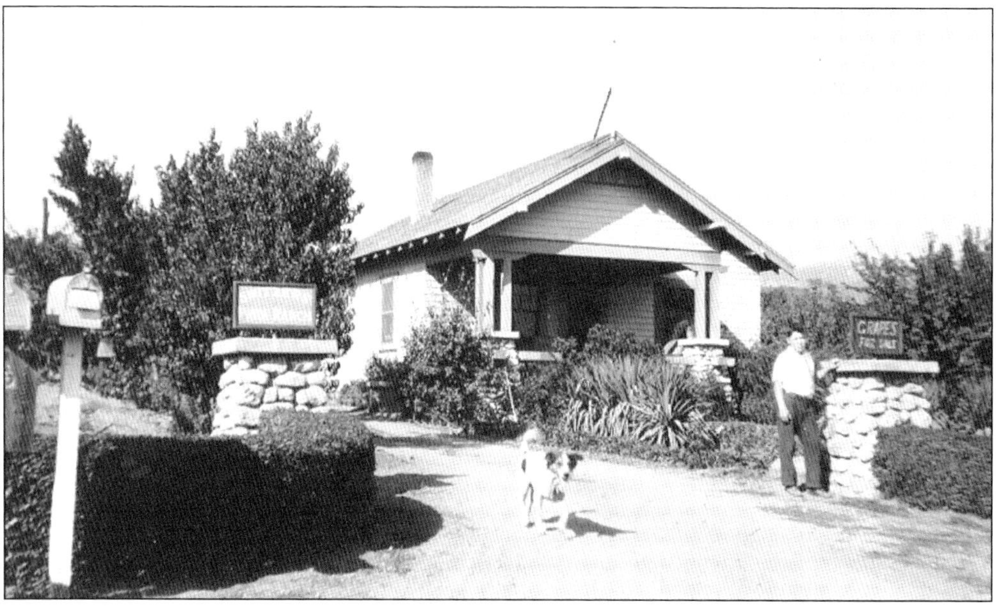

Around the Beaumont area were numerous small farms, such as the Switzer Farm, seen here. Many typical endeavors were quite successful, as the climate was ideal for growing many types of fruit, such as prunes, plums, apples, and especially cherries. Fruit grown in this area even won prizes at the Chicago Exposition of 1893. (Courtesy of SGPHS.)

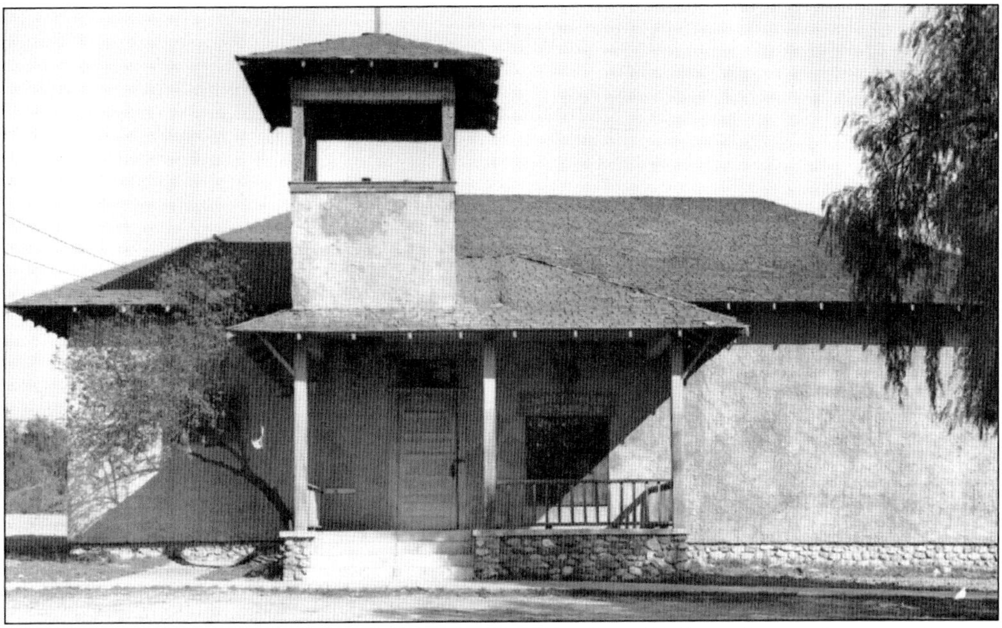

This is an early photograph of the grammar school built in 1905 on the northern outskirts of Beaumont, shortly after another grammar school was built in the heart of town. The Grange began after the Civil War in 1867 to protect against dangers on the western frontier. By 1950, the Grange had bought this vintage schoolhouse to become its meeting place. It still acts as a meeting hall for other functions. (Courtesy of SGPHS.)

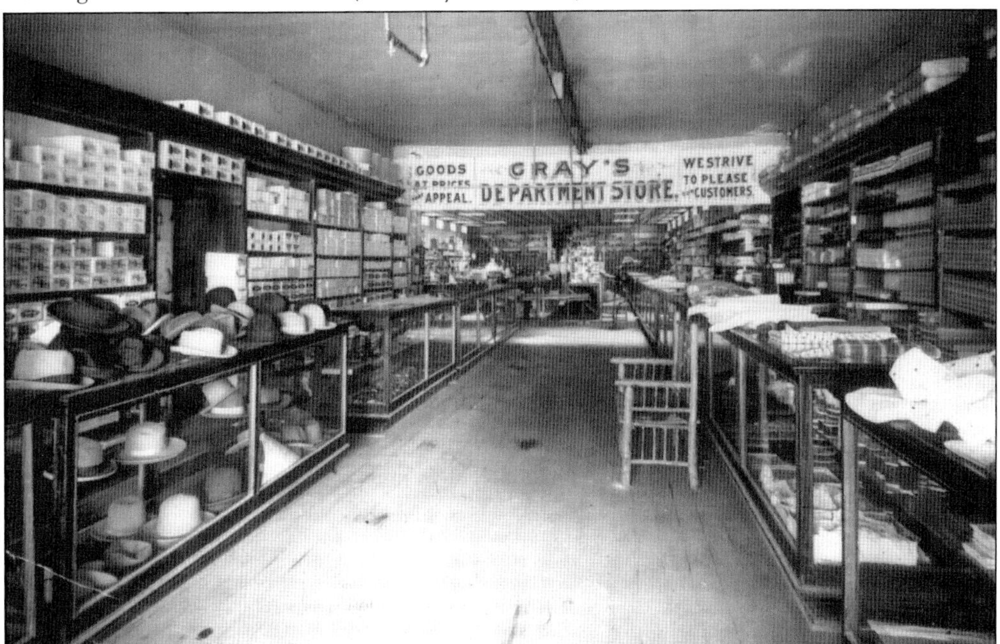

The merchandise at Gray's Department Store in Beaumont was arranged in an orderly manner, except perhaps for the large selection of hats. It is obvious hats were a popular item. The store advertised "foods at prices that appeal, and we strive to please our customers." Gray's was a popular department store with its closest competition in nearby Banning. (Courtesy of SGPHS.)

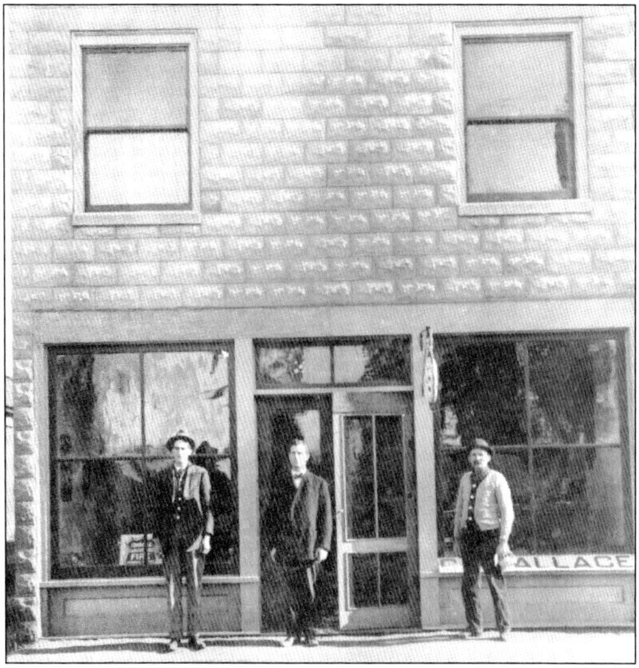

Endeavors to establish new businesses in Beaumont were rampant during its early years, when it was becoming populated. This is a typical business building that was constructed in 1908 with its proprietors proudly posing outside. Many of the buildings along Egan Avenue were constructed with this conventional block scheme typical of the era. (Courtesy of Nara Haskell.)

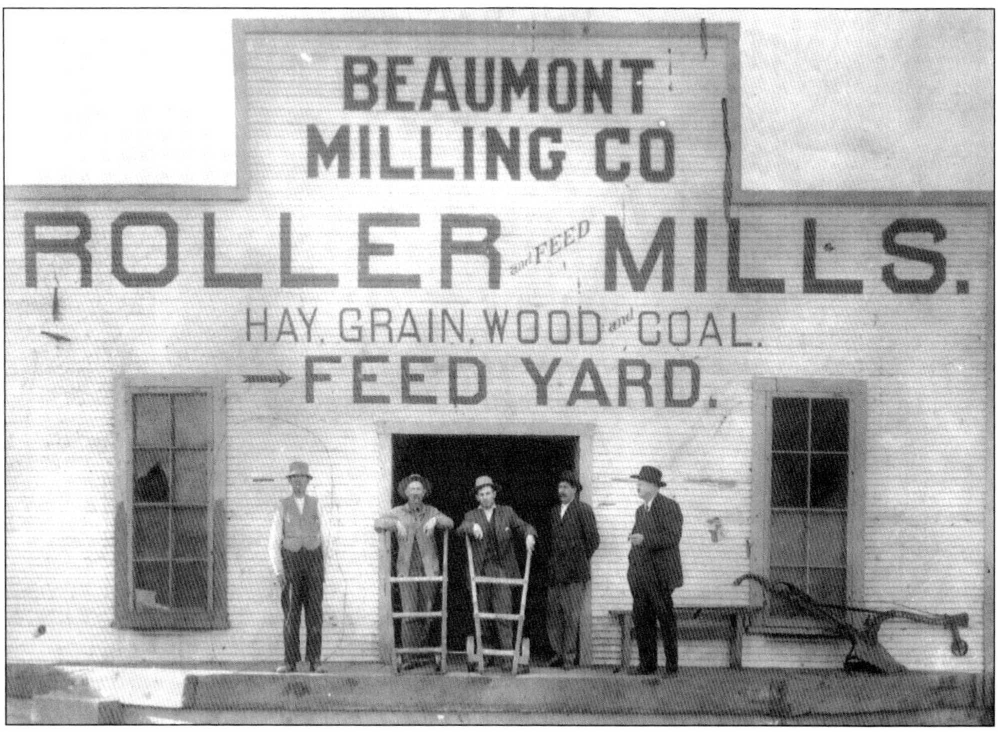

This is the Beaumont Milling Company, which was important because hay and grain farming had become such a large endeavor in the Beaumont area. The staff of the Beaumont Milling Company is gathered outside, proudly representing the establishment. The milling company, the roller mill, and the feed yard provided hay and grain as well as wood and coal commodities. (Courtesy of SGPHS.)

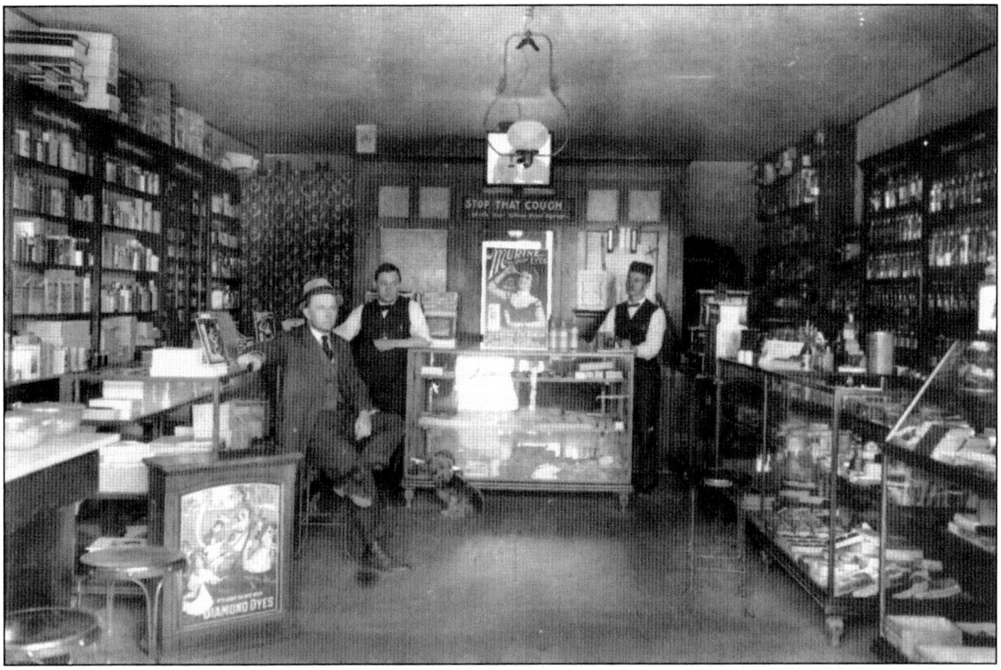

This view is of the inside of the Fulton Drug Store in Beaumont in its early years. The man standing at the counter at right in a skullcap is Robert Fulton, the proprietor. The two other men are perhaps employees, with one maybe being the druggist. It is interesting to note the poster on the counter advertising Murine for the eyes, an advertisement that could still be seen in today's drugstores. (Courtesy of SGPHS.)

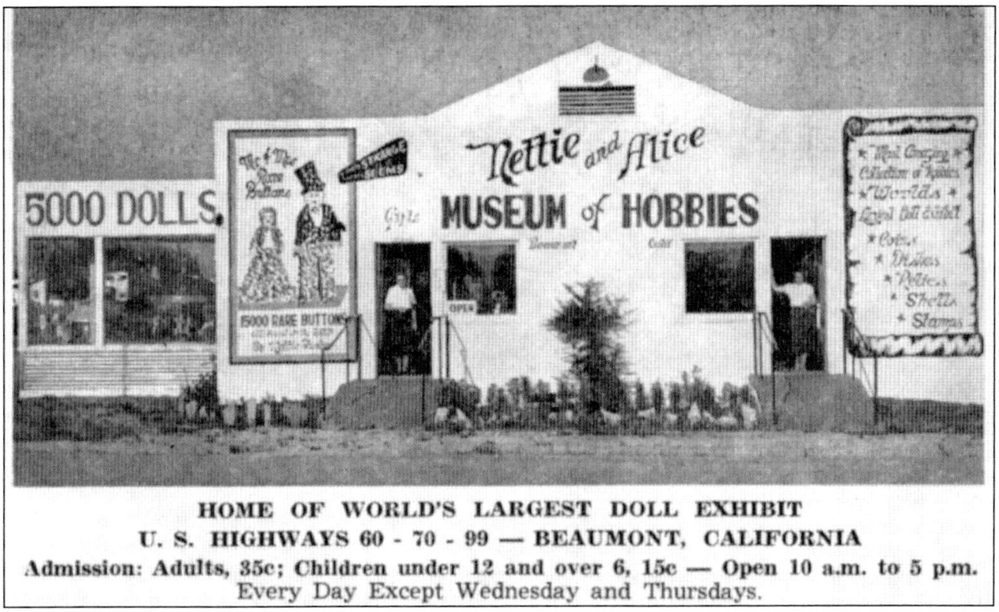

This is the Nettie and Alice Museum of Hobbies, located within Beaumont on the main route through the town off of U. S. Highways 60, 70, and 99. It prided itself in claiming to have the world's largest doll collection. Nettie is standing in the doorway at the left of the museum, and Alice is in the doorway at the right. (Courtesy of Steve Lech.)

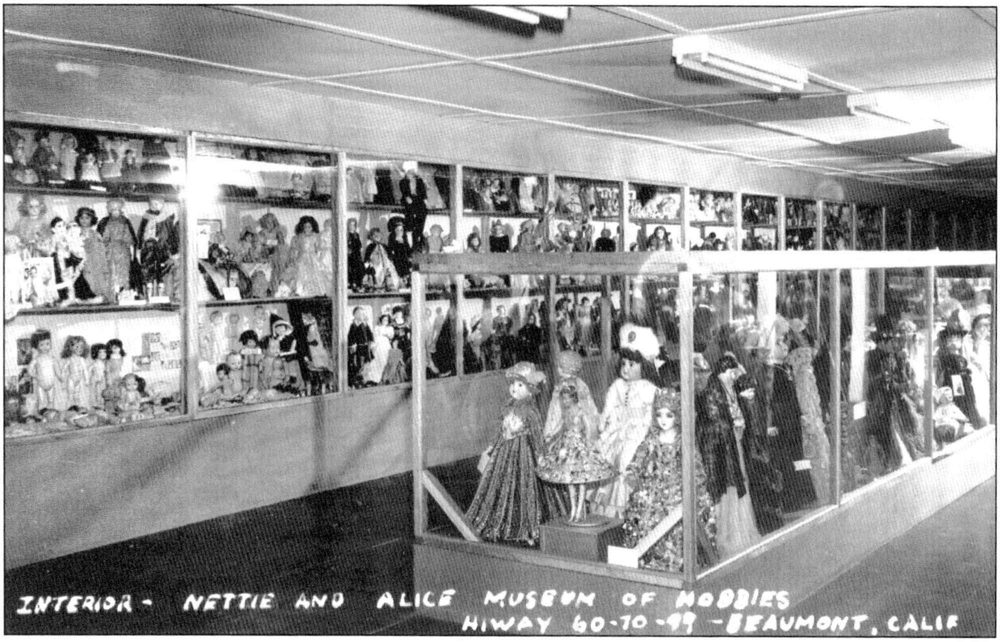

This photograph depicts the large doll exhibit within the interior of the Nettie and Alice Museum of Hobbies in Beaumont. The museum was a very popular attraction for many years, serving the community well, as schools from Beaumont and elsewhere often visited it. It eventually fell by the wayside, and its dolls were acquired by private collectors. (Courtesy of Steve Lech.)

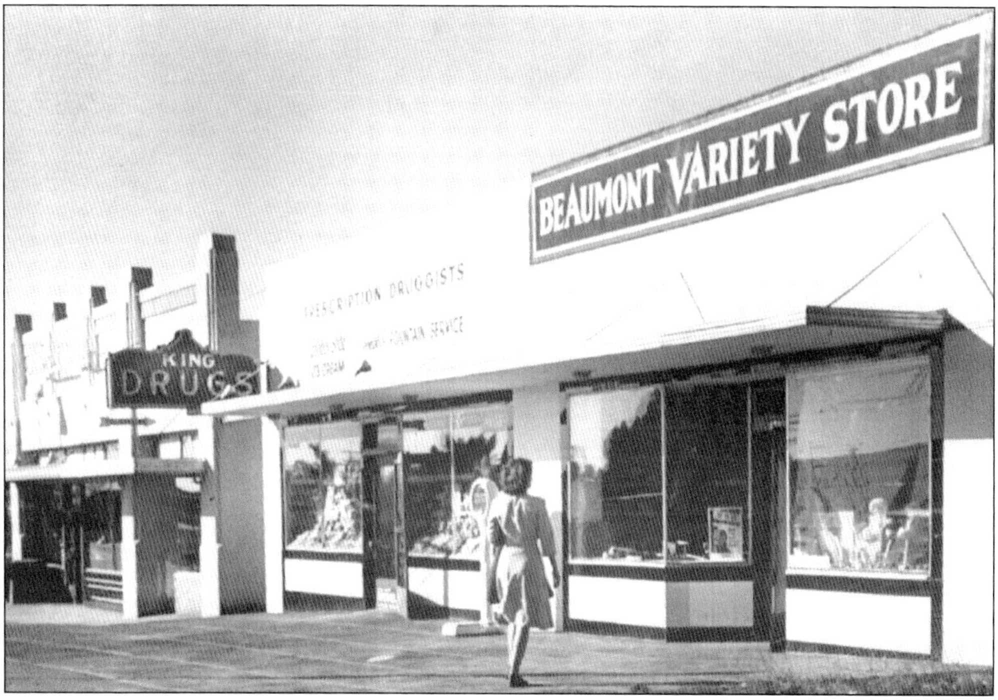

In this photograph are two popular businesses of many that inhabited Sixth Street in Beaumont. King Drugs was not only a popular drug store, but its fountain service was a great attraction, especially for school children, who gathered there frequently. (Courtesy of Nara Haskell.)

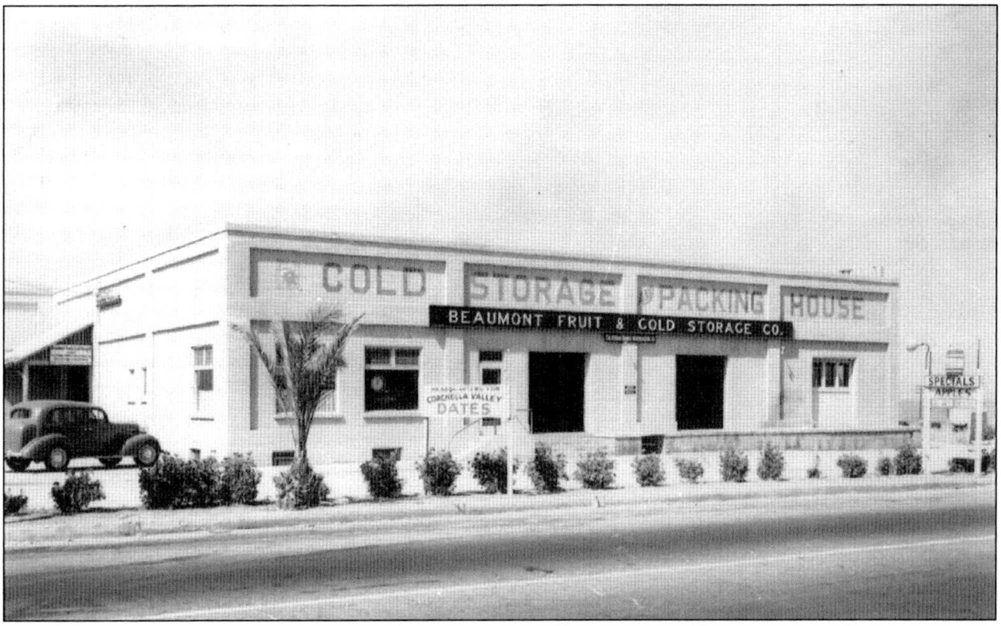

After the introduction of fruit orchards in Beaumont, fruit growing became quite lucrative. Over time, as the population of the town grew, so did the acreage of fruit trees in the area. Some of the fruit grown was sold locally, but much of it was exported. Thus the Beaumont Fruit and Cold Storage Company, seen here, was an important entity in town. (Courtesy of Nara Haskell.)

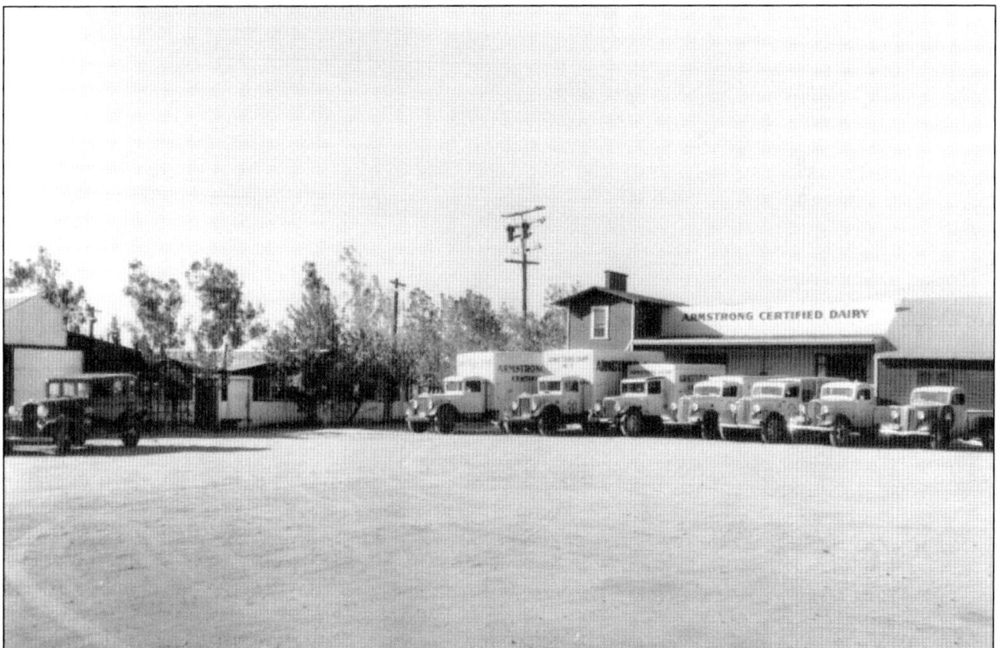

This is the Armstrong Certified Dairy that prospered so well during Beaumont's early years. The magnitude of the operation is perhaps illustrated by the number of delivery trucks parked in a row in front of the dairy headquarters. Milk delivery was popular during this era and was as reliable as the newspaper is today. (Courtesy of Nara Haskell.)

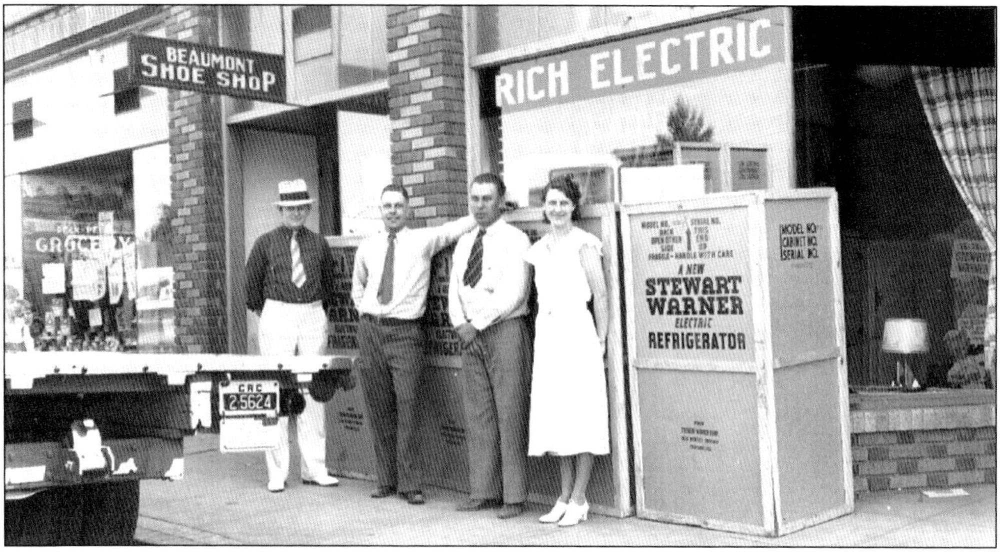

The delivery of refrigerators perched on the sidewalk, as depicted in this photograph, may capture the viewer's interest. Those posing in front of the delivery are perhaps the owner and staff of the Rich Electric Company. It is evident that they are proud of the refrigerator, an item that was less affordable then than it is in today's business climate. (Courtesy of SGPHS.)

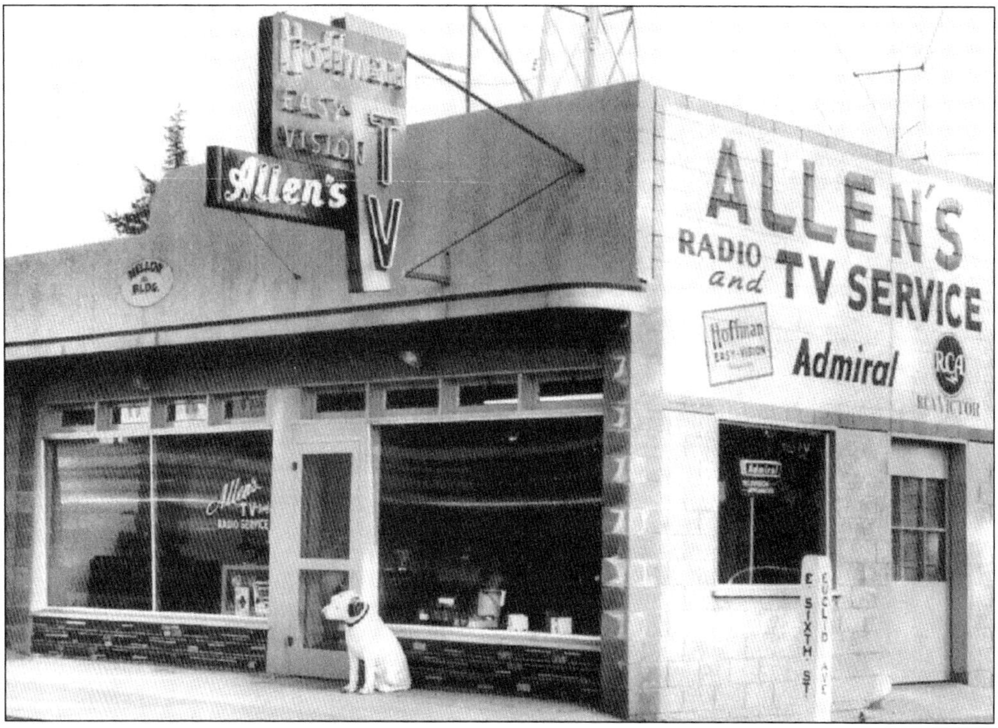

This is Allen's Radio and TV Service in Beaumont on the corner of East Sixth Street and Euclid Avenue. Note the RCA dog, the icon for RCA Records, standing guard at the entrance. This was an era when televisions, like the Hoffman Easy Vision advertised on the overhanging neon sign, were repaired when they became inoperative instead of being discarded like they are today. (Courtesy of Bud Mathewson; Leonard McCulloh, photographer.)

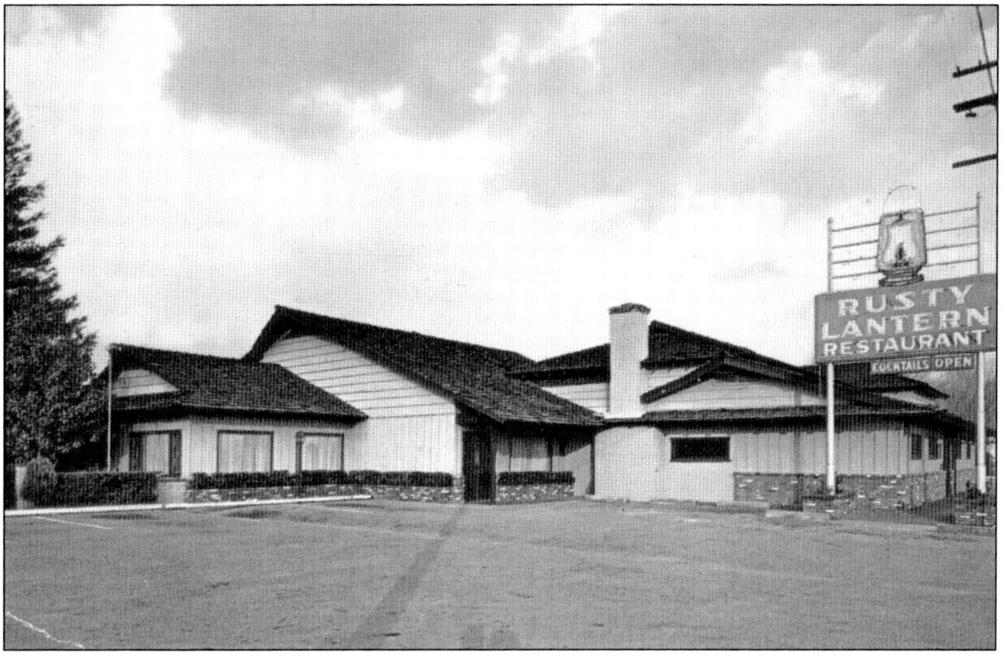

The Rusty Lantern was once one of Beaumont's prized restaurants until it closed its doors a number of years ago. It was a popular stop for many Hollywood celebrities passing through Beaumont on their way to Palm Springs. For years, it drew many from far and near and was considered one of Beaumont's best dining places. (Courtesy of Steve Lech.)

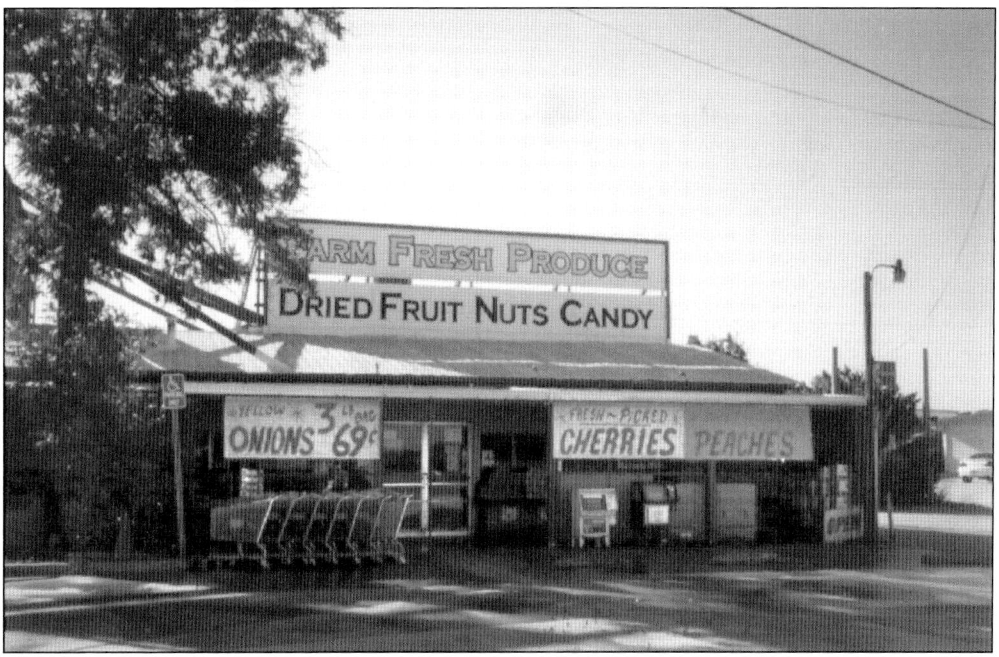

Dowling's fruit stand was established in Beaumont over a half century ago. Its owner, Francis Dowling, is a fruit grower who still manages his 61-acre ranch. One set of his grandparents came to Cherry Valley in 1908 and planted some of the first cherries there. Francis was born in Cherry Valley in 1925 and moved to Beaumont in 1951. (Courtesy of authors.)

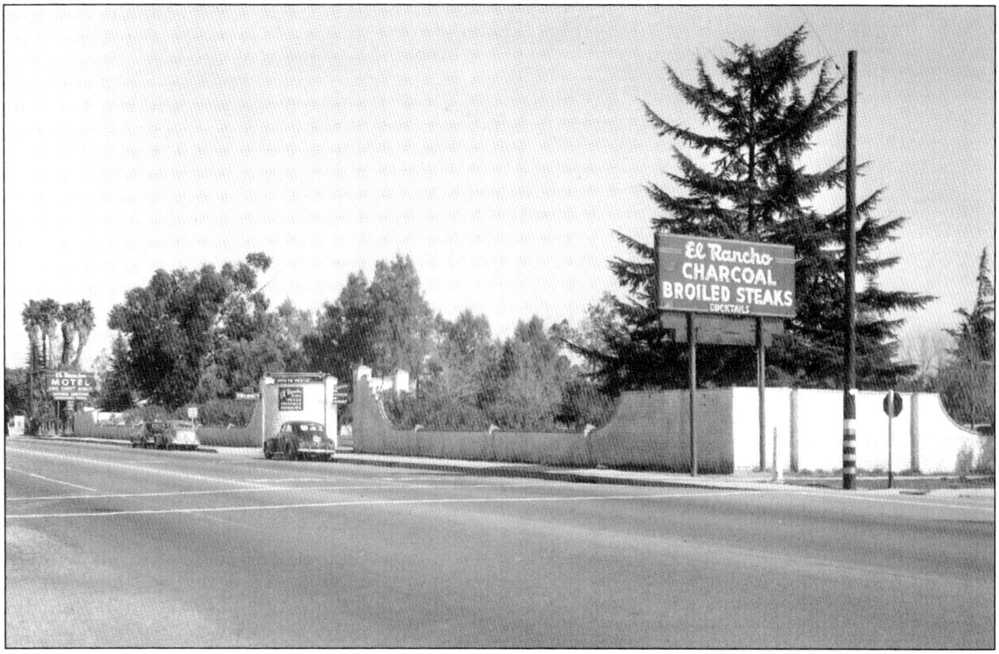

This is the attractive block wall that once surrounded the compound where the popular El Rancho Motel once stood. Today the wall is gone and the motel has been replaced by a two-story, modern version known by the same name. Its operation has been a continuing endeavor, and there still remains a restaurant on the grounds next to the motel as before. (Courtesy of Steve Lech.)

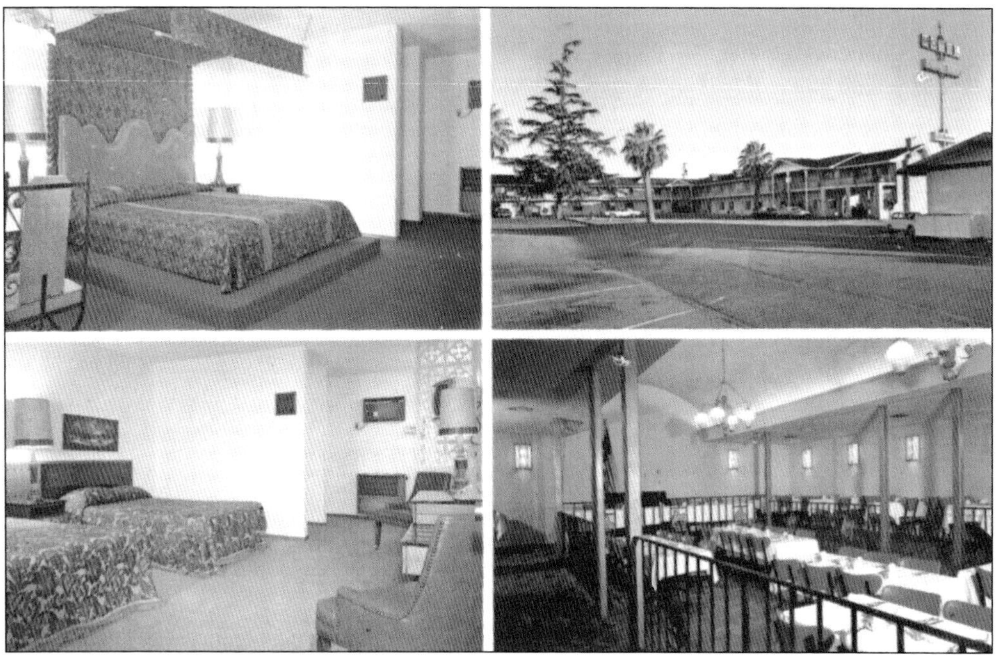
This photograph depicts the modern version of the El Rancho Motel, illustrating its elaborate rooms and its appealing dining room. Today it sits approximately on the same site where the large Beaumont Hotel once stood, at the corner of Beaumont Avenue and Fifth Street. (Courtesy of Steve Lech.)

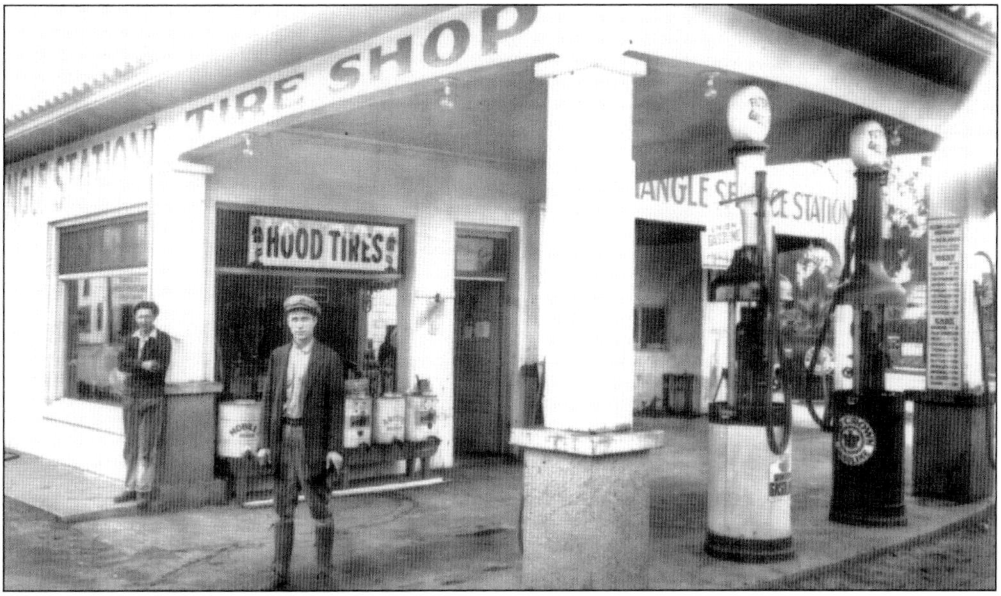

Endeavors to establish and operate small gas stations like the Triangle Service Station in Beaumont, as seen here, were quite popular. Some were strung along Sixth Street to accommodate the traffic in Beaumont's early years. Notice that just one brand of tires is being advertised on the sign in the window of the Triangle station unlike the numerous smatterings of listings seen today. (Courtesy of Steve Lech.)

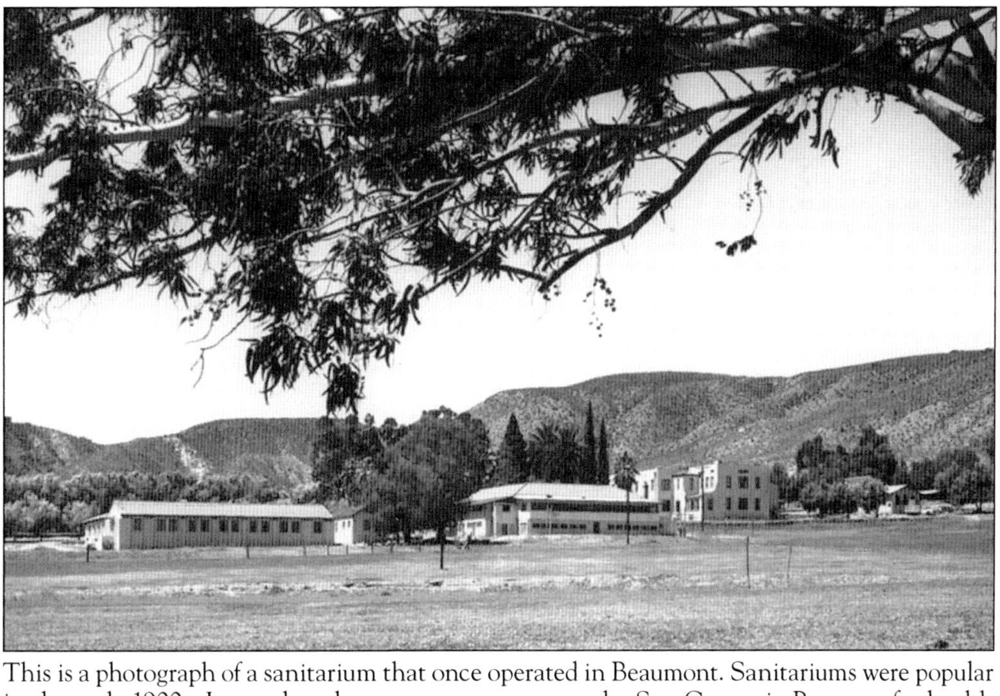

This is a photograph of a sanitarium that once operated in Beaumont. Sanitariums were popular in the early 1900s. It was thought necessary to come to the San Gorgonio Pass area for health reasons, especially as a cure for lung ailments. Note that the facility's buildings were spread out over a large area and separated from one another, implementing a quarantine-type atmosphere. (Courtesy of Steve Lech.)

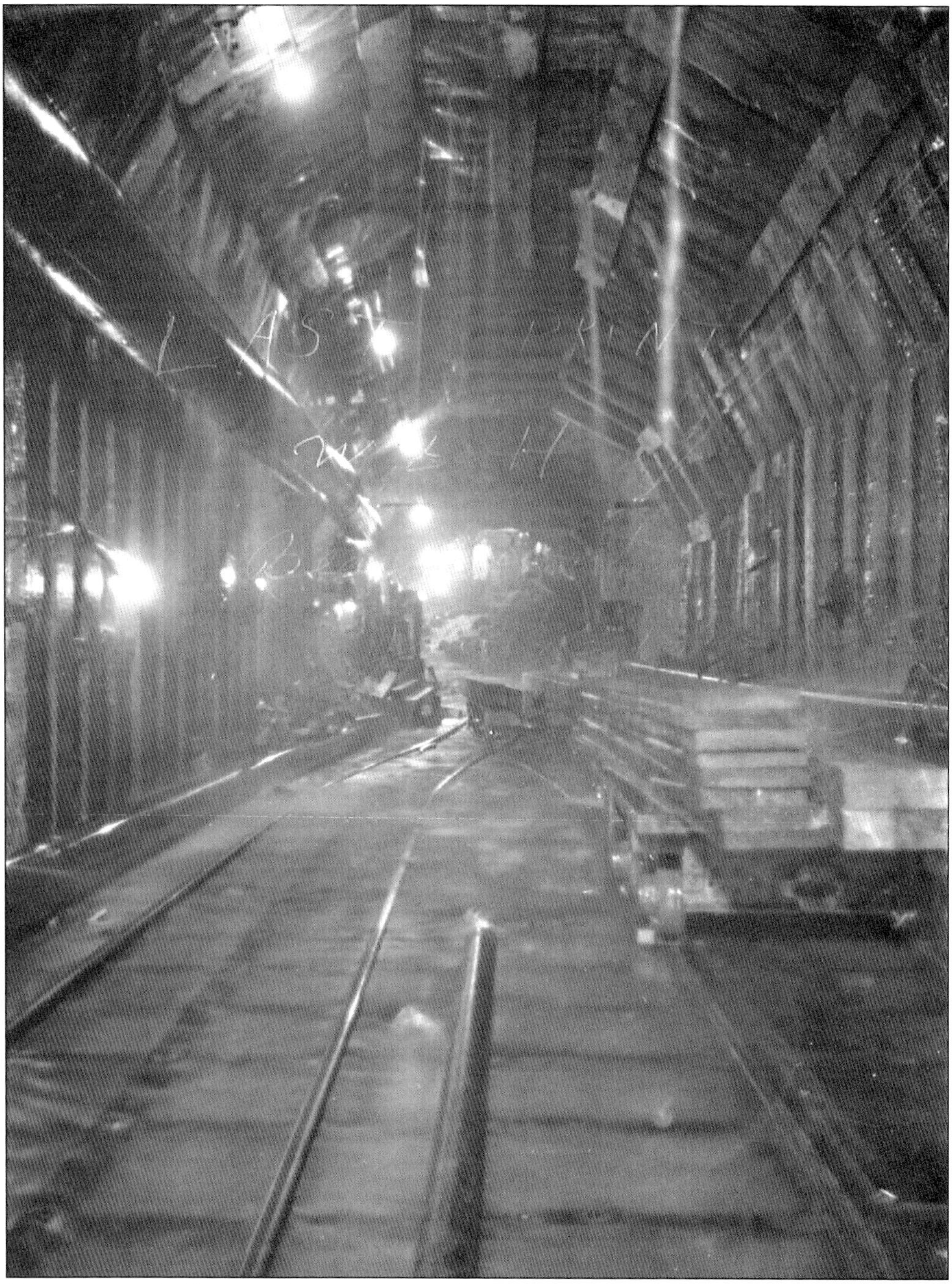

This photograph illustrates the massiveness of the 17-foot-diameter, three-mile tunnel through the San Jacinto Mountain Range being constructed southeast of Beaumont, a project of the Metropolitan Water District's Colorado Aqueduct in the early 1930s. Today water flows through it from the Colorado River to supply water to Southern California. (Courtesy of SGPHS.)

These are men actively working on shoring the tunnel after a section of the passage had been drilled and carved and the rock and soil removed. Note the complexity of the heavy overhead shoring that had to be used. In some cases, though, the tunnel overhead consisted of solid granite, making the venture easier. (Courtesy of SGPHS.)

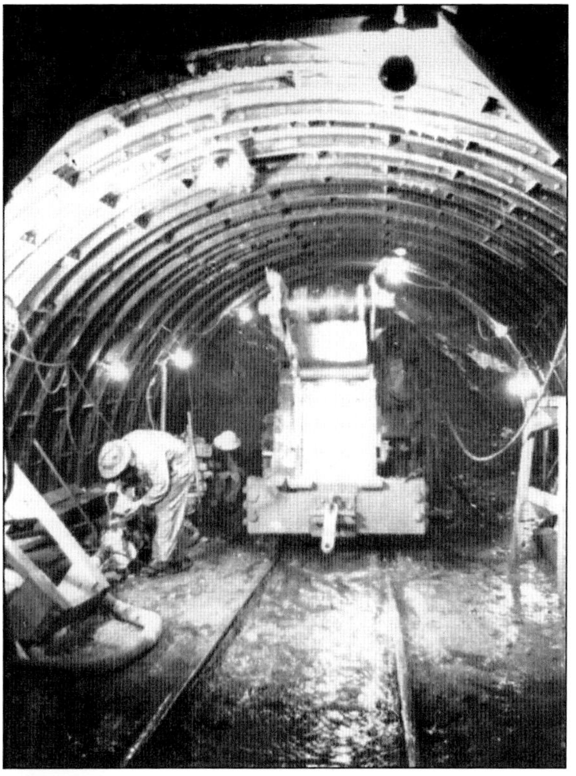

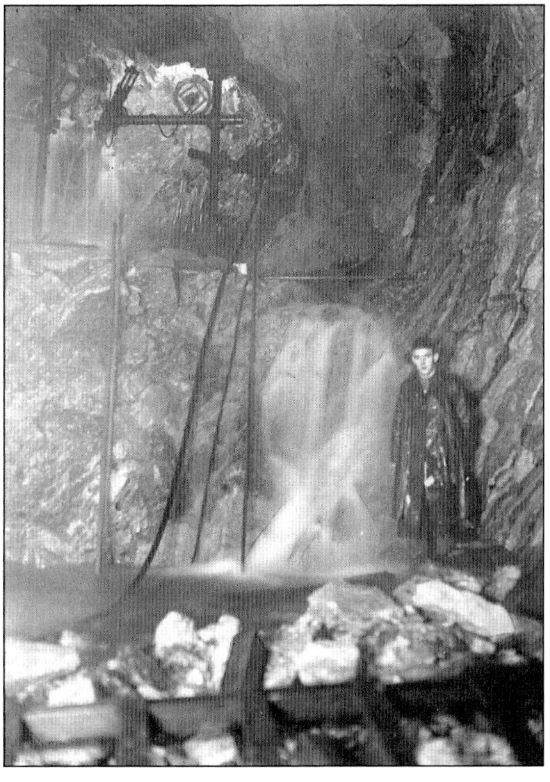

It was a surprise when the drilling crew broke through an aquifer while drilling, imploding thousands of gallons of water that flooded their path. A worker decked in a raincoat poses for a photograph as water from the aquifer pours onto the floor of the tunnel at a fast rate. (Courtesy of SGPHS.)

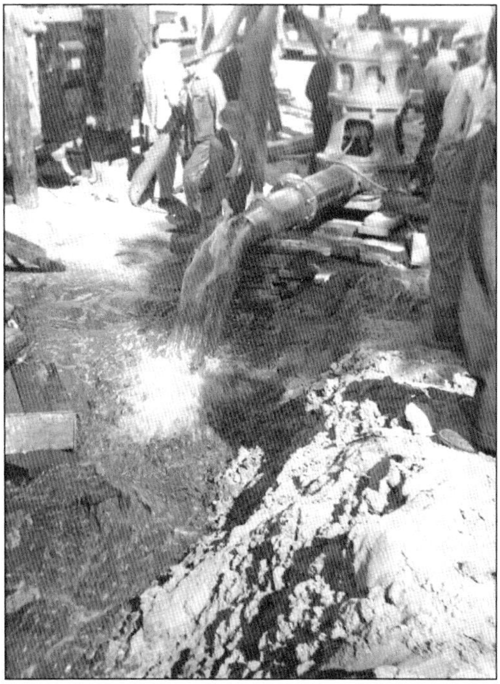

This is a multi-horsepowered pump that was brought to the drill site and shafted down into the tunnel cavity to begin pumping water away, thereby alleviating the flooding of the tunnel. Land owners below this site were later quite disturbed, because they discovered that much of their previous water availability on their land was lost due to the aquifer's diversionary action. (Courtesy of SGPHS.)

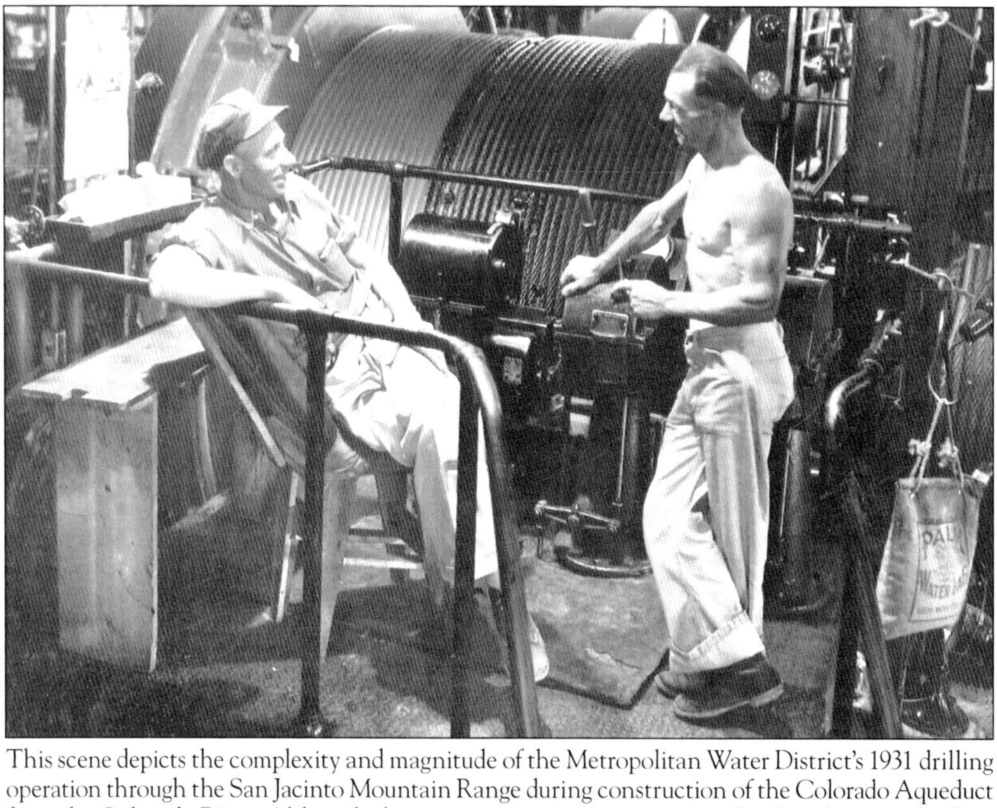

This scene depicts the complexity and magnitude of the Metropolitan Water District's 1931 drilling operation through the San Jacinto Mountain Range during construction of the Colorado Aqueduct from the Colorado River. Although the two men appear at ease posing for this photograph, their jobs were quite strenuous and required great expertise. (Courtesy of Marianne Bailiff.)

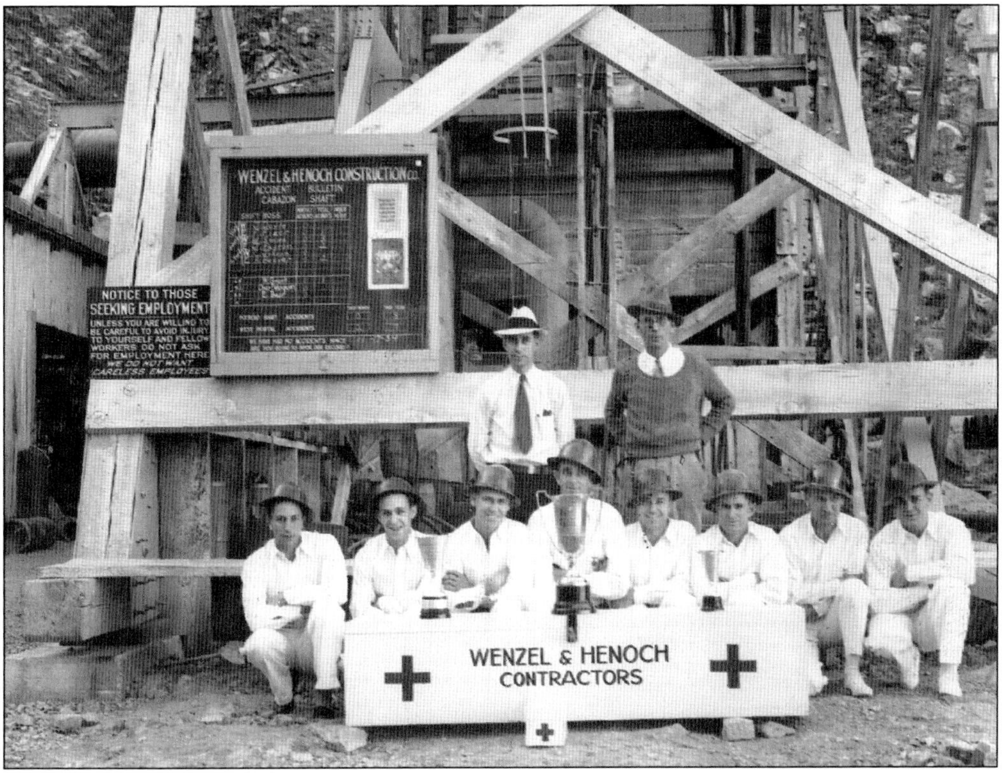

The contracting crew in this photograph made up much of the workforce of Wenzel and Henoch Contractors, whose men were involved in tunnel drilling for the Metropolitan Water District's tunnel through the Mount San Jacinto Mountain Range. Perhaps their smiles are due to the fact that they are employed in the midst of a nationwide depression. (Courtesy of Marianne Bailiff.)

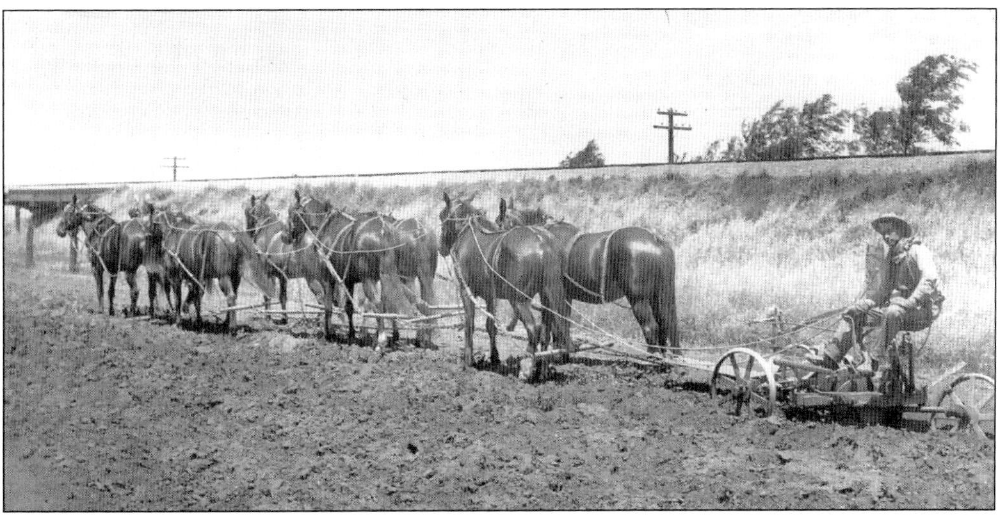

Farming during the early era in and around Beaumont was a venture attempted by many farming speculators, some of whom were quite successful. In this photograph is Earl E. Beasley, a farmhand on the very successful Stewart Ranch who is preparing the soil for planting. Notice the number of horses required to pull the farm equipment. (Courtesy of Marilyn Vonderheide and LMSF.)

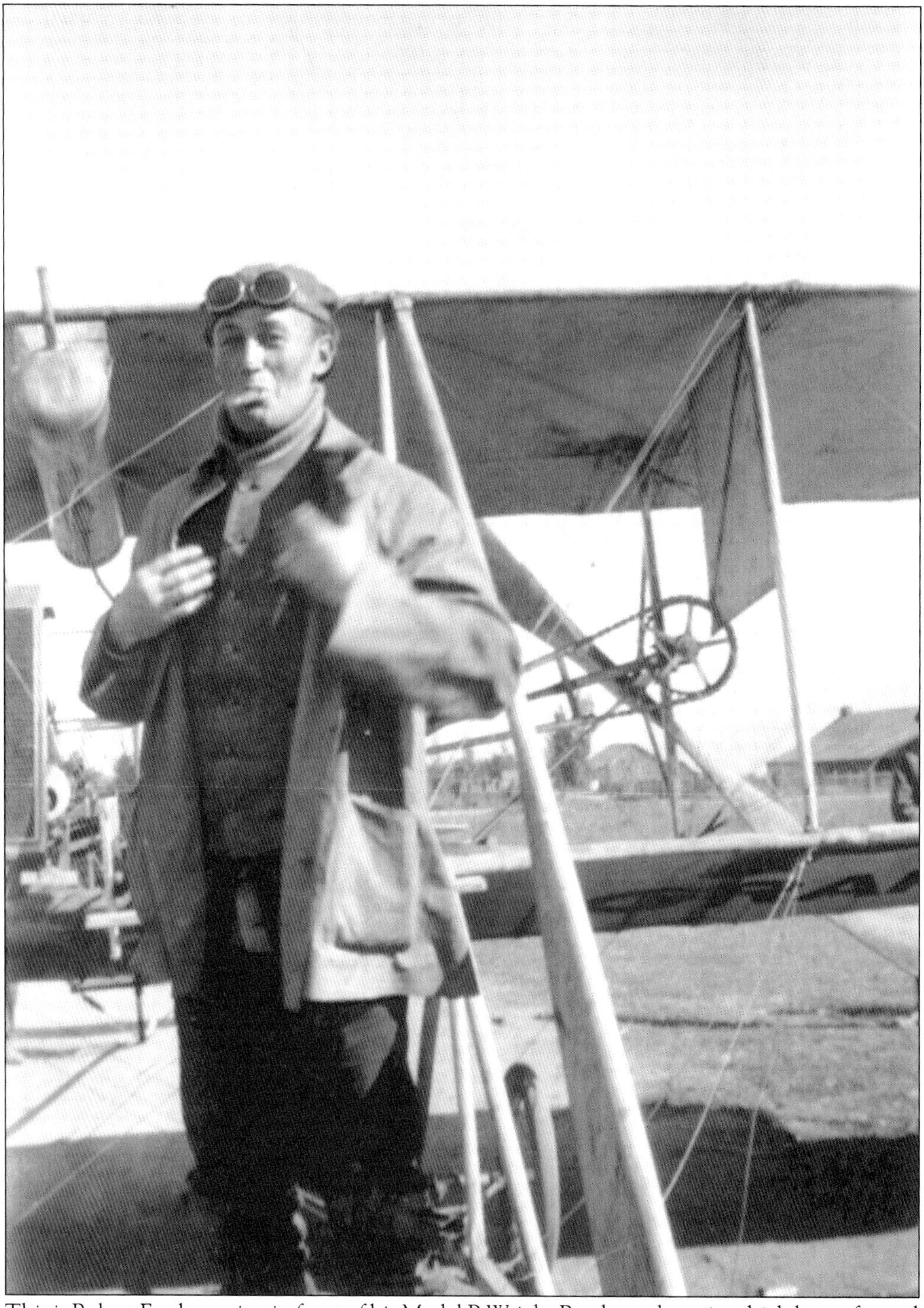

This is Robert Fowler posing in front of his Model B Wright Brothers plane, in which he performed an emergency landing on the Stewart Ranch. He was competing for prize money offered by William Randolph Hearst, who offered $50,000 for the first pilot to make a transcontinental flight in 30 days. He did not complete the endeavor in time but certainly stirred excitement in Beaumont and the surrounding area. (Courtesy of LMSF.)

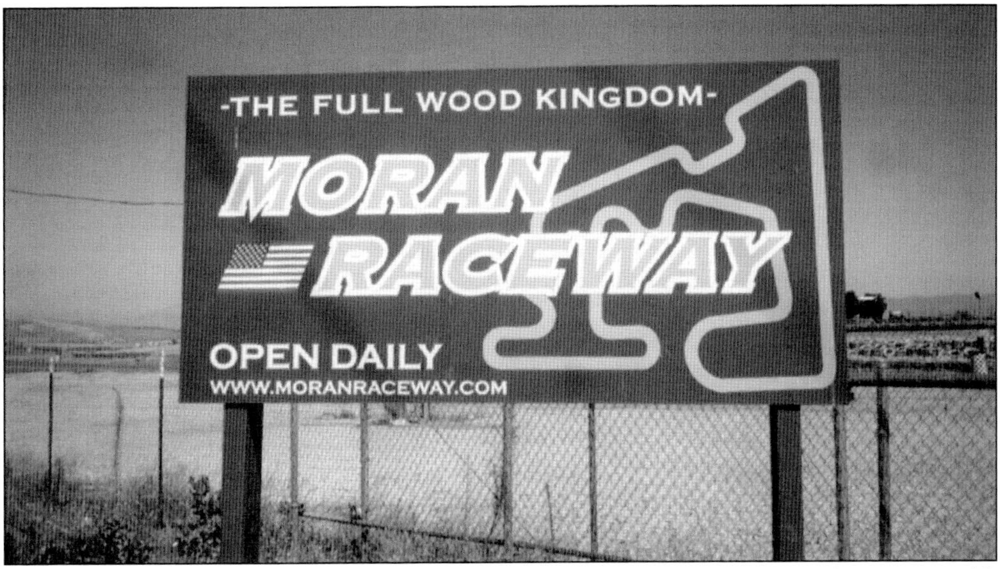

Moran Raceway in Beaumont is owned and operated by two famous names in the racing world: Rocky Moran Sr. and Rocky Moran Jr. Both men have spent most of their lives in the racing world and have brought all of their knowledge into operating Moran Raceway. The raceway is an endeavor that has produced the largest kart track in the world, which sponsors corporate events and a racing school. (Courtesy of the authors.)

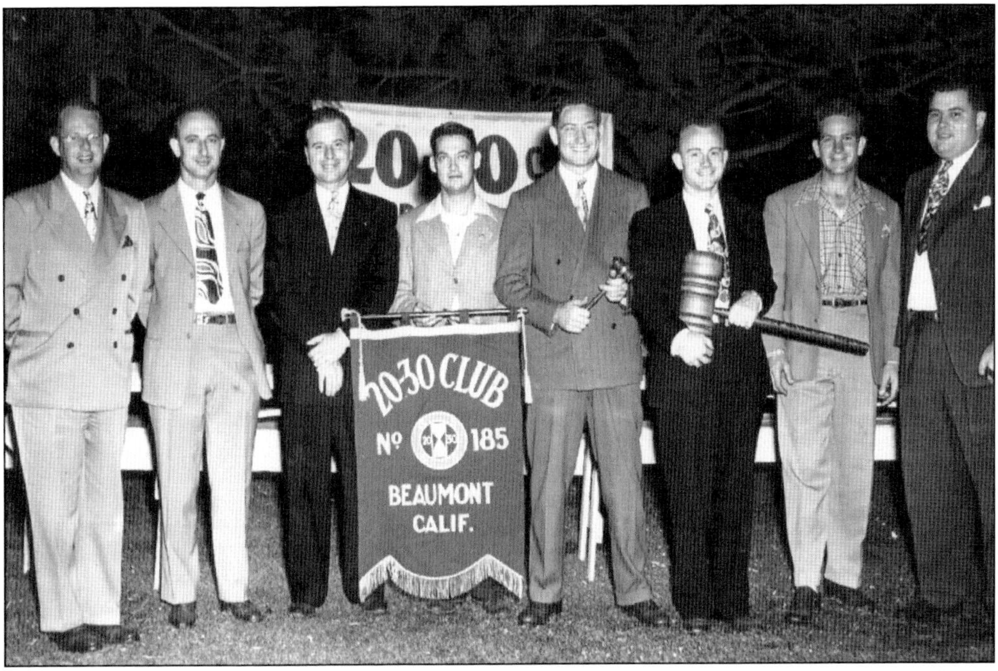

Pictured here are eight of Beaumont's past leading businessmen who formed the 20/30 Club of Beaumont, composed of men from ages 20 to 30, all with the goal of promoting good business. Banning also had a 20/30 Club and once sponsored Bob Hope's live radio show, broadcast from the Banning Theater, which is now known as the Fox Cineplex Theater. (Courtesy of Beverly Lewis.)

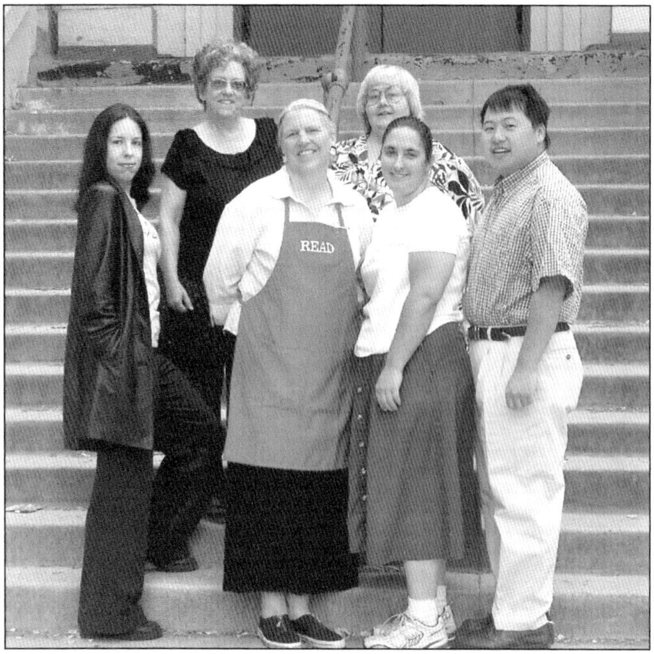

This is the Beaumont Library District staff. Pictured from left to right are (first row) reference librarian Melissa Walter, senior librarian and early childhood specialist Nancy Wood, administrative assistant Laura Cook, and head of adult services Edmund Ye Kiang; (second row) library director Clara DiFelice and children's librarian Linda Johnson. Their endeavor is to make reading available to all in the area, as suggested on Nancy's apron. (Courtesy of Beaumont Library District.)

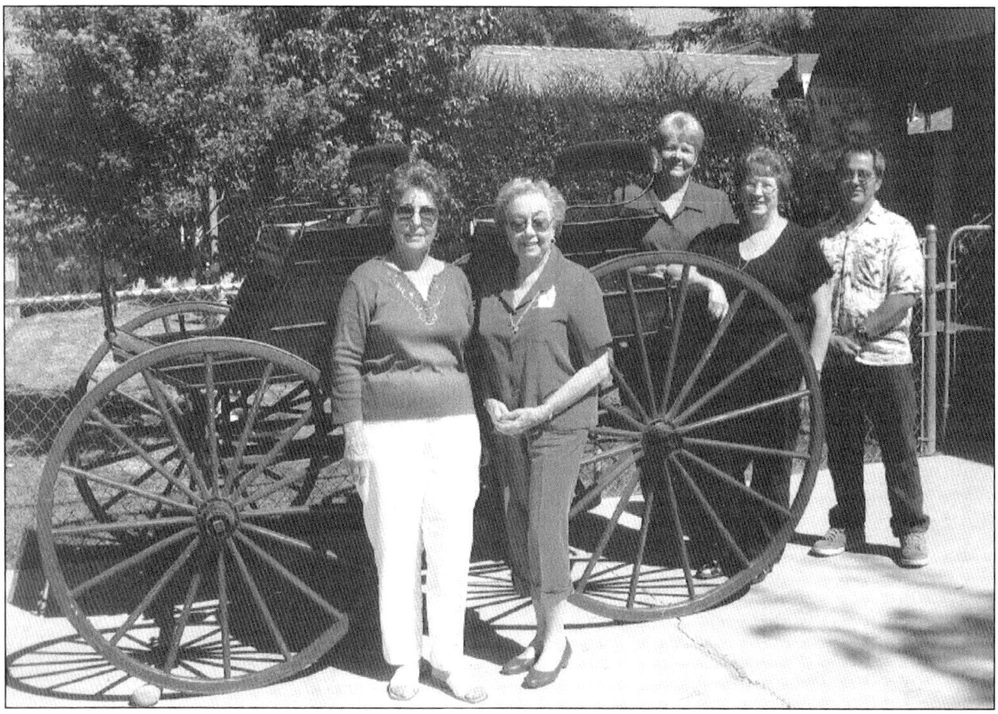

This is a recent photograph of the Stewart family buggy. It was originally a gift from Clara Stewart Beasley and was recently donated to the Laura May Stewart Foundation (LMSF) by the Donald L. Sumner family. Pictured here from left to right are Peggy Sumner; Margaret Hanson, LMSF committee member; Jan Wages, LMSF chair; Marilyn Vonderheide, LMSF program manager; and Les Racadio, LMSF committee member. Their endeavor is to find a permanent home for the buggy. (Courtesy of Bill Lopez.)

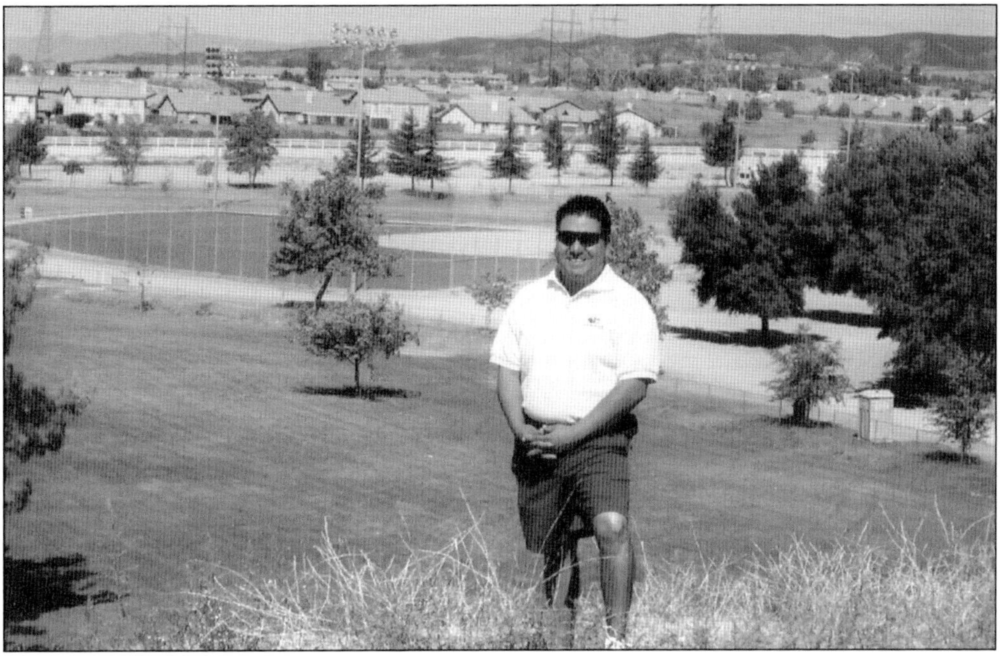

Seen here is Michael "Mickey" Valdevia, the Beaumont–Cherry Valley Recreation and Park District's Noble Creek Regional Park manager. Valdevia, whose family spans four generations in Beaumont, has been an intrepid overseer in making the park a success. The panoramic view includes a new baseball park to the left. Recently the 17th Annual Octoberfest was held on part of the 60-acre park grounds to the right. (Courtesy of the authors.)

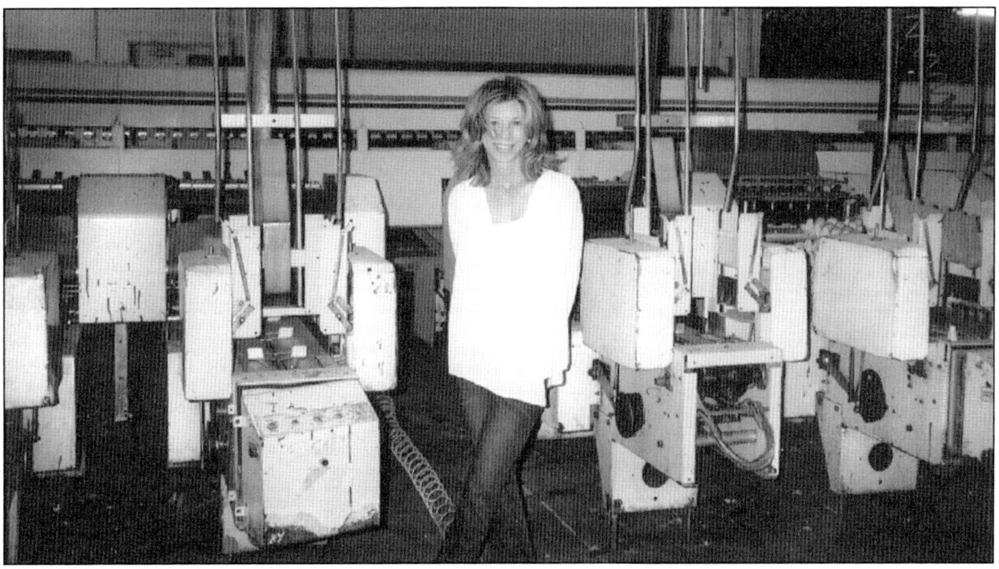

This is Cathy Burham, daughter of Bud Manheim, who bought Gorges George's turkey ranch in 1964, which then contained purple-painted turkey houses. Cathy is giving a tour of the egg-processing facility, one of the few buildings that still remain after the closure of their chicken ranch in 2005. The ranch contained 100 chicken houses, which were 399 feet long and contained 15,000 birds each. The 1.5 million chickens were replenished whenever the current stock died or became nonproductive. (Courtesy of authors.)

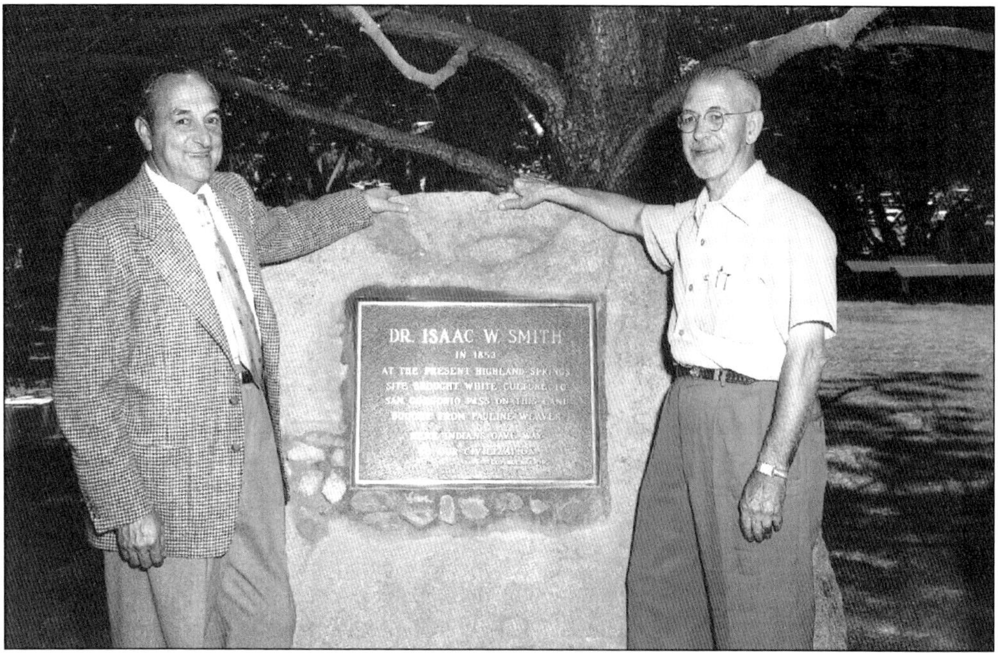

This plaque was presented to Highland Springs Resort by Guy Bogart, standing at right, in honor of Dr. Isaac W. Smith. Fred Hirsch, owner of the facility at the time, appears to be accepting it graciously. It reads, "Dr. Isaac W. Smith in 1853, at the present Highland Springs site brought white culture to San Gorgonio Pass on this land bought from Pauline Weaver. Here Indians gave way to our civilization." It is dated 1953. (Courtesy of SGPHS.)

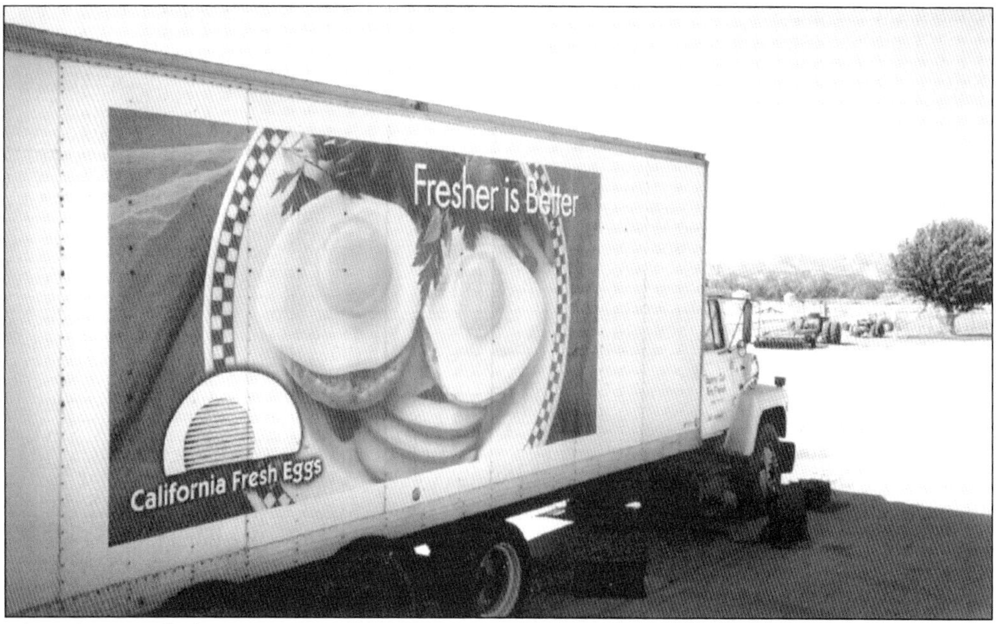

This photograph depicts a Sunny Cal egg-delivery truck. The processing plant was capable of producing 500 cases of eggs per hour, each containing 30 dozen eggs, so the truck was often seen on the nearby highways. However, it now stands idle beside the processing plant. Notice at right the razed chicken houses with only feed tanks still standing. (Courtesy of the authors.)

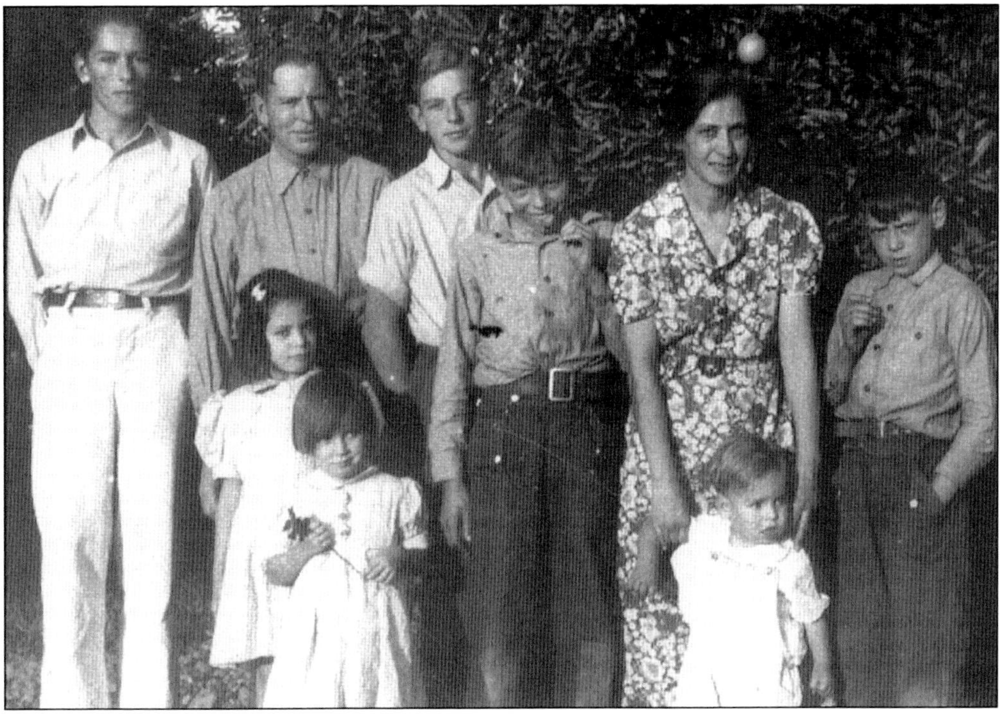

This is the Charles L. Barrett family in 1938, one of Beaumont's early families and descendents of pioneer Lucy Christian Sabin. Pictured here from left to right are (first row) Barbara, Margaret, and Charles W.; (second row) James, Charles L. (dad), Fred, Wade, Barbara (mom), and Jack. It was a great endeavor for pioneer Lucy Christine Sabin to come to what would be Beaumont in 1875, for there was no town there then. Grading for the railroad had reached San Timoteo Canyon around 1873, and the railroad came through a year or so afterwards. Land was taken up, and settlers such as Sabin moved in. Two years later, she married James L. Barrett, who had come to California in 1850 at age four. (Courtesy of Jim Barrett.)

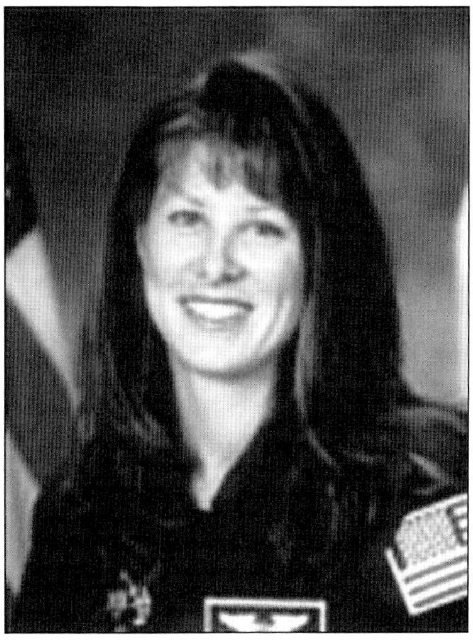

This is a photograph of Dr. Tracy E. Caldwell, who hails from Beaumont but is now residing at the Lyndon B. Johnson Space Center at Houston, Texas, since being selected by NASA in June 1998 as an astronaut candidate for training there. Previously she received a doctorate in physical chemistry from the University of California at Davis in 1997. She is assigned to the crew of STS-118 and targeted for launch in 2007, an endeavor that will deliver to the space station the third starboard truss segment, an external stowage platform. (Courtesy of Betty Warren and Mary Ellen Caldwell.)

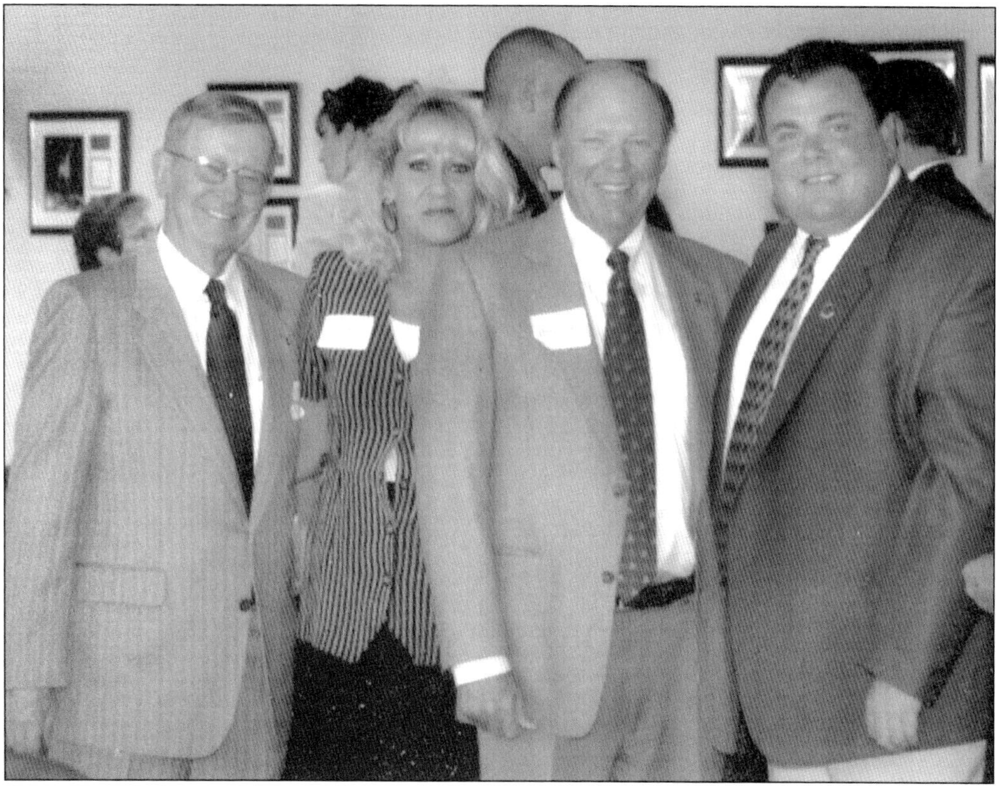

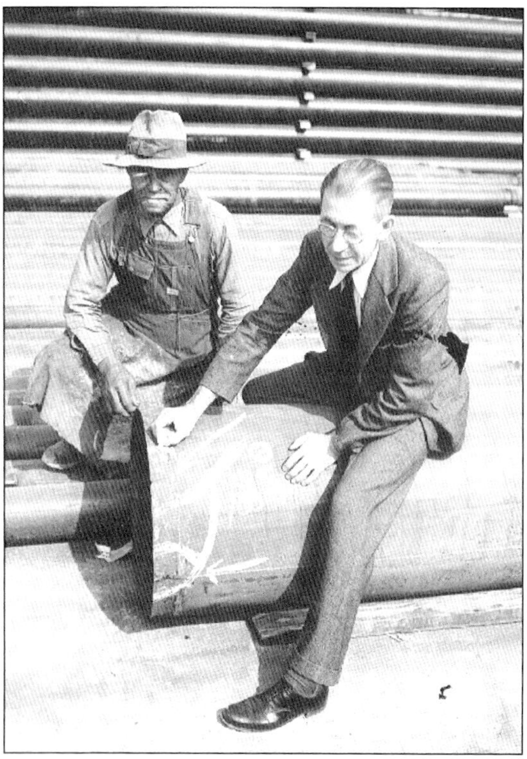

This group was photographed during a recent fund-raising event. Endeavors like this for important causes are popular in Beaumont. Pictured here from left to right are Bill Jenkins, former Banning City Council member; Lori Fox, wife of Mayor Jeff Fox; Marian Ashley, supervisor of the Fifth District of Riverside County; and Mayor Jeff Fox of Beaumont. (Courtesy of Mayor Jeff Fox.)

Guy Bogart, one of Beaumont's model citizens, is seen here instructing a worker in preparation for the installation of pipe casing. Endeavors like this were important, because water was a necessary commodity in the Beaumont area. Notable is Bogart's torn jacket, and it can only be surmised what happened. (Courtesy of SGPHS.)

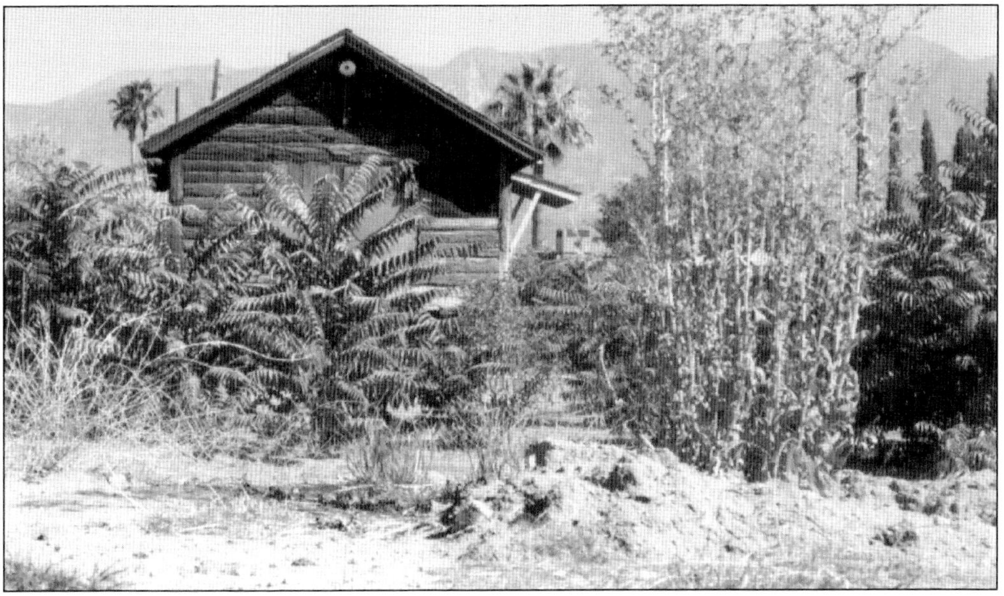

This is the old log cabin schoolhouse that allegedly once was in old Hall City, the precursor to Cabazon. It was first moved to Cabazon and then Beaumont, donated to the San Gorgonio Historical Society, and has stood at this site for several years awaiting a home. However, the building is now in dire shape, so the society has prudently decided to build a replica of the structure at Noble Creek Park instead of moving it there and trying to restore it. (Courtesy of authors.)

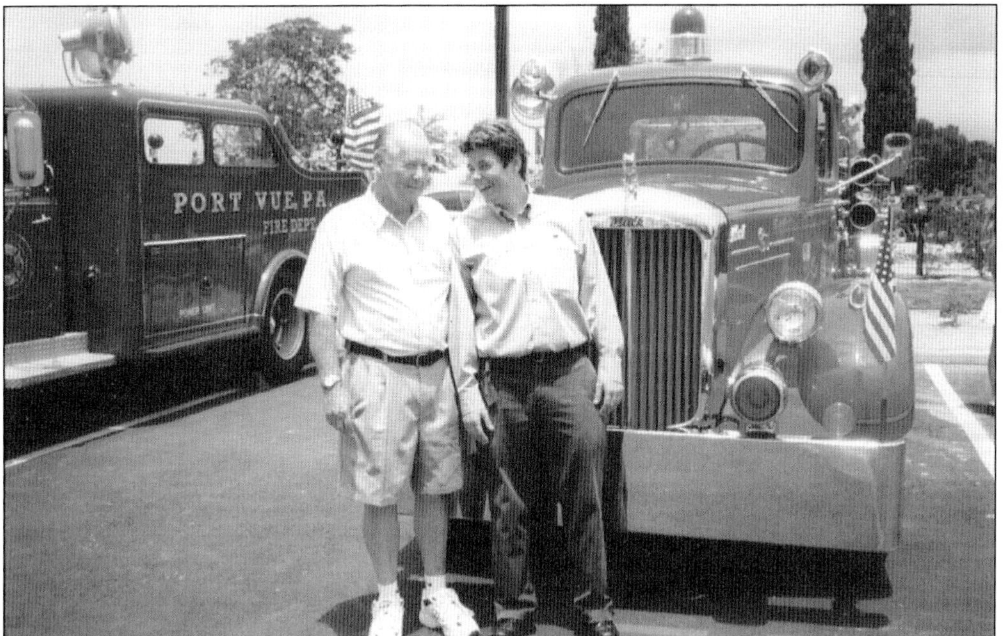

The recent arrival of an Applebee's restaurant to Beaumont is an endeavor that has been a great success. Seen here on opening day is author Ken Holtzclaw (left) and Janet Cherpes, the general manager of the new restaurant. For the opening, the Beaumont Fire Department lined Sixth Street in front of the establishment with a collection of vintage fire trucks, providing a spectrum of color for the gala event. (Courtesy of Ken Holtzclaw.)

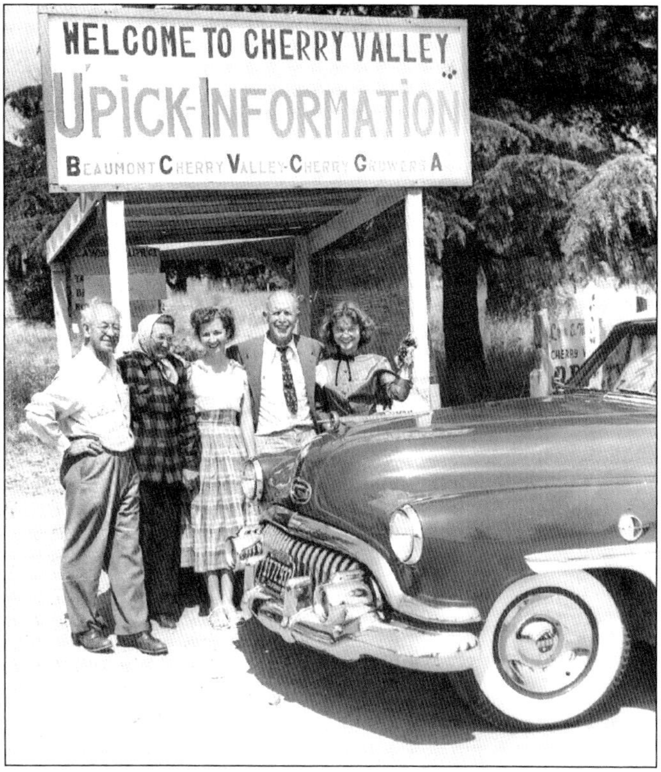

Standing at left, with a group of people promoting the cherry-growing industry, is Guy Bogart, a Beaumont citizen who greatly supported fruit growing. The sign above advertises the Beaumont and Cherry Valley Cherry Growers Association, an endeavor that was launched in the area quite successfully. (Courtesy of SGPHS.)

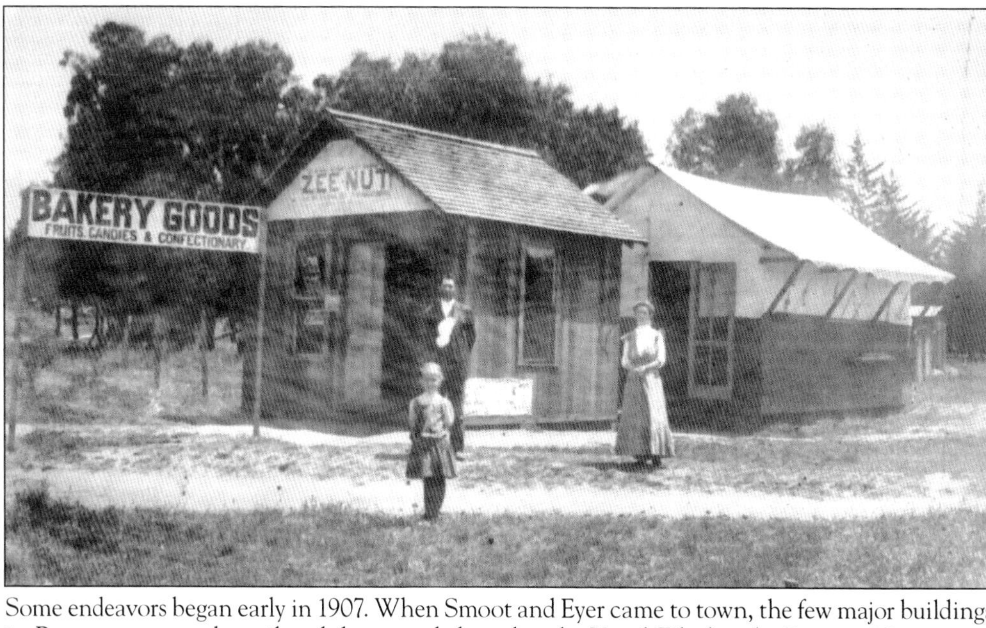

Some endeavors began early in 1907. When Smoot and Eyer came to town, the few major buildings in Beaumont were the railroad depot and three hotels: Hotel Edinburgh, Summit House, and Del Paso Hotel. Rooms went for about 50¢, while meals were 25¢. This is a 1907 photograph of the bakery business and home of the G. M. Kimball family during this era, but the town also boasted a post office, general store, lumberyard, funeral parlor, two livery stables, and two pool halls. (Courtesy of SGPHS.)

Five

The Stewarts

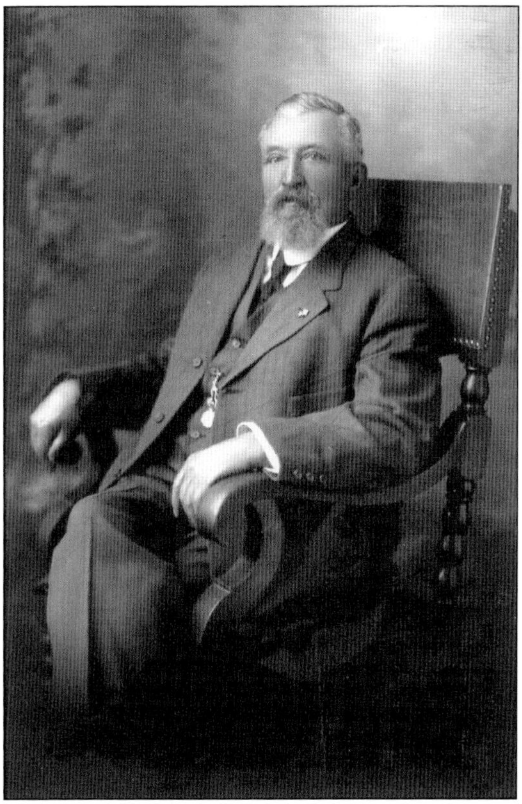

This photograph was taken of Reznor Perry Stewart some years after the Stewart Ranch was firmly established. He was born in Illinois on November 3, 1845. At age five, he and his mother crossed the Plains and stopped at Hangtown, California, now Placerville. Stewart became foreman of the vast George Scott Ranches, remaining there 21 years, before establishing his own ranch in Beaumont. (Courtesy of Marilyn Vonderheide and LMSF.)

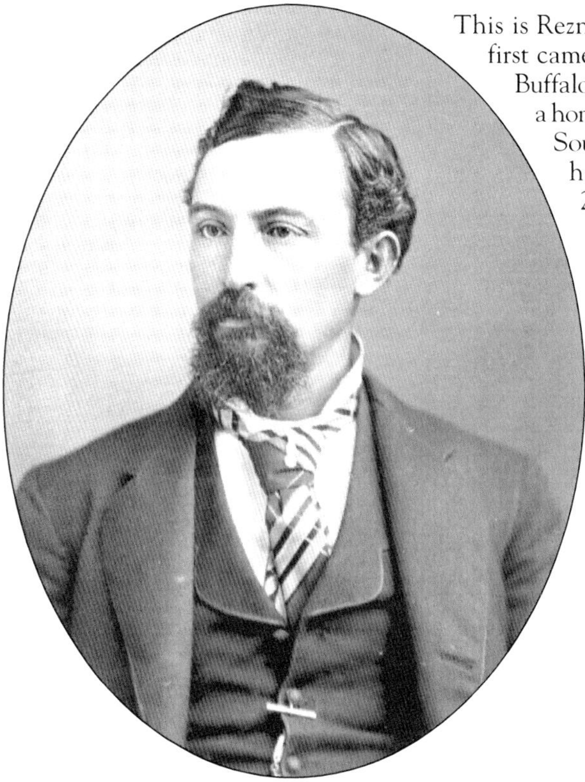

This is Reznor Stewart as a young man. When he first came to California, he met Kit Carson and Buffalo Bill. It was in 1883 that Reznor took up a homestead in Beaumont. He later purchased Southern Pacific Railroad land to add to his holdings, forming a ranch of around 2,200 acres on which he dry farmed grain and grew hay. (Courtesy of Marilyn Vonderheide and LMSF.)

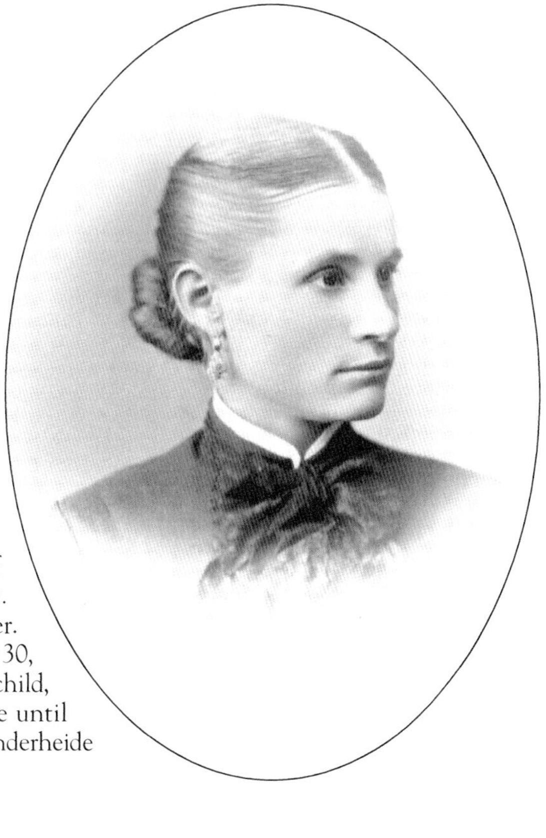

Pictured here is Reznor's wife, Mary Christensen, whom he married on December 30, 1880. She was the stepdaughter of prominent Banning resident, C. F. Jost. Three boys and two girls were born to her. She succumbed to an early death on August 30, 1890, a few months after the birth of her fifth child, Reznor Perry Jr., but her husband didn't die until November 12, 1933. (Courtesy of Marilyn Vonderheide and LMSF.)

Pictured here are the three sons of Reznor and Mary Stewart. They are, from left to right, Emery Ross, Reznor Perry, and Arthur. All lived relatively short lives, with Reznor Perry dying in 1907 at the young age of 17. Arthur died in 1913 in Lima, Peru, in a mining accident at age 27, and Emery Ross lived to be 45, dying at sea in 1925. Through a span of only 18 years, Stewart lost all three sons. (Courtesy of Marilyn Vonderheide and LMSF.)

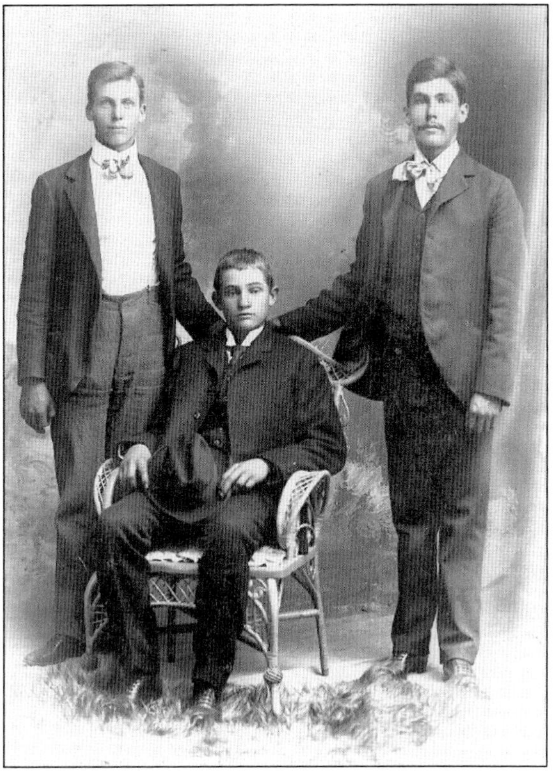

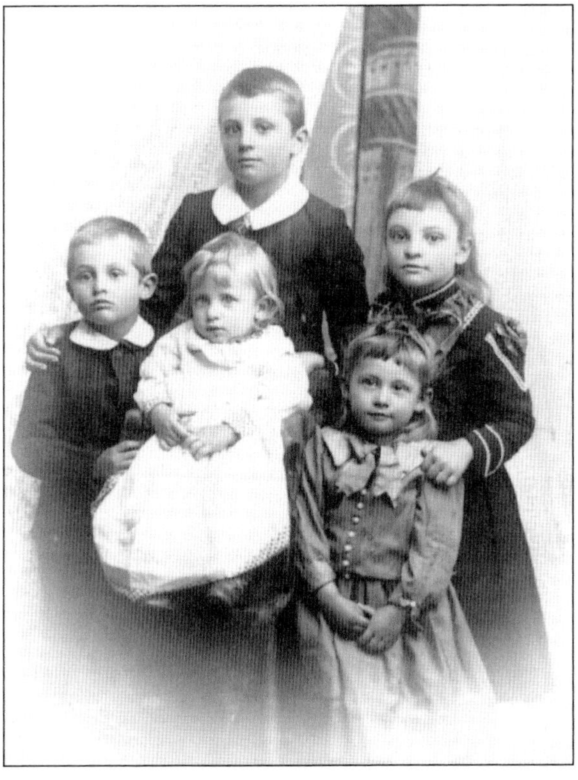

This photograph goes back to the early childhood of all three Stewart children, taken in the late 1880s. By this time, their mother had been deceased for several years. It appears from this photograph that Reznor Stewart was doing a great job in caring for them. Pictured from left to right are (first row) Arthur, Reznor Perry Jr., and Clara; (second row) Emery and Laura Mae. (Courtesy of Marilyn Vonderheide and LMSF.)

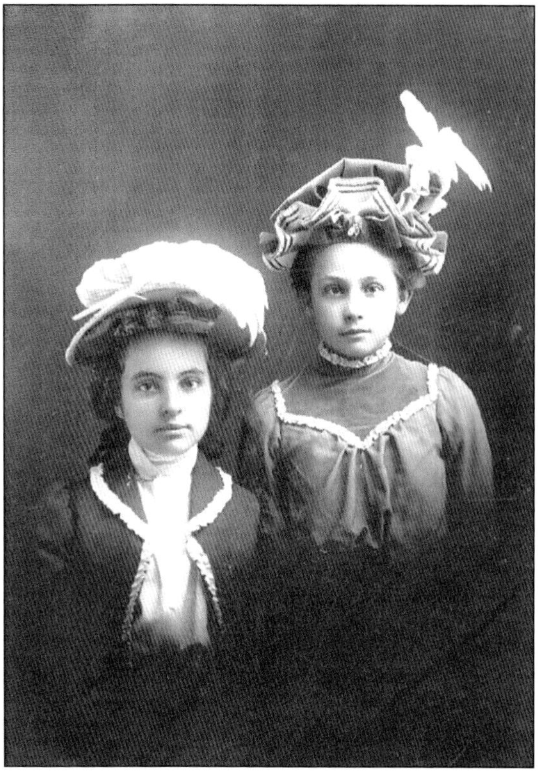

Pictured here are Laura Mae Stewart, at left, and her sister Clara. By this time, they had reached an age when they had begun to be a great help to their father. They helped care for the ranch, following in the footsteps of their mother in maintaining an orderly and happy household. They adapted well to farm life and were an indispensable twosome to their father. (Courtesy of Marilyn Vonderheide and LMSF.)

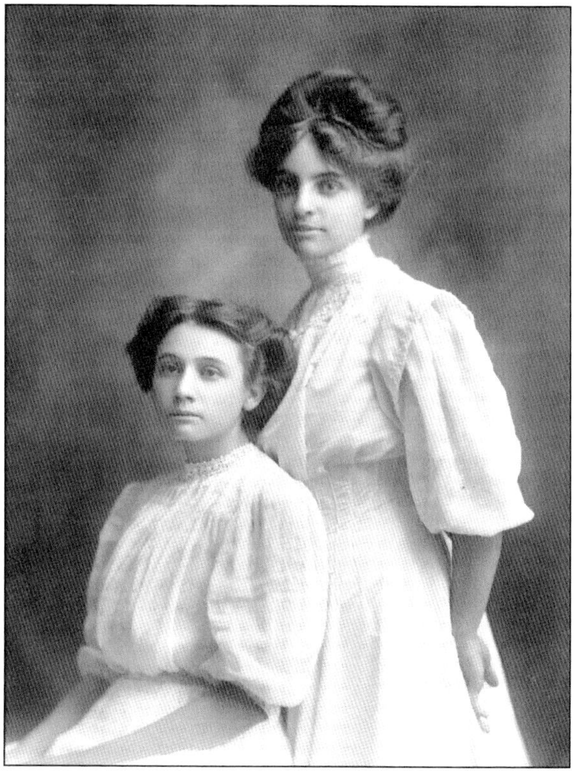

The two Stewart sisters, Clara (left) and Laura, are seen here nearing adulthood. By this time, the Stewart Ranch was a well-known entity in Beaumont and added much to its economy. The girls were a welcome sight during grain harvest when they often appeared in a buggy in the fields to supply lunch for the crew. (Courtesy of Marilyn Vonderheide and LMSF.)

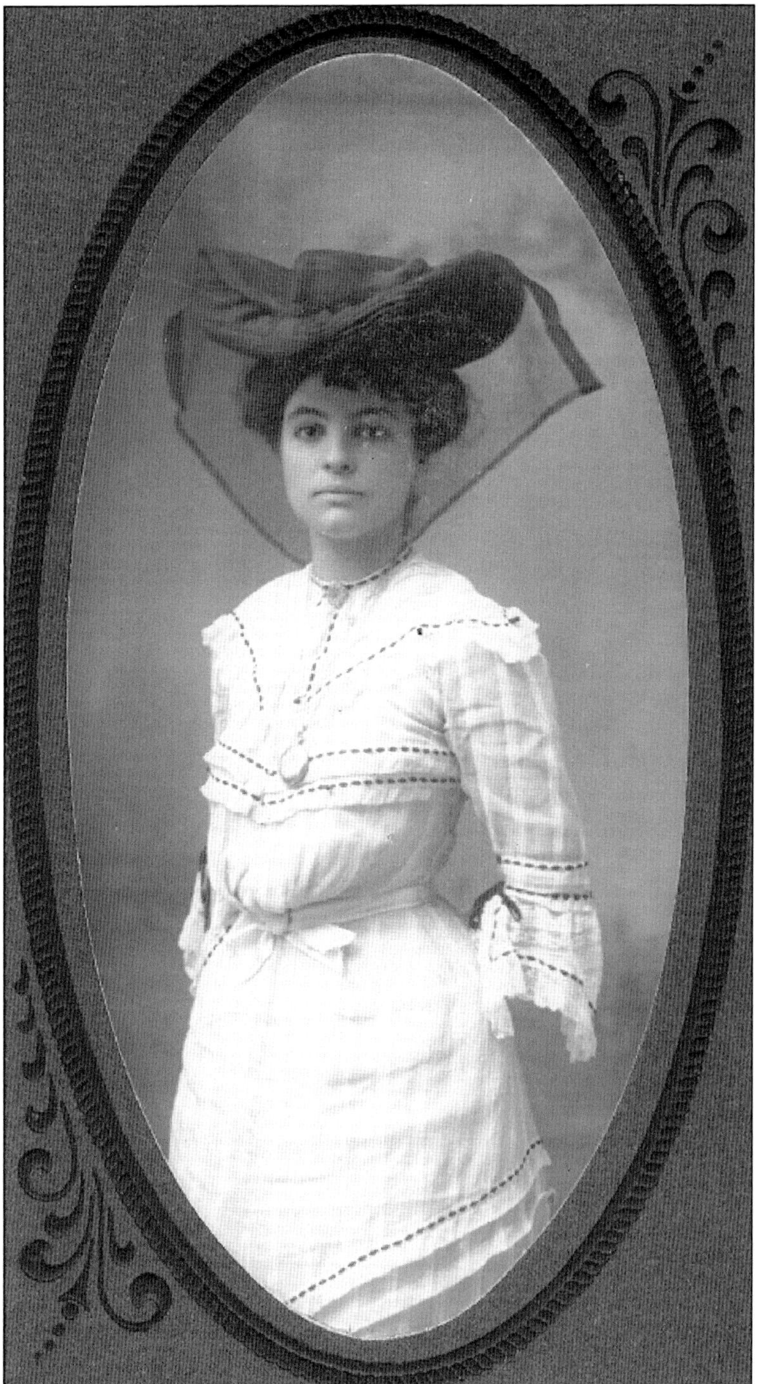

This is a portrait of Laura Mae Stewart that once hung in the family residence of the Stewart Ranch. Her beauty perhaps justified her in receiving the first title of Cherry Queen of the Cherry Festival celebration held in Beaumont in 1919, over which she presided with grace and dignity. A big, six-cylinder Studebaker was handsomely decorated for her and her maids of honor for the parade. (Courtesy of Marilyn Vonderheide and LMSF.)

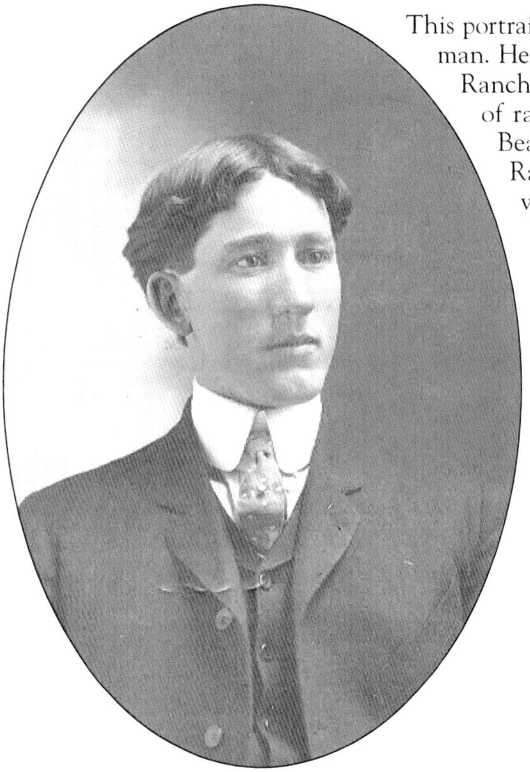

This portrait is of Earl E. Beasley when he was a young man. He became the top ranch hand of the Stewart Ranch and later married Clara Stewart, daughter of ranch owner and pioneer Reznor Stewart. Beasley was dedicated to making the Stewart Ranch successful, and his expertise was of great value toward that goal. (Courtesy of Marilyn Vonderheide and LMSF.)

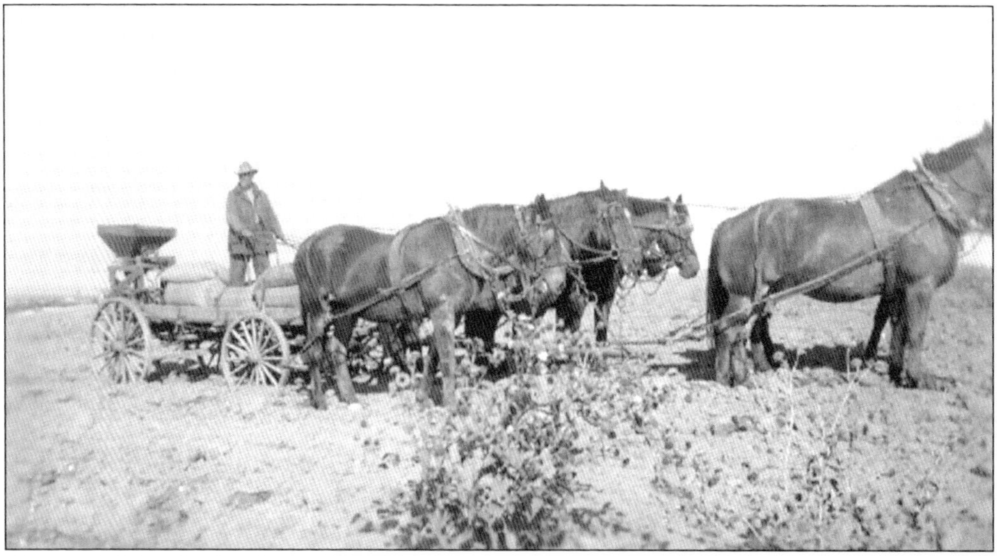

This is Earl Beasley hard at work on the Stewart Ranch. It was a rush to get the many acres of grain planted on the ranch each season before the first rains, and Beasley was quite successful in accomplishing the feat, as seen here, with his team of horses pulling the large seeder rig. Note the sacks of grain stacked hip high on the seeder. (Courtesy of Marilyn Vonderheide and LMSF.)

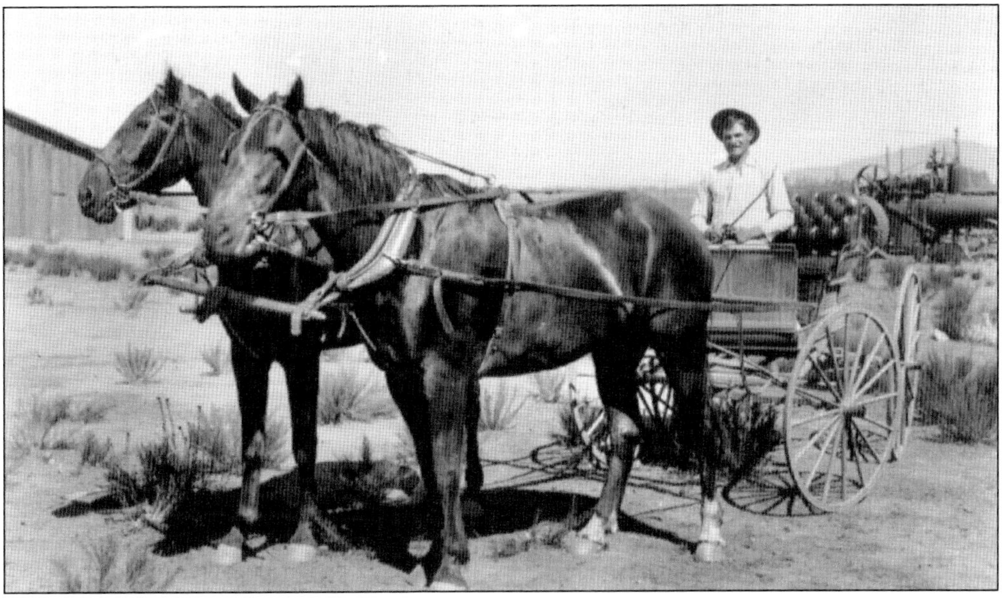

Emery Stewart, the oldest son of the Reznor and Mary Stewart family, adapted well to farm life on the ranch. In this photograph, he is in the family buggy, perhaps ready for a trip to town for shopping or a business event. He became quite adept in harnessing the horses driving the carriage. (Courtesy of Marilyn Vonderheide and LMSF.)

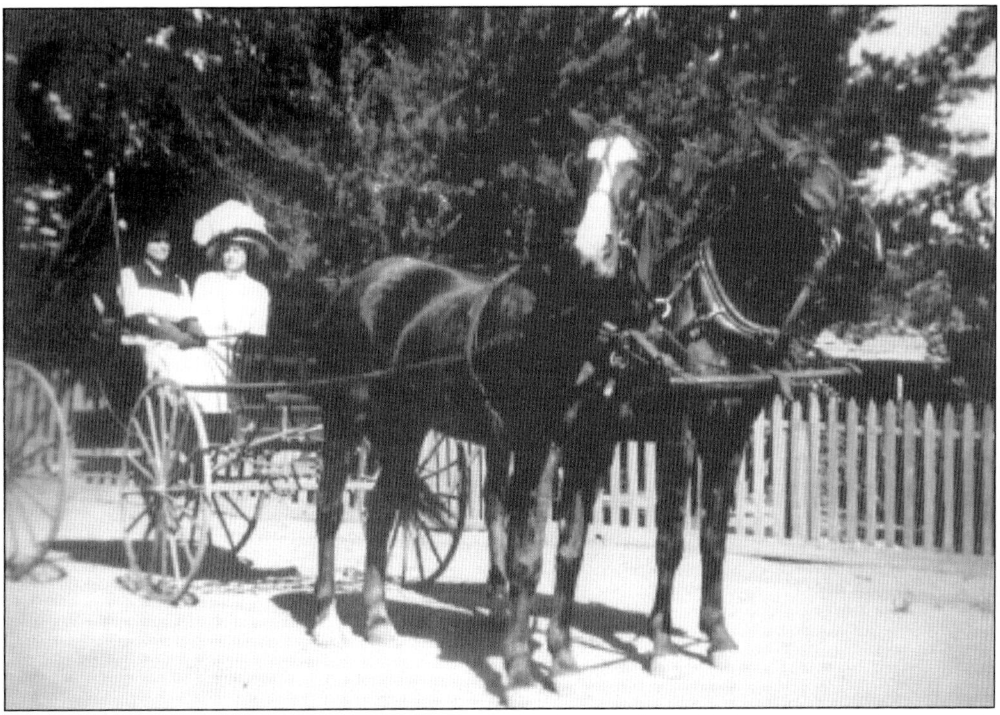

Laura Mae Stewart and her friend Blanch are seen here in June 1911, sitting in a buggy with the horses harnessed, perhaps en route to church or some special event. Laura is seated at left with reins in hand. The scene was captured in front of the Stewart Ranch House. (Courtesy of Marilyn Vonderheide and LMSF.)

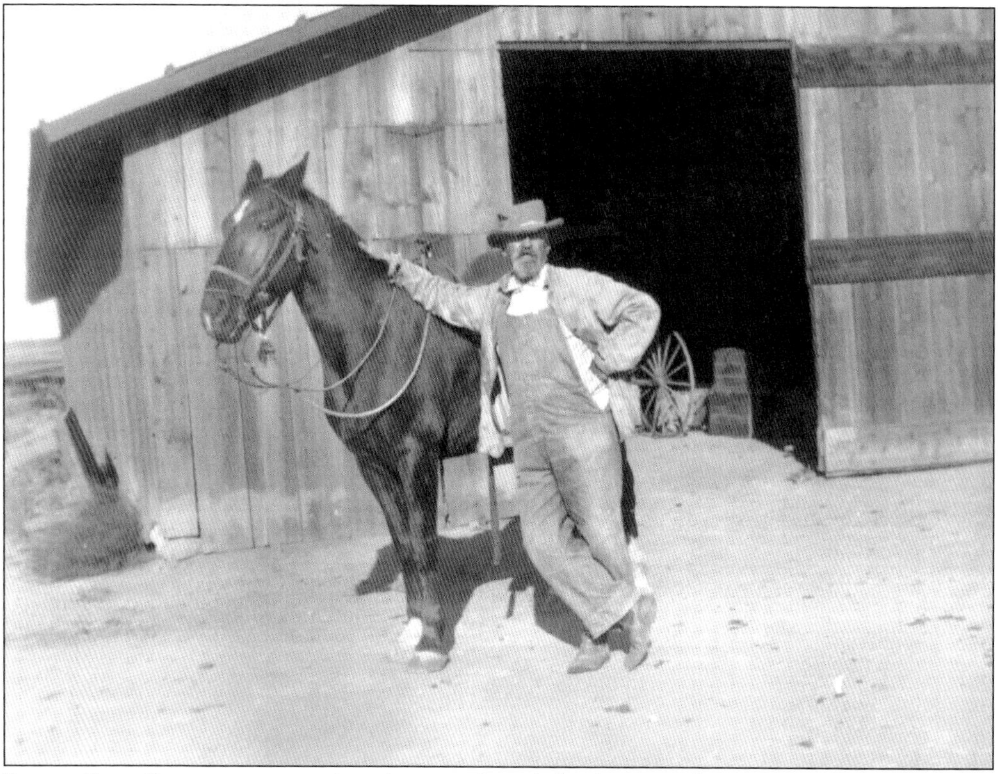

Reznor Perry Stewart poses in this photograph with his horse in front of the barn he built on his ranch shortly after he homesteaded land south of today's Interstate 10. He worked hard at farming his large acreage, becoming one of the most successful farmers in Beaumont. (Courtesy of Marilyn Vonderheide and LMSF.)

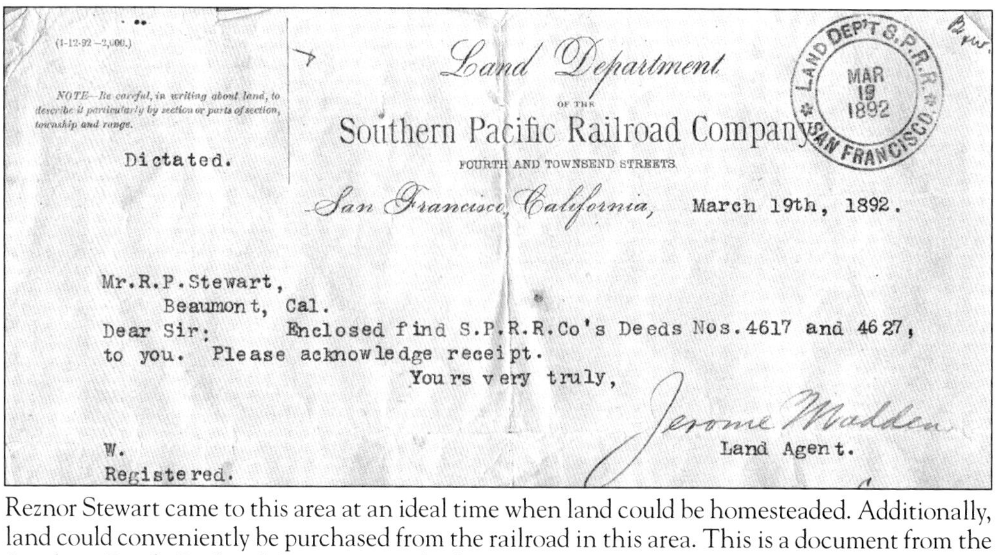

(1-12-92—2,000.)

NOTE—Be careful, in writing about land, to describe it particularly by section or parts of section, township and range.

Dictated.

Land Department
OF THE
Southern Pacific Railroad Company
FOURTH AND TOWNSEND STREETS.

LAND DEP'T S.P.R.R. MAR 19 1892 SAN FRANCISCO

San Francisco, California, March 19th, 1892.

Mr. R. P. Stewart,
Beaumont, Cal.
Dear Sir: Enclosed find S.P.R.R.Co's Deeds Nos. 4617 and 4627, to you. Please acknowledge receipt.
Yours very truly,
Jerome Madden
Land Agent.

W.
Registered.

Reznor Stewart came to this area at an ideal time when land could be homesteaded. Additionally, land could conveniently be purchased from the railroad in this area. This is a document from the Southern Pacific Railroad Company in which Reznor had purchased two parcels of land from the railroad, descriptive of deeds 4617 and 4627. (Courtesy of Marilyn Vonderheide and LMSF.)

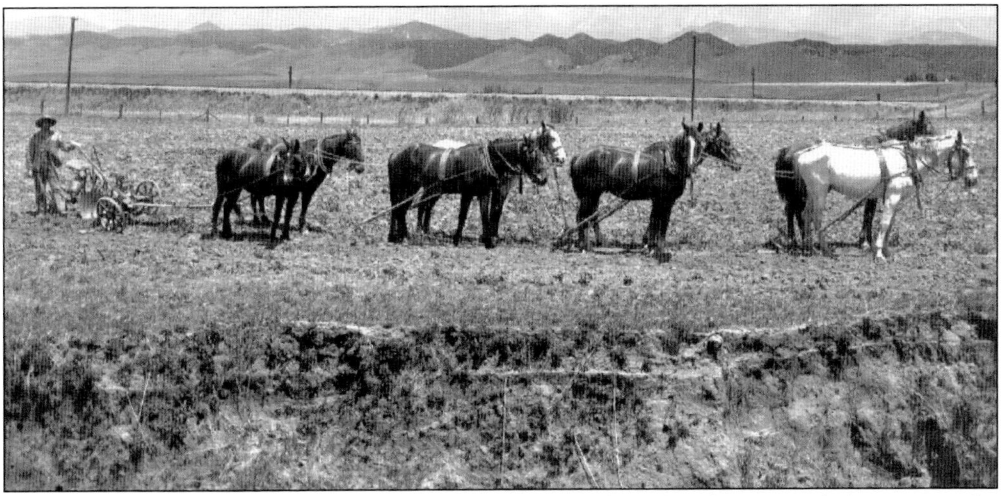

A team of horses, such as the one pictured here, did much of the plowing and planting on the Stewart Ranch. Adequate horsepower was required to pull the large plow blade through some of the hard-packed soil. Standing at the plow is ranch hand Earl Beasley, who married Clara Stewart. (Courtesy of Marilyn Vonderheide and LMSF.)

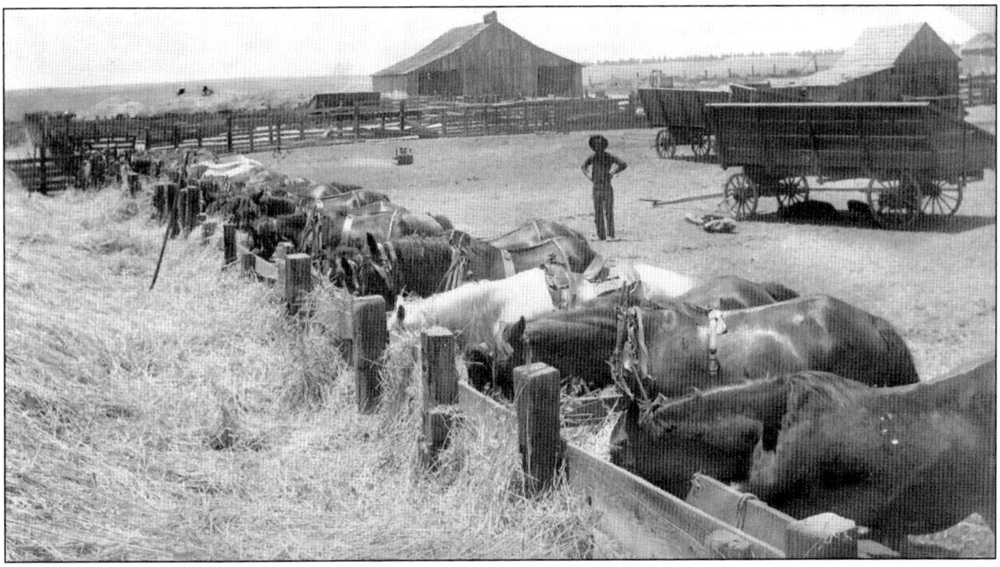

Here Reznor Stewart's horses are in the barn corral and are feeding on hay grown on the ranch. It was a tedious task caring for the horses, for they had to be kept in top condition to perform the numerous ranch tasks. The ranch hand at center, with hands on hips, is anxiously waiting for the feeding to finish. (Courtesy of Marilyn Vonderheide and LMSF.)

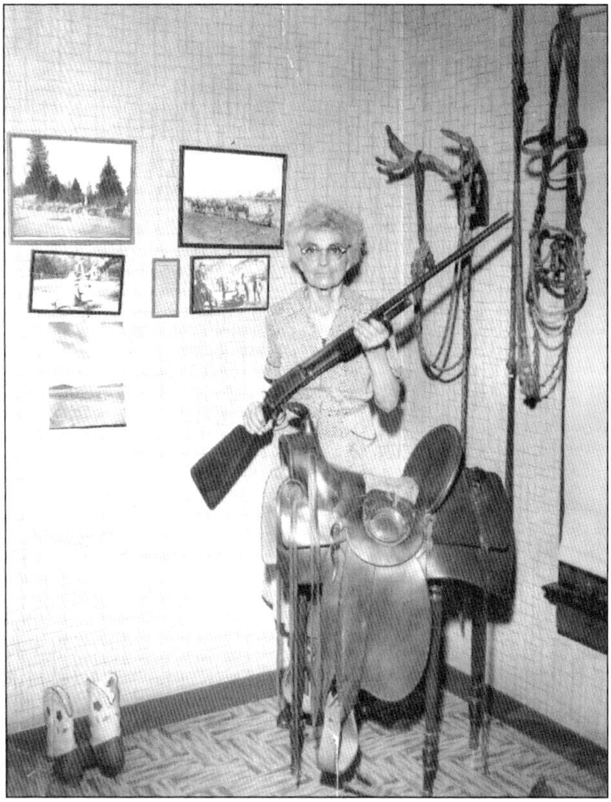

Laura Mae Stewart is seen here in the house where she was born. A humorous story arose from the event when a Wright Brother's Model B plane landed on her father's ranch. Apparently Reznor Stewart rushed into the house and jovially yelled, "Get your gun, Laura. The biggest hawk I have ever seen just landed out in our barley field!" (Courtesy of Marilyn Vonderheide and LMSF.)

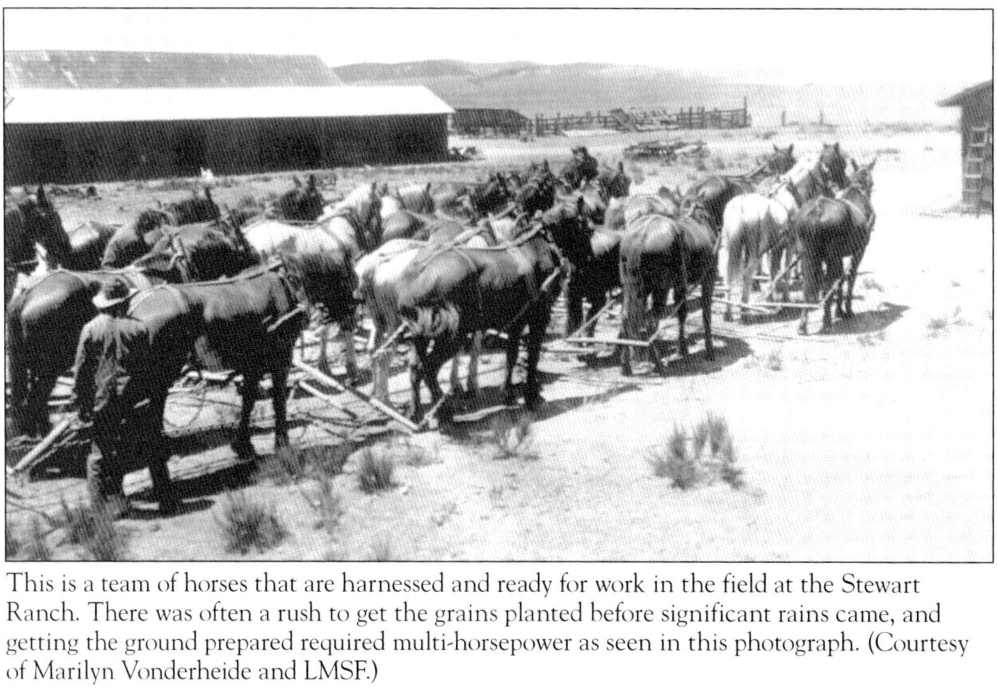

This is a team of horses that are harnessed and ready for work in the field at the Stewart Ranch. There was often a rush to get the grains planted before significant rains came, and getting the ground prepared required multi-horsepower as seen in this photograph. (Courtesy of Marilyn Vonderheide and LMSF.)

Six

The Guy Bogart Era

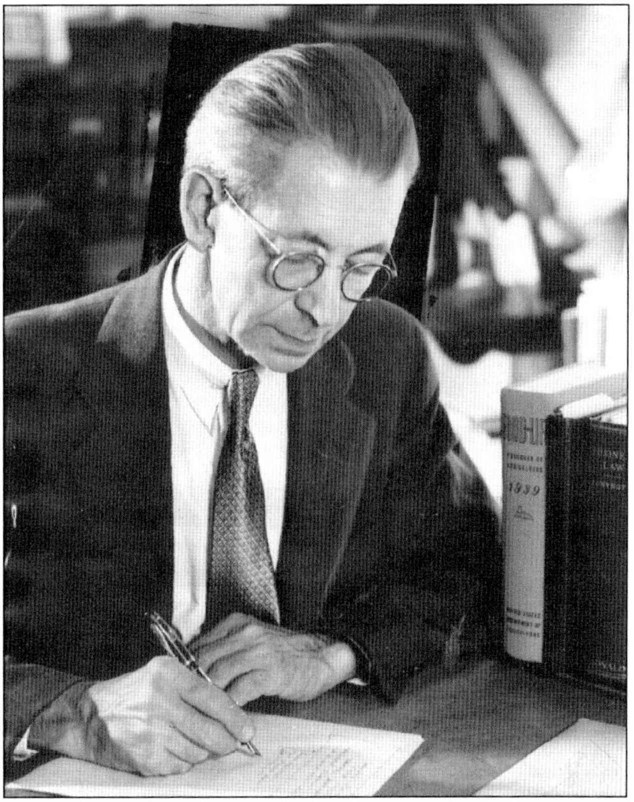

Community builder Guy Bogart is pictured after he had come from Los Angeles in 1924 to settle in Beaumont. He immediately went to work to improve the Beaumont community, and he developed a deep interest in the general area. He was successful in many of the endeavors he undertook, including becoming one of Beaumont's mayors. (Courtesy of SGPHS.)

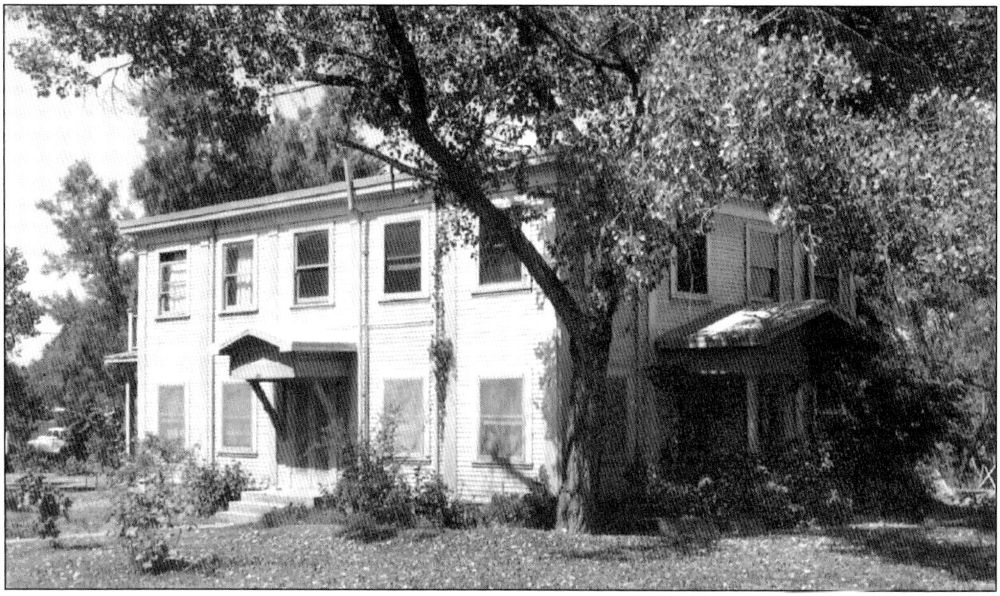

This is the original home of Dr. Guy Bogart in Beaumont, which he built soon after arriving. Today it is listed on the National Register of Historic Homes. William and Deborah Lash recently bought the Bogart House, an example of Colonial Revival architecture, and are now restoring it. (Courtesy of SGPHS.)

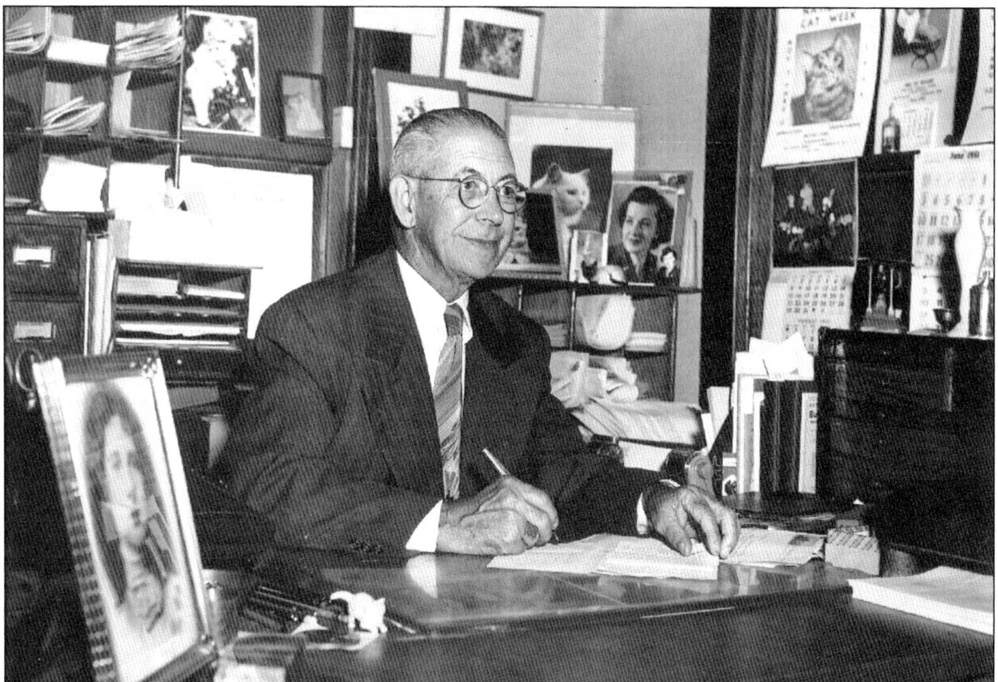

This photograph depicts Guy Bogart at his desk at home in Beaumont on Euclid Avenue. By now, Guy, along with his son Bobbie, had established a CPA business that kept them quite busy. Guy also had become a member of the Beaumont Chamber of Commerce and was involved in other civil duties. (Courtesy of SGPHS.)

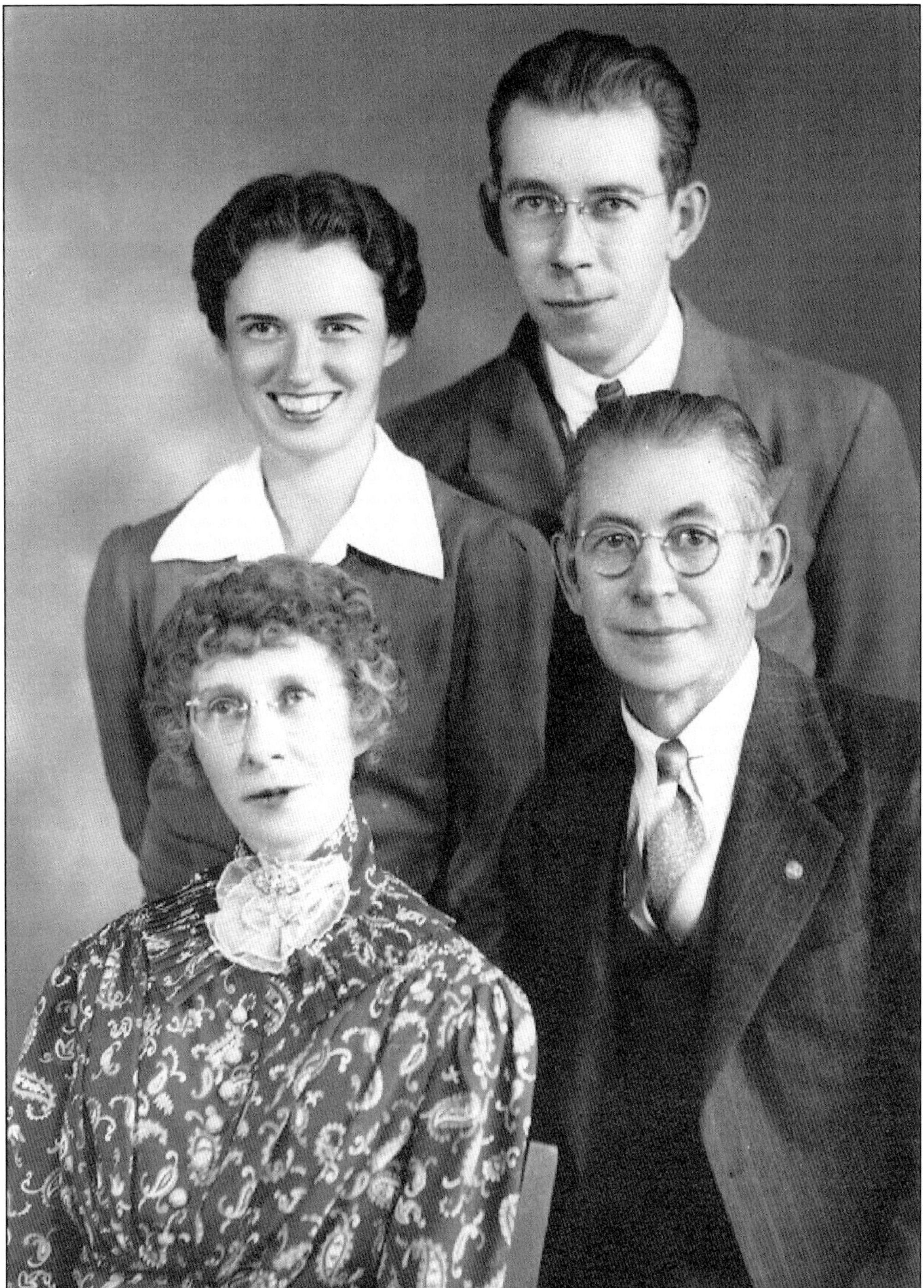

This photograph of the Bogart family of Beaumont was taken in the early years that they lived in town. Pictured here from left to right are (first row) concert violinist and wife of Guy Bogart, Lucy P. Bert Bogart, and Guy Bogart; (second row) wife of Bobbie Bogart, Edna Ann Bogart, and Bobbie, son of Guy and Lucy Bogart. (Courtesy of SGPHS.)

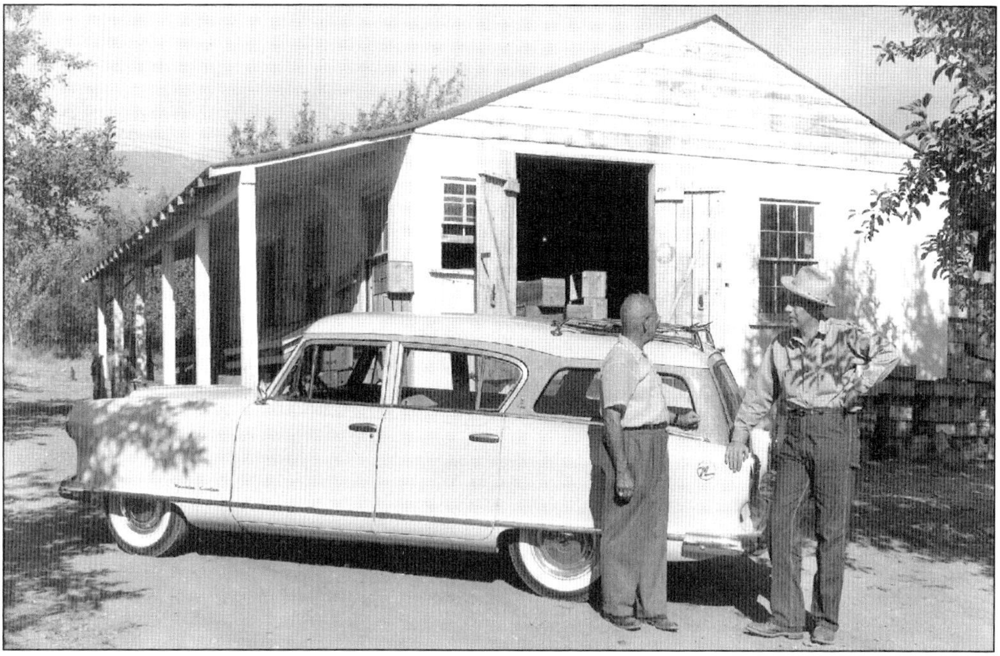

This is Guy Bogart (left) visiting with Dan Bedford of Sleepy Hollow Ranch at Oak Glen in October 1954. Bogart held an extraordinary ambassador relationship with Beaumont's surrounding fruit growers, as well as with Beaumont itself. He was very influential in promoting the best means of fruit production. (Courtesy of SGPHS.)

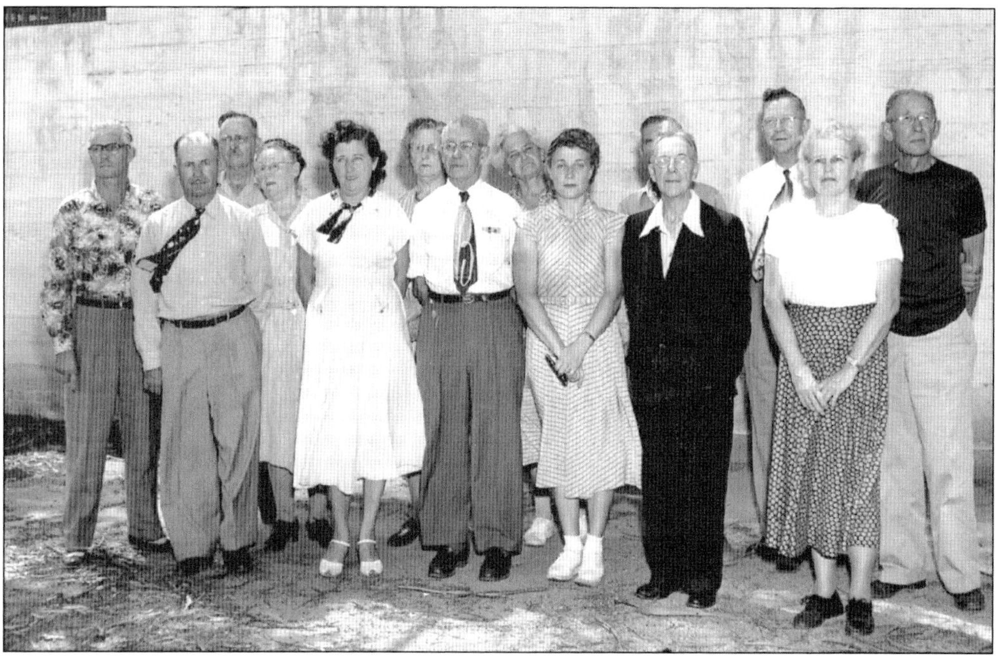

This group of citizens represents both the Banning and Beaumont Civil Defense teams that joined forces during dire war years. Guy Bogart is pictured in the middle of the group sporting his emblematic tie embossed with the letter B. It is possible that this letter could denote the town of Beaumont. (Courtesy of SGPHS.)

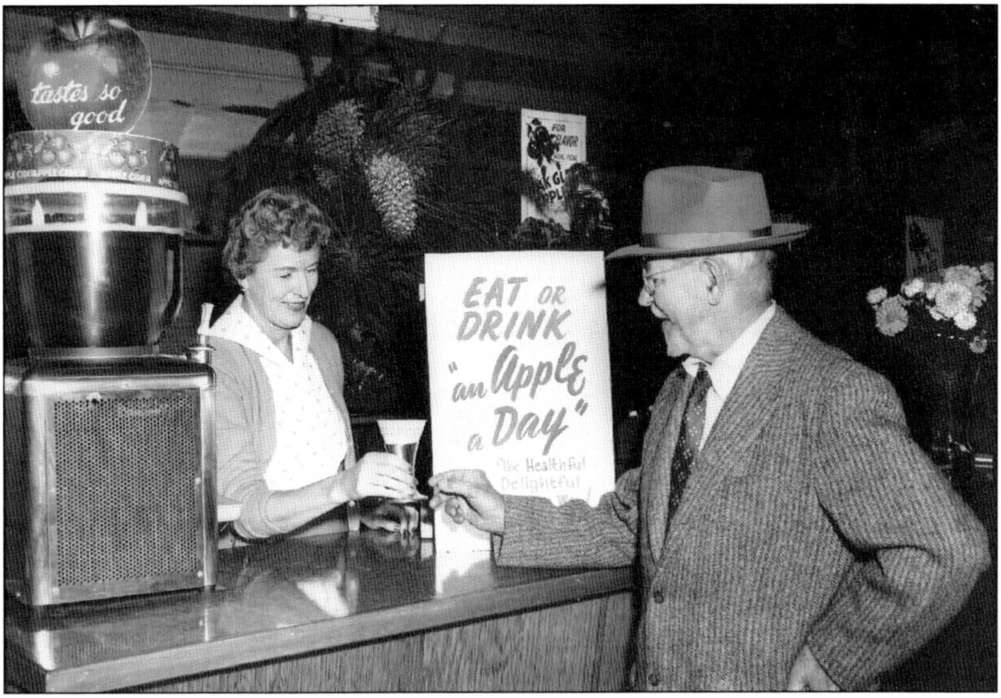

Guy Bogart is seen here reaching for a glass of apple juice being presented by an unidentified server at one of the Oak Glenn ranches. Apples were highly promoted in Oak Glen, and Guy would often support the agricultural industry. (Courtesy of LMSF.)

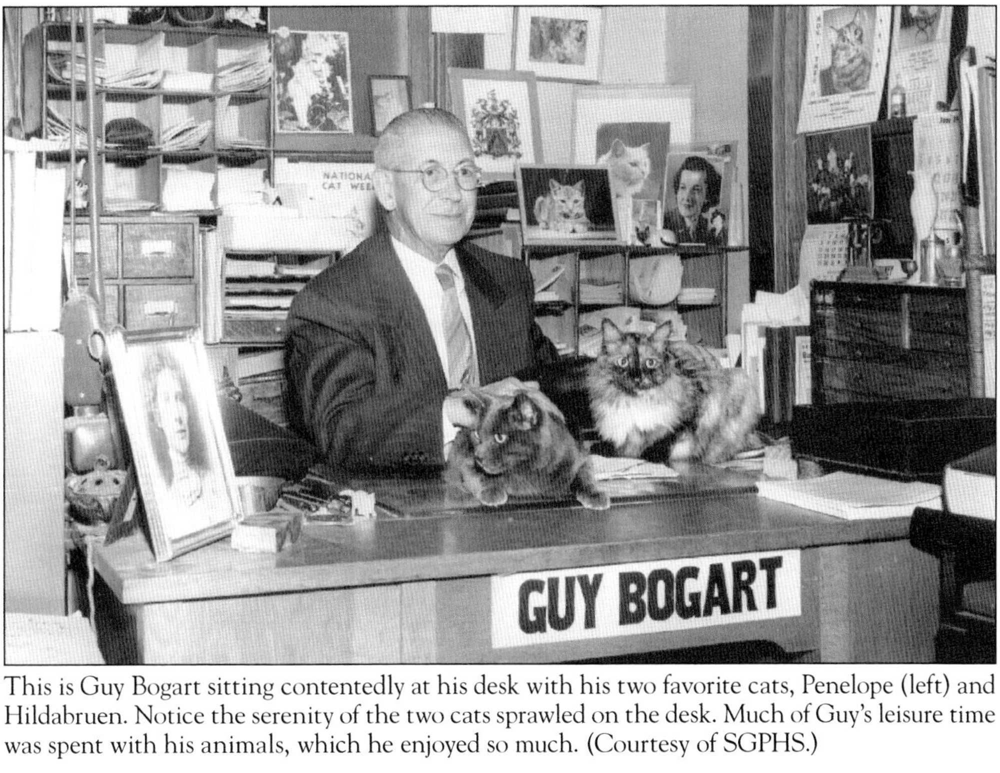

This is Guy Bogart sitting contentedly at his desk with his two favorite cats, Penelope (left) and Hildabruen. Notice the serenity of the two cats sprawled on the desk. Much of Guy's leisure time was spent with his animals, which he enjoyed so much. (Courtesy of SGPHS.)

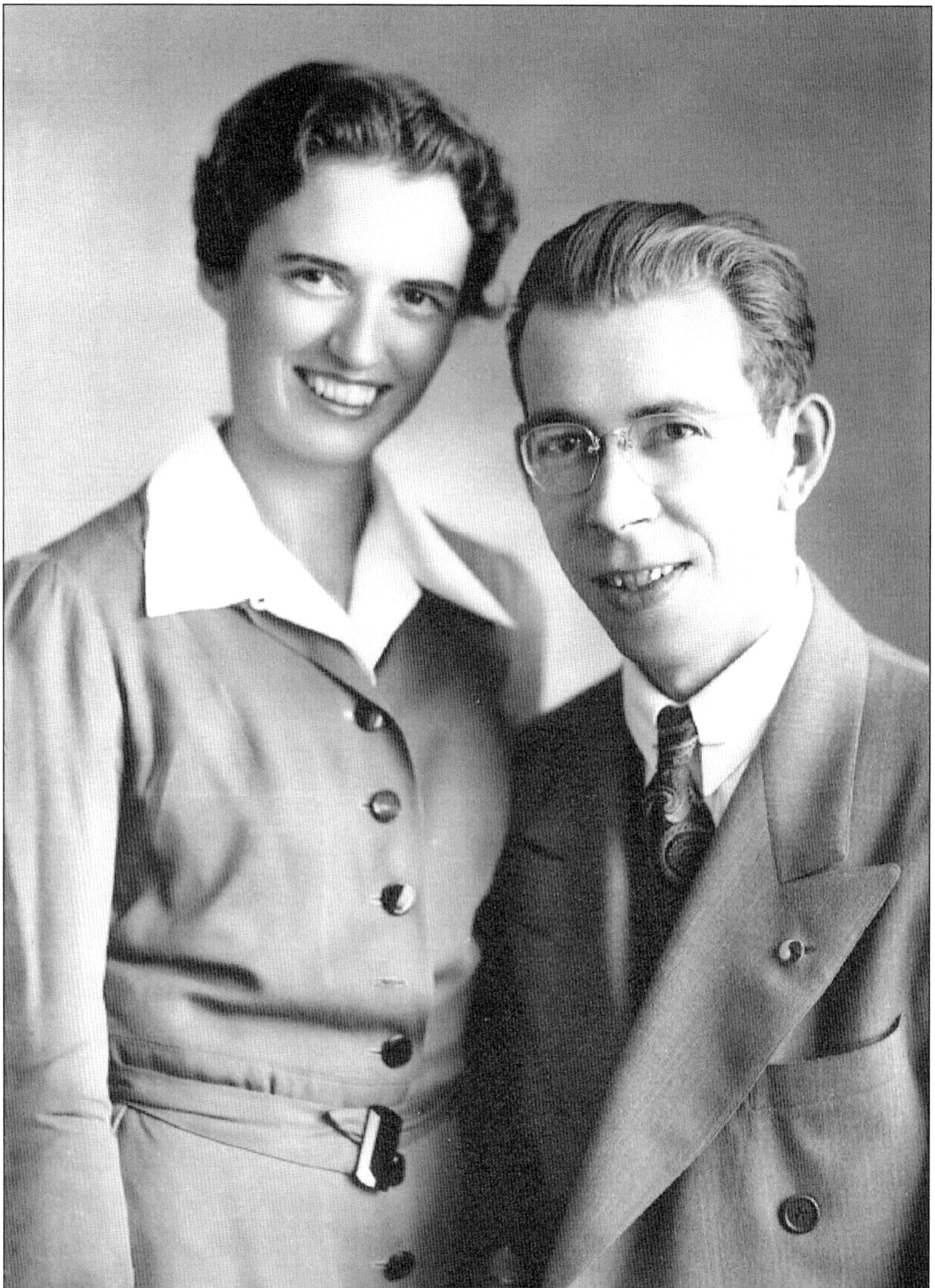

Bobbie Bogart and his wife, Edna Ann, are seen here after living in Beaumont for a number of years. They loved the area and the rural scenes that abounded everywhere in the San Gorgonio Pass, especially during the winter months with snowcapped mountains to the north and south, which encouraged Bobbie's photographic inclinations. (Courtesy of SGPHS.)

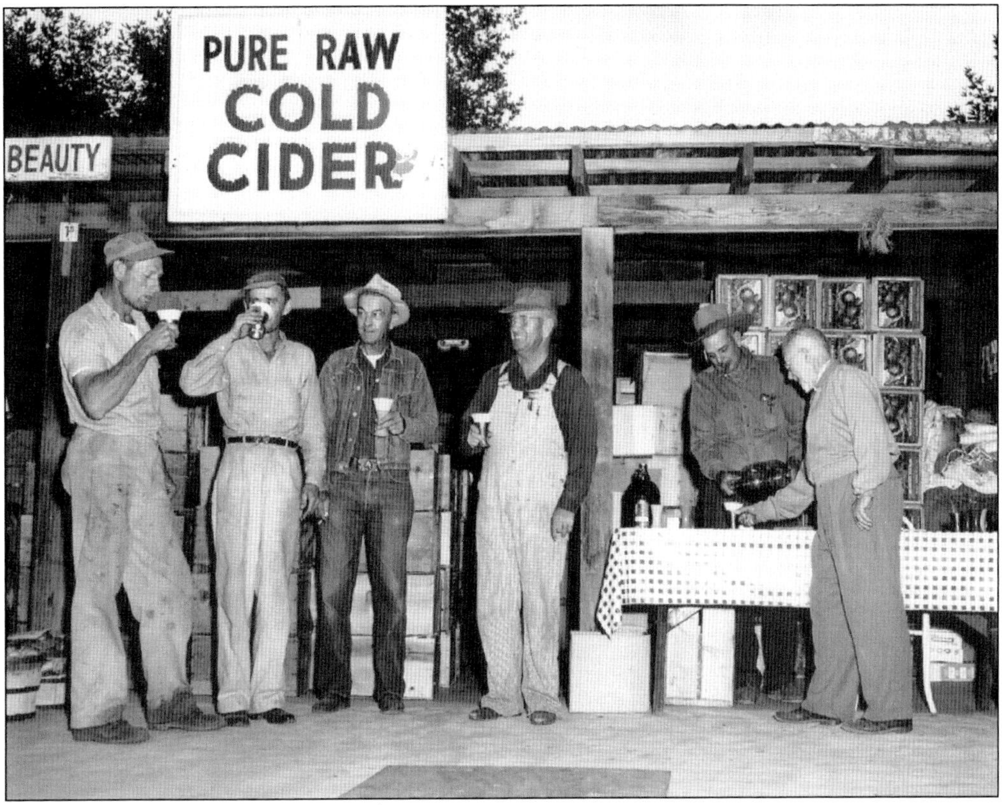

Guy Bogart is seen here at right with Blackie Wiltshire, who is pouring him a glass of pure raw cider. The four farm workers at left also appear to be immensely enjoying the cold cider. Here again, Bogart is giving his support to fruit growers in the area, this time at the Wilshire Ranch in Oak Glen. (Courtesy of SGPHS; Leonard McCulloh, photographer.)

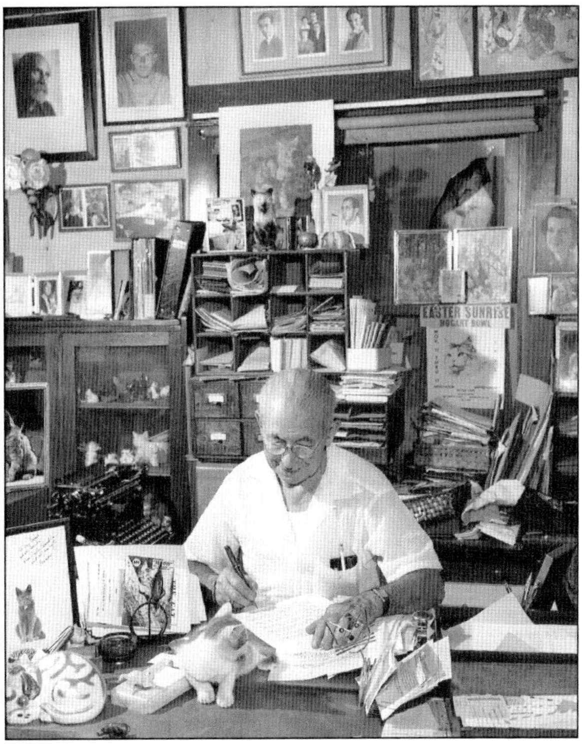

This is Guy Bogart hard at work at his desk. By scrutinizing the photograph, it is quite evident that he is an admirer of cats with the collection of cat figurines in the cabinet at left and the cat calendar at right. The cliché that a cluttered desk portrays the abundance of work performed by its owner certainly was accurate in Bogart's case. (Courtesy of SGPHS.)

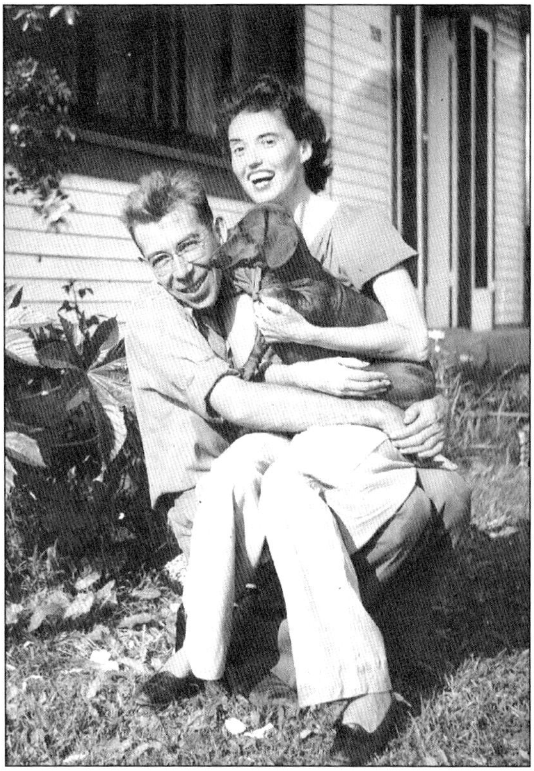

Pictured here are Bobbie Bogart and his wife, Edna Ann, jovially posing for the camera with their pet Daschund dog. Bobbie was kept busy working with his father in their CPA business, as well as with exploring his own photographic interests. However, he had relaxed and enjoyable moments as expressed here. (Courtesy SGPHS.)

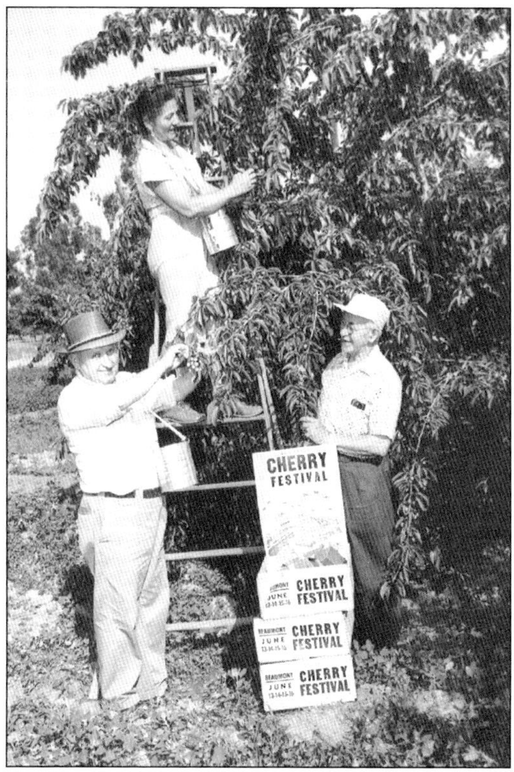

Picking cherries during the Cherry Festival is a community activity connected with the festival. Scenes like this can be seen throughout the many groves in Beaumont and its surrounding area during Cherry Festival time. Seen here is Guy Bogart (right), who was an ardent promoter of the Cherry Festival, with two unidentified friends. (Courtesy of SGPHS; Leonard McCulloh, photographer.)

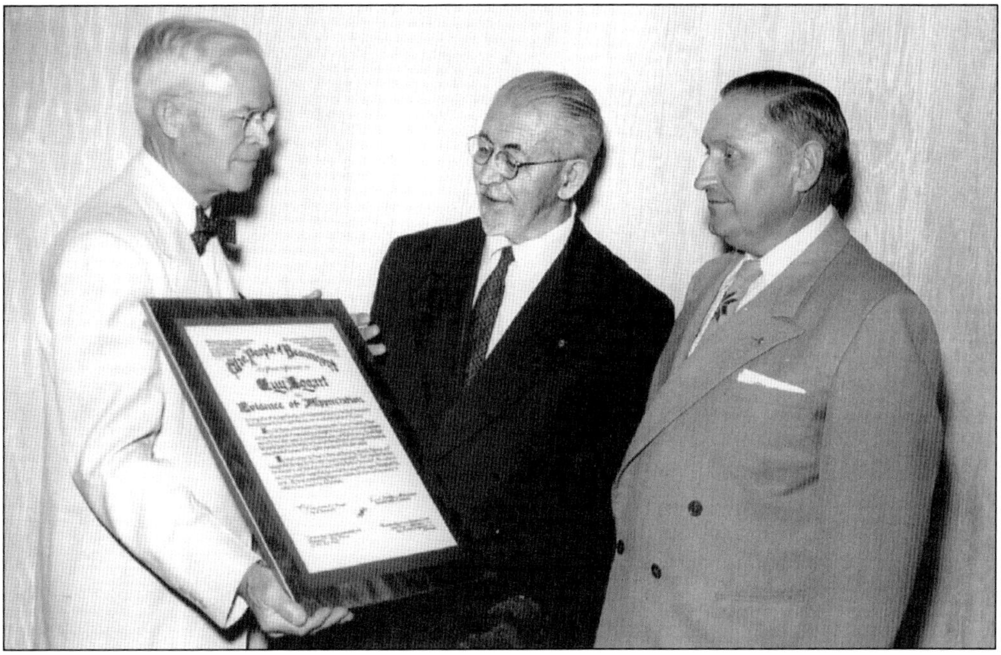

This is Guy Bogart in July 1948 being presented an award that highlighted his many civic duties in Beaumont. He devoted much of his time up until that point to writing and public relations work. In the 32 years he lived in Beaumont, as described in the award plaque, Bogart held multiple official and civic posts, all devoted to community. He was a former mayor and served the chamber of commerce for 25 years—serving 18 of them as president, director, and secretary. (Courtesy of SGPHS.)

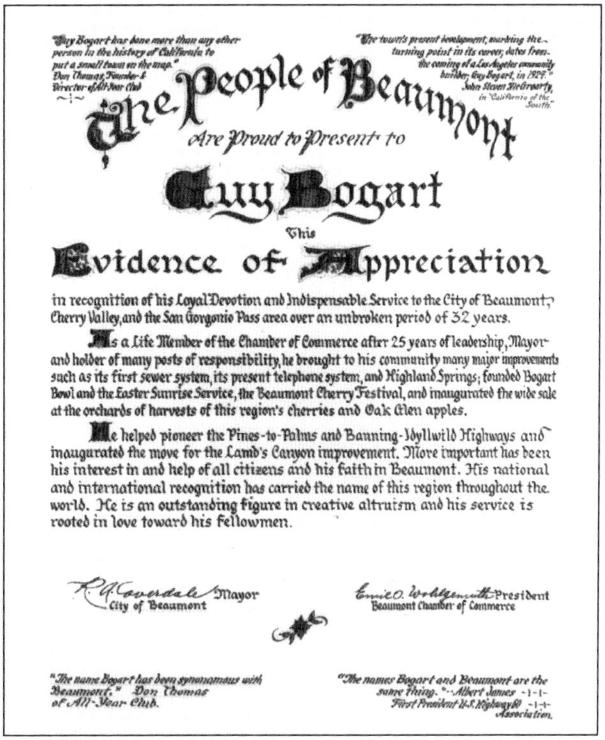

"Guy Bogart has done more than any other person in the history of California to put a small town on the map." Don Thomas, Founder & Director of All-Year Club

"The town's present development, marking the turning point in its career, dates from the coming of a Los Angeles community builder, Guy Bogart, in 1929." John Steven McGroarty, in "California of the South."

The People of Beaumont

Are Proud to Present to

Guy Bogart

This

Evidence of Appreciation

in recognition of his Loyal Devotion and Indispensable Service to the City of Beaumont, Cherry Valley, and the San Gorgonio Pass area over an unbroken period of 32 years.

As a Life Member of the Chamber of Commerce after 25 years of leadership, Mayor and holder of many posts of responsibility, he brought to his community many major improvements such as its first sewer system, its present telephone system, and Highland Springs; founded Bogart Bowl and the Easter Sunrise Service, the Beaumont Cherry Festival, and inaugurated the wide sale at the orchards of harvests of this region's cherries and Oak Glen apples.

He helped pioneer the Pines-to-Palms and Banning-Idyllwild Highways and inaugurated the move for the Lamb's Canyon improvement. More important has been his interest in and help of all citizens and his faith in Beaumont. His national and international recognition has carried the name of this region throughout the world. He is an outstanding figure in creative altruism and his service is rooted in love toward his fellowmen.

Mayor, City of Beaumont

President, Beaumont Chamber of Commerce

"The name Bogart has been synonamous with Beaumont." Don Thomas of All-Year Club.

"The names Bogart and Beaumont are the same thing." Albert James, First President U.S. Highway 60 Association.

This award was presented to Guy Bogart in 1948 for his many contributions to the city of Beaumont. As noted on the plaque, Don Thomas, founder and director of All-Year Club, said that Guy Bogart had done more than any other person in the history of California to put a small town on the map. (Courtesy of SGPHS.)

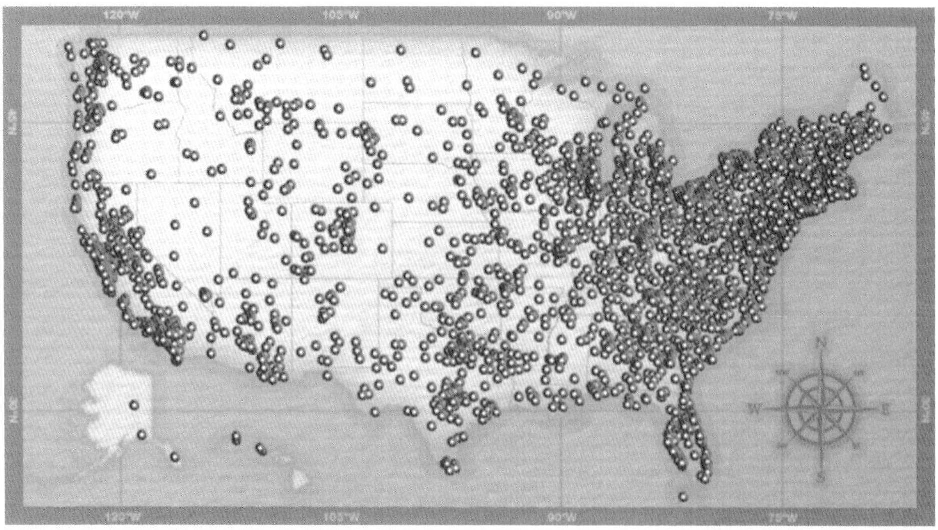